THE COUNSELOR-AT-LAW: A COLLABORATIVE APPROACH TO CLIENT INTERVIEWING AND COUNSELING

Second Edition

ROBERT F. COCHRAN, JR.
Louis B. Brandeis Professor of Law
Pepperdine University

JOHN M.A. DIPIPPA
Distinguished Professor of Law and Public Policy
University of Arkansas at Little Rock
William H. Bowen School of Law

MARTHA M. PETERS, PH.D.
Director of the Academic Achievement Program
University of Iowa College of Law
Professor of Legal Education
Elon University School of Law

LexisNexis™
Matthew Bender®

Library of Congress Cataloging-in-Publication Data

Cochran, Robert F., 1951–
    The counselor-at-law : a collaborative approach to client interviewing
    and counseling / Robert F. Cochran, Jr., John M.A. Dipippa, Martha
    M. Peters—2nd ed.
        p. cm.
    Includes index.
    ISBN 0-8205-6473-7 (perfectbound)
    1. Attorney and client—United States. 2. Interviewing in law practice—
    United States. I. DiPippa, John M. A. II. Peters, Martha M. III. Title.
    KF311.C63 2006

    347.73'504—dc22

                                                            2006003094

This publication is designed to provide accurate and authoritative information in regard to the subject matter covered. It is sold with the understanding that the publisher is not engaged in rendering legal,accounting, or other professional services. If legal advice or other expert assistance is required, the services of a competent professional should be sought.

Editorial Offices
744 Broad Street, Newark, NJ 07102 (973) 820-2000
201 Mission St., San Francisco, CA 94105-1831 (415) 908-3200
701 East Water Street, Charlottesville, VA 22902-7587 (434) 972-7600
www.lexis.com

(Pub. 3116)

DEDICATION

To my mentors, Tom Shaffer and John Acuff, who taught me to love my clients. — R.F.C.

To Karen, who brings light to my day, and Joel, Andrew, Micah, and Nikolai, who make the day worthwhile, and for my parents, John and Theresa DiPippa, whose love and devotion I can never repay. — J.D.P.

To Don, for opening many worlds to me and experiencing them through mutual and collaborative learning and teaching, including, but not limited to, legal education; to my uncle, Douglas Drysdale, my first model of a collaborative counselor-at-law; and to John, Michael, and Tim, who have deepened my appreciation for the value of differences and the importance of effective communication. — M.M.P.

ACKNOWLEDGMENTS

Many hands have helped bring this book to fruition. We want to thank: Karen DiPippa, Margot Barg, Gail Harris, Jessie Cranford, Terri Yeakley, Rod Smith, Lynn Foster, Tony Baker, Lee Boyd, Paul Zwier, Don Peters, Michelle Jacobs, Nancy Lyn Jones, Kenneth Nunn, Lynda Ruf, Gretchen Viney, Raymond Rinkol, and Kristy Jackson.

SUMMARY TABLE OF CONTENTS

TABLE OF CONTENTS

CHAPTER 1

THREE MODELS OF LEGAL COUNSELING

§ 1-1. INTRODUCTION

Our popular culture is obsessed with the courtroom. Movies and television shows focus, almost exclusively, on litigation. Of course, lawyers roll their eyes at the popular portrayal of lawyers. In real life, even litigators spend a small percentage of their time in the courtroom. Ninety percent of their cases are settled. Litigators typically spend much more time counseling clients, negotiating, researching, answering interrogatories, taking depositions, etc. than they do in trial.

Though lawyers scoff at the portrayal of lawyers in popular culture, the portrayal of lawyers in law school is not much more realistic. Law students spend most of their time reading appellate court cases. Most research and writing classes and moot court competitions focus on brief writing and appellate advocacy. The law school's obsession with appellate cases is even more unrealistic than the media's obsession with litigation; only a minuscule portion of litigated cases are appealed. Of course, to be fair, study of appellate cases does more than train lawyers for appellate work. An appellate opinion serves as a window on the litigation in the case that has gone on before and it can generate consideration of legal theory. Moot court trains students in writing and advocacy skills that can be used in other contexts. Nevertheless, traditional law school education is clearly skewed toward the appellate courtroom.

The rise of interest in skills training and alternative dispute resolution has brought a more balanced approach to law school. There has been a new interest in litigation, negotiation, and mediation skills, but the focus of such courses is often primarily on advocacy. Law students are likely to leave law school with an education that consists of four parts legal theory and one part advocacy skills. They are likely to have no exposure to one of the most important and most frequently used lawyer skills, legal interviewing and counseling. Coming out of law school, many young lawyers see clients merely as occasions for advocacy. Both in the culture at large and within the profession, there is little recognition of the lawyer's role as counselor.

It has not always been this way. At one time, the most lofty title a lawyer could claim was that of "Counselor-at-Law." Lawyers had this title printed below their names on their business cards and on the entrances to their offices. There was a recognition of the importance of this lawyer task. In our obsession with advocacy and legal theory, we may have lost sight of it.

Legal interviewing and counseling is not only one of the most common of lawyer tasks, it is also the basis on which clients are most likely to judge their lawyers. Studies have shown that clients judge lawyers primarily, not by their advocacy skills and not even by the results obtained, but by their relational skills with clients.[1]

More importantly, effective legal interviewing and counseling is foundational to effective performance of almost all other lawyer tasks. A lawyer who does not have good interviewing and counseling skills will not be a good advocate. A litigator who is a poor interviewer will miss facts that she should know at trial; a negotiator who is a poor counselor will not know what settlement terms will best meet his client's needs. The lawyer as advocate speaks for the client in many settings. The purpose of legal interviewing and counseling is to make a thoughtful determination of what the lawyer should say.

Defining legal interviewing and counseling is a complex task. A definition requires an understanding of the attorney's responsibility as an advocate, counselor, advisor, negotiator, and officer of the court, as well as a picture of the clients. This definition also needs a theory of what lawyers should do for clients, as well as an understanding of what clients should expect from lawyers.

These orientations influence how lawyers represent clients. In particular, they influence the degree to which lawyers share control of the representation with clients. Three basic models of client interviewing and counseling have emerged: authoritarian, client-centered, and collaborative models. In the remainder of this chapter, we will consider each of these models. Our preference and our focus in this book is on the collaborative model.

§ 1-2. THE AUTHORITARIAN MODEL

In his classic study of personal injury lawyers and clients, David Rosenthal asked "Who's In Charge?"[2] He found that many lawyers are authoritarian in orientation.[3] The authoritarian lawyer exercises "predominant control over and responsibility for the problem-solving delegated to him rather passively by the client."[4] The Authoritarian Model assumes that:

- Lawyers give adequate and effective service;

- Lawyers are able to be disinterested and make objective decisions;

- The solutions to legal problems are primarily technical;

- Ordinarily, there is a correct solution to a legal problem; and

---

[1] *See* Stephen Feldman & Kent Wilson, *The Value of Interpersonal Skills in Lawyering*, 5 L. & HUM. BEHAV. 311 (1981). For further discussion see Chapter 4.

[2] DOUGLAS E. ROSENTHAL, LAWYER AND CLIENT: WHO'S IN CHARGE? (1974).

[3] Rosenthal referred to this as the traditional model.

[4] *Id.* at 2.

- Lawyers are experts in the technical information that is needed to arrive at the correct conclusion.[5]

There are four basic problems with the authoritarian model of client-counseling. First, it is inconsistent with client dignity. There is a broad consensus within Western ethical systems in support of the principle that, to the extent reasonably possible, individuals should control decisions that affect them. This principle finds support in utilitarian, Kantian, and Judeo-Christian theories of ethics.[6] A right of client control is based on what Gerald Dworkin refers to at the "the intrinsic desirability of exercising the capacity for self-determination."

> [N]otions of creativity, of risk-taking, of adherence to principle, of responsibility are all linked conceptually to the possibility of autonomous action. These desirable features of a good life are not possible (logically) for nonautonomous creatures. In general, autonomy is linked to activity, to making rather than being, to those higher forms of consciousness that are distinctive of human potential.[7]

Client control provides the client with an opportunity to be good, to make moral choices, and to grow in moral understanding.[8] The attorney should enable the client, within the law, to understand and exercise the full range of choices that might otherwise be limited by the state or other people. A relationship that should expand the client's autonomy, should not merely substitute one limit on the client's autonomy (the attorney), for other limits (the state and other people).

Not only should the client control the representation because of the intrinsic value of control of one's life, the client should control the representation because client control is likely to yield better results than attorney control, whether we measure the results based on the subjective goals of the individual client, or based on goals held by clients generally.

Client control is likely to provide more satisfying results to the client because clients, in general, are likely to be the best judges of their own interests. The goals of an individual client may be quite different than an attorney would expect, in part because a client may have different values than the attorney;[9] the lawyer may assume that the client is concerned with money, the client may be more concerned with relationships. In addition, a client's risk preferences may be different than those of the attorney; a client might have a great fear of going to trial, whereas a lawyer may enjoy the thrill of trial.

---

[5] *Id.* at 169.

[6] GERALD DWORKIN, THE THEORY AND PRACTICE OF AUTONOMY 110 (1988).

[7] *Id.* at 112.

[8] *See* IMMANUEL KANT, FOUNDATIONS OF THE METAPHISICS OF MORALS 59, 67-68, 73 (1959) (trans. by Lewis Beck).

[9] *See* GARY BELLOW & BEATRICE A. MOULTON, THE LAWYERING PROCESS 1055 (1978) *and* GEOFFREY C. HAZARD, ETHICS IN THE PRACTICE OF LAW 136-37 (1978).

Even as to goals that lawyers and clients commonly share, client control of the representation is likely to yield better results. Rosenthal's study found that plaintiffs who are actively involved in their cases obtain higher settlements and higher verdicts, than plaintiffs who allow their lawyers to control the representation.[10]

Finally, the authoritarian model is inconsistent, at least in spirit, with the professional responsibility rules. Model Rules 1.2 and 1.4 give the client authority to make "decisions concerning the objectives of representation" and require the lawyer to "consult with the client as to the means by which [the objectives] are to be pursued."[11] These rules give broad authority to clients, but authoritarian lawyers can often control representation in spite of the rules. The authoritarian lawyer can control decisions either by pushing the client to approve the lawyer's decision or by presenting the options to the client in a way that leads the client in the way that the lawyer would have him to go.

§ 1-3.   THE CLIENT-CENTERED COUNSELING MODEL

Legal academics responded to the problems of the authoritarian model with the client-centered model. Client-centered concepts made their way into the legal profession in 1977 with the publication of *Legal Interviewing and Counseling* by David Binder and Susan Price.[12] The elements of client-centered counseling are:

- The lawyer helps identify problems from a client's perspective;

- The lawyer actively involves a client in the process of exploring potential solutions;

---

[10] ROSENTHAL, *supra* note 2, at 36-46.

[11] The Model Rules present a division-of-authority model. The client decides the ends, the lawyer (in consultation with the client) decides the means. But there are problems with the ends/means division of authority. First, the ends/means line is an unclear line. In many cases, it will be difficult to distinguish the ends from means. As David Luban has said:

> [T]he client may want to win acquittal *by* asserting a certain right, because it vindicates him in a way that matters to him; or he may wish to obtain a settlement without using a certain tactic, because he disapproves of a tactic. In the end, what the lawyer takes to be mere means are really part of the client's ends.

David Luban, *Paternalism and the Legal Profession*, 1981 WIS. L. REV. 454, 459 n.9.

A second difficulty with the ends/means line is that clients will often have many ends. *See* Mark Spiegel, *Lawyering and Client Decisionmaking: Informed Consent and the Legal Profession*, 128 U. PA. L. REV. 41, 41 (1979). A means that is designed to meet one of those ends may be likely to yield results that are inconsistent with one of the other ends. For example, a plaintiff may both want to settle a case, to avoid having to testify, and to get as much money as possible. Should the lawyer use negotiation tactics that are likely to gain the highest recovery, but which carry a greater risk of deadlock?

[12] DAVID A. BINDER & SUSAN C. PRICE, LEGAL INTERVIEWING AND COUNSELING: A CLIENT-CENTERED APPROACH (1977). The Binder and Price approach was updated with the publication of DAVID A. BINDER ET AL., LAWYERS AS COUNSELORS: A CLIENT-CENTERED APPROACH (1991) and a second edition in 2004. Others advocating a client-centered approach include ROBERT M. BASTRESS & JOSEPH D. HARBAUGH, INTERVIEWING, COUNSELING, AND NEGOTIATING: SKILLS FOR EFFECTIVE REPRESENTATION (1990) and Robert D. Dinerstein, *Client-Centered Counseling: Reappraisal and Refinement*, 32 ARIZ. L. REV. 501 (1990).

- The lawyer and client identify the likely consequences to the client of each option;

- The lawyer encourages a client to make all decisions which are likely to have a substantial legal or non-legal impact on the client;

- The lawyer accepts the client's values and gives advice based on them;

- The lawyer acknowledges a client's feelings and recognizes their importance;

- The lawyer repeatedly conveys a desire to help.

Binder and Price urge lawyers to expand their view of the client's "case" to include non-legal aspects. The lawyer's role "involves having clients actively participate in identifying their problems, formulating potential solutions and making decisions. Thus, client-centered lawyering emanates from a belief in the autonomy, intelligence, dignity, and basic morality of the individual client."[13] Lawyers are asked to convey "empathic understanding" of their clients. Lawyers invite clients to define the goals of the case, to suggest alternatives to pursue those goals, and to make decisions to advance the case. In client-centered counseling, the lawyer maintains an appearance of neutrality and refrains from providing direct advice. Whereas the client has a very limited role in the authoritarian model, the lawyer has a very limited role in the client-centered model.

In many respects, client-centered counseling was an improvement to the way lawyers related to clients under the authoritarian model. It removed the barriers to client participation identified by Rosenthal, and it opened the way for a more comprehensive resolution of the client's problems.

But the client-centered model has its own problems. One problem with the client-centered counseling model is signified by its name. Under the client-centered approach, all decisions are made solely in terms of client interests. "Because client autonomy is of paramount importance, decisions should be made on the basis of what choice is most likely to *provide a client with maximum satisfaction*."[14] Client-centered counselors steer clients toward self-centered decision-making. We agree that lawyers should not dictate decisions in the client-counseling relationship, but lawyers should raise and discuss with clients the interests of those who might be hurt by client decisions. For an extended discussion of the client-centered approach to moral issues in the law office and our proposed alternative, see Chapter 9.

A second problem with the client-centered model is its one-size-fits-all approach. Under the client-centered approach, every significant issue is to be resolved by the client after an elaborate decision-making process. At times, some clients want lawyers to make decisions for them. In the original client-centered counseling book, Binder and Price suggest that when a

---

[13] BINDER ET AL. (1991), *supra* note 12, at 18.

[14] *Id.* at 261 (original emphasis). *See also* BINDER ET AL. (2004), *supra* note 12, at 272 *and* BASTRESS & HARBAUGH, *supra* note 12, at 256.

client has difficulty making a decision, "providing the client with the option of choice by the lawyer should usually be a last resort,"[15] and that when asked their opinion "lawyers should refrain from stating what they would do."[16] Binder and Price want attorneys to actively discourage the client from allowing the attorney to control the representation because of a legitimate concern that the client will come to the attorney with preconceived notions that the attorney is to make the decisions. However, as one commentator suggested, Binder and Price encourage the attorney to "unilaterally, manipulatively impose the goal of full participation." We believe that the client should be able to have the attorney give advice and even make decisions during representation. The lawyer can ensure that a choice for attorney control is an informed one. Attorney control of choices during legal representation does not violate the client's autonomy, so long as the client makes an informed choice for attorney control.[17] Recent client-centered counseling books suggest that lawyers present clients with their opinion when the client asks.[18]

Finally, the client-centered lawyer may be so fearful of influencing the client that she fails to provide the central thing that the lawyer brings to the counseling process: practical wisdom. Lawyers should be careful not to overpower clients, but they should not deny to clients the primary thing that the client may have come for: help in making decisions. The following section discusses the central role that practical wisdom plays in lawyering in general, and the client-counseling process in particular.

§ 1-4.   THE COLLABORATIVE DECISION-MAKING MODEL

We believe that the authoritarian model provides too small a role for clients, the client-centered approach provides too small a role for lawyers, and that clients will be best served when lawyers and clients resolve problems in the law office through collaborative decision-making. Under this model, the client controls decisions, but the lawyer structures the process and provides advice in a manner that is likely to yield wise decisions.[19]

---

[15] BINDER & PRICE, *supra* note 12, at 154.

[16] *Id.* at 186.

[17] *See* DWORKIN, *supra* note 6, at 108-09.

[18] BINDER ET AL. (1991), *supra* note 12, at 347-50 *and* BINDER ET AL. (2004), *supra* note 12, at 368-70.

[19] It appears that the first use of the term "collaborative" to describe how a lawyer and client might resolve issues arising in representation was in JAMES E. MOLITERNO & JOHN M. LEVY, ETHICS OF THE LAWYER'S WORK 86 (1993). They describe this model as follows:

> The lawyer and client say, "let's work together to reach the objective." They share responsibility for diagnosis, action and implementation. They divide responsibility along sensible lines accounting for the lawyer's training and experience and the client's concern about the representation matter.

This model avoids the problems of the authoritarian model. The client's control of the decisions assures client dignity. It is also likely to yield superior results to the authoritarian model. In his study of personal injury cases, Rosenthal found that the more varied the forms of client participation and the more persistently the client employed them, "the better his chances of protecting his emotional and economic interests in the case outcome."[20] We share Rosenthal's call for lawyers and clients to engage in "mutual participation in a cooperative relationship in which the cooperating parties have relatively equal status, are equally dependent, and are engaged in activity 'that will be in some ways satisfying to both [parties].'"[21]

A collaborative client counseling model also avoids the weaknesses of the client-centered counselors. It provides the lawyer and client with an opportunity to consider the effects of their decisions on other people. It provides the lawyer the flexibility to counsel the client in a wide variety of ways. Finally, it enables the client and lawyer to engage in collaborative deliberation that is likely to yield practical wisdom.

Several of the most thoughtful observers of the legal profession have suggested that the central characteristic of a good lawyer is the ability to exercise practical wisdom.[22] This ability goes by many names: practical reasoning, prudence, deliberative wisdom, and practical judgment. Aristotle described it as the ability to deliberate well. According to John Finnis, "Practical reasonableness is reasonableness in deciding, in adopting commitments, in choosing and executing projects, and in general in acting."[23] In short, it is the ability to make wise judgments.

Practical wisdom plays an important role in almost all of the questions a lawyer must address. Determining whether to raise an objection at trial, whether to make an argument in a brief, and whether to provide for a contingency in a contract all require the exercise of practical reason. Practical wisdom is *central* to the job of client counseling, for client counseling is primarily a matter of making decisions. Practical wisdom in client counseling is not merely a matter of *the lawyer* exercising practical wisdom, however; it is a matter of enabling *the client* to exercise practical wisdom.

One of the most forceful proponents of practical wisdom in the life of a lawyer is former Yale Law School Dean Anthony Kronman. In *The Lost Lawyer*, Kronman argues that the modern lawyer is "lost" because he no longer has the ability or the opportunity to exercise practical wisdom. Kronman identifies the ability to "combine the opposing qualities of

---

[20] *See* ROSENTHAL, *supra* note 2, at 57.

[21] *Id.* at 10.

[22] *See, e.g.,* THOMAS L. SHAFFER, AMERICAN LEGAL ETHICS 114-125 (1985) (including excerpts on lawyers and practical wisdom from Aristotle, philosopher Alasdair MacIntyre, and novelist Anthony Trollope); ANTHONY T. KRONMAN, THE LOST LAWYER: FAILING IDEALS OF THE LEGAL PROFESSION 14-17 (1993); *and* MARY ANN GLENDON, A NATION UNDER LAWYERS: HOW THE CRISIS IN THE LEGAL PROFESSION IS TRANSFORMING AMERICAN SOCIETY 231 (1994).

[23] JOHN FINNIS, NATURAL LAW AND NATURAL RIGHTS 12 (1980).

sympathy and detachment" as necessary components of practical wisdom. The lawyer must understand the client and yet retain "the spirit of aloofness on which sound judgement also critically depends."[24]

Kronman contrasts his view with "the narrow view":[25]

> If a lawyer is simply an instrument for effecting his client's desires, as the narrow view suggests, then there is no need for him to deliberate at all. The client does whatever deliberating is required. It only remains for his lawyer to calculate the consequences of the client's decisions and to construct an efficient path to the end that he selects.

In contrast, Kronman argues that lawyers' "responsibilities to a client go beyond the preliminary clarification of his goals and include helping him to make a deliberatively wise choice among them."[26]

> In many cases, it is only through a process of joint deliberation, in which the lawyer imaginatively assumes his client's position and with sympathetic detachment begins to examine the alternatives for himself, that the necessary understanding can emerge. . . .[27]

Kronman joins those[28] who have suggested that the good counselor-at-law is like a friend to a client:

> Friends take each other's interests seriously and wish to see them advanced; it is part of the meaning of friendship that they do. It does not follow, however, that friends always accept uncritically each other's accounts of their own needs. Indeed, friends often exercise a large degree of independent judgement in assessing each other's interests, and the feeling that one sometimes has an obligation to do so is also an important part of what the relation of friendship means. What makes such independence possible is the ability of friends to exercise greater detachment when reflecting on each other's needs than they are often able to achieve when reflecting on their own. A friend's independence can be of immense value, and is frequently the reason why one friend turns to another for advice. Friends of course expect sympathy from each other: it is the expectation of sympathy that distinguishes a friend from a stranger. But they also want detachment, and those who lack either quality are likely to be poor friends.[29]

---

[24] KRONMAN, *supra* note 22, at 304.

[25] *Id.* at 128.

[26] *Id.* at 129.

[27] *Id.* at 133.

[28] *See* Thomas L. Shaffer, *A Lesson From Trollope*, 35 WASH. & LEE L. REV. 727 (1978); Thomas D. Morgan, *Thinking About Lawyers as Counselors*, 42 FLA. L. REV. 439, 453 (1990); *and* THOMAS L. SHAFFER & ROBERT F. COCHRAN, JR., LAWYERS, CLIENTS, AND MORAL RESPONSIBILITY (1994).

[29] KRONMAN, *supra* note 22, at 131-132. For a further discussion of the lawyer/friend analogy, see Chapter 2.

Practical wisdom is in part a skill. We try in this book to introduce you to that skill. But practical wisdom is much more. It also requires innate ability, habit, age, knowledge, breadth of experience,[30] education, and character.[31] To some extent, practical wisdom comes only with age and experience. To a young lawyer-to-be, that fact might be frustrating. On the other hand, you have a lifetime to look forward to growing in your ability as a counselor-at-law. We hope that this book can be an introduction to that process.

As is no doubt apparent, of the three models that we have discussed, the traditional "lawyer-centered" model, the individualistic "client-centered" model, and the collaborative decision-making model, we prefer the collaborative model. It is the model that is most likely to draw on the resources of both lawyer and client. In our opinion, it is the model most likely to yield practical wisdom.

The collaborative model requires much of the lawyer. To be wise and effective legal counselors, lawyers must be legal technicians, trusted advisors, moral counselors, servants, and decision-process guides. This means lawyers must learn how to make their clients feel comfortable, how to ask questions of and listen to clients, and how to guide clients through a sound decision making process. Lawyers must be legally and morally competent, raising critical legal and moral issues with the client when appropriate.

This book borrows techniques from a wide variety of sources to construct an approach to legal interviewing and counseling. Empathy and information gathering, positive regard and sound legal advice, and genuine personal warmth and professional distance are all necessary ingredients. We explore the major approaches to legal interviewing and counseling and outline the available research on the psychology and the sociology of clients and lawyers. This book explores communication and decision-making theory, memory and recall, power and submission, personality types, and ethics. From this base, we construct a model of interviewing and counseling based on the techniques that are effective in real-life encounters. Thus, elements of both traditional and client-centered lawyering find their way into this book.

In the end, we want this book to provide a template for effective legal interviewers and counselors. The individual lawyer should adapt that template to fit her personality, the client, and the circumstances of each case. The most effective legal counselors are those who are instilled with respect for the client, cognizant of building rapport, aware of the psychological dynamics of the lawyer-client relationship, and equipped with technical communication skills which enable them to gather information without sacrificing rapport. These are the lawyers who are likely to enable the client to make wise decisions.

---

[30]Aristotle taught that age and experience were necessary, though not sufficient components. See KRONMAN, *supra* note 22, at 31, *citing* Nicomachean Ethics I, 3:1094b28-a12; 4:1095a31-b13.

[31]According to Aristotle, the practically wise person is one who has "the right kind of likes and dislikes." Nicomachean Ethics 1179b29-30, *quoted in* KRONMAN, *supra* note 22 at 41.

CHAPTER 2

THE GAMES LAWYERS PLAY: HOW LAWYERS CONTROL CLIENTS

§ 2-1. INTRODUCTION

Before constructing a method of interviewing and counseling, we will first look at how lawyers actually interview and counsel clients. By looking at what lawyers do, we can choose techniques that work well and avoid techniques that do not.

Although there is a great deal of information about how other professionals counsel their clients, relatively little has been produced about lawyers.[1] The data that has been gathered shows that clients are most satisfied with lawyers who have the best personal skills. Clients are more satisfied with them, they consider them the best lawyers, and they will refer clients to them.[2]

The studies also show that lawyers in many different practice settings continue to dominate their clients. Rosenthal's authoritarian lawyer appears to be alive and well. Lawyers control the content, sequence, and structure of face-to-face meetings with their clients. By doing this, they control the frame in which the client's case is presented. Cases are placed in the lawyer's template and the conversation is steered toward an option that is both comfortable and familiar to the lawyer.

In many settings, lawyers choose the outcome even before the client has fully explained the case. Lawyers often function as agents of social control, smoothing out rough clients to ensure efficient processing by the legal system. In the end, clients often are dissatisfied with their representation and disillusioned with the legal system. Some have no alternative but to engage in guerilla warfare with the lawyer for control of their cases.

---

[1] The attorney-client evidentiary privilege is thought to be largest obstacle to this work. *See* Brenda Danet, Kenneth B. Hoffman & Nicole C. Kermish, *Obstacles to the Study of Lawyer-Client Interaction: The Biography of a Failure,* 14 LAW & SOC'Y REV. 905, 918 (1980). Other factors also work against empirical studies of lawyer client interaction. They are:

- The unwillingness of lawyers to impose on their clients

- Lack of incentives for lawyers' participation in studies

- Lawyers' general reluctance to be observed.

See DOUGLAS E. ROSENTHAL, LAWYER AND CLIENT: WHO'S IN CHARGE? 179-180 (1974).

[2] Stephen Feldman & Kent Wilson, *The Value of Interpersonal Skills in Lawyering,* 5 LAW & HUM. BEHAV. 311 (1981). See Chapter 4 for more discussion on this.

There is one exception to this picture of lawyer dominance: corporate representation where the picture is almost reversed.[3] Corporate clients tend to dominate their attorneys to the point of making the lawyer's professional autonomy almost non-existent. Corporate clients tend to tell their attorneys what goals they want to achieve and what means will be used to pursue those goals. The corporate setting may be the place where "client-centered" lawyering is alive and well. However, in most other settings — divorce, legal aid, consumer bankruptcy, and criminal — the traditional model reigns; lawyers are in charge.

This chapter looks at what these studies tell us about how lawyers interview and counsel their clients.

§ 2-2.   TRANSFORMING THE CLIENT'S CASE

The first way that lawyers control the client's case is by transforming the definition of it. The conventional view is that lawyers are experts in legal rules who use those rules to champion their client's causes. Lawyers have specialized knowledge that sets them apart as professionals. They are said to have a singular interest — to serve their clients. They know how to manipulate the law to achieve the best for their clients. They simply listen to a summary of the client's case, pull out the right legal rule for the situation, and then proceed to handle the matter for the client.

If the conventional view is true, then interviewing and counseling is a simple task. The lawyer only needs to hear the basic category in which the client's case falls. Once the case is properly categorized, the lawyer starts the "law machine" to take over the case.

Stewart Macaulay surveyed lawyers concerning the way they handled consumer protection cases.[4] He wanted to see if the conventional view of lawyer-client relationships held up in consumer protection cases. He found that the conventional view is naive and inaccurate. Lawyers "often operate in situations where they do not know much about the relevant legal norms or where those norms do not play a significant part in influencing what is done."[5] At these times, lawyers act more like mediators. They seek to work out solutions that satisfy not only the clients' interests, but also the interests of the lawyer, the legal system, and others.[6] In this way lawyers transform their clients cases. Legal rules only play a background part in the eventual resolution of their clients' cases.

---

[3] *Compare* Robert L. Nelson, *Ideology, Practice, and Professional Autonomy: Social Values and Client Relationships in the Large Law Firm,* 37 STAN. L. REV. 503 (1985) (corporate practice dominated by clients) *with* Richard W. Painter, *The Moral Interdependence of Corporate Lawyers and Their Clients,* 67 S. CAL. L. REV. 507 (1994) (corporate lawyers are not morally independent from their clients).

[4] Stewart Macaulay, *Lawyers and Consumer Protection Laws,* 14 LAW & SOC'Y REV. 115 (1979).

[5] *Id.* at 117.

[6] *Id.*

Macaulay's consumer protection lawyers played a number of roles, including "the gatekeeper who teaches clients about the costs of using the legal system, the knowledgeable friend or therapist, the broker of information or coach, the go-between or informal mediator, the legal technician, and the adversary bargainer-litigator."[7] These roles transform the client's perception of their problem and their goals.

Lawyers serve as gatekeepers to the legal system by screening out cases that, in their view, are not worth pursuing. These lawyers may only talk to the client briefly (in person or on the phone) or they may screen cases through office procedures.[8] At other times, the lawyer may simply explain the cost of legal services. These lawyers "see their role as educating would-be clients to see that they cannot afford to pursue that matter."[9]

The lawyer may serve as a trusted friend or therapist and allow the client to blow off steam about a matter. Once the client's anger has dissipated, the lawyer then helps the client redefine their problem: "What appeared to the client to be a clear case of fraud or bad faith comes on close examination to be seen as no more than a misunderstanding."[10] This may lead the lawyer and the client to pursue non-legal solutions to the client's problem.

The lawyer may also assume the role of an "information broker or coach."[11] The lawyer hears the client's complaint but, instead of taking on the representation, refers the client someplace else. This might mean an administrative agency, a private body, or self-help. In connection with this referral, the lawyer may give the client information about legal rules or agency procedure. The lawyer may also coach the client in ways to present the matter.

Few of Macaulay's lawyers took on the role of advocate. More often, the lawyers served as mediators or go-betweens. The lawyer's status often gets the client's complaint heard at a higher level than if the client complained on his own. What happens from this point gets complex, however. The lawyer may simply relay information from the seller to the client or may negotiate the claim on behalf of the client. As this situation develops, lawyers often balance multiple interests. They balance their personal preferences, their professional reputation, their economic interests against their client's needs. The balance works against overly aggressive representation of their clients.

Transforming client disputes has important benefits. Lawyers put client disputes into a language that is shared and understood by other lawyers and the legal system. This commonality helps all parties craft an agreeable solution. It mediates between the client's perceptions of the matter, the other side's perceptions, and the legal system's tools.

---

[7] *Id.* at 152.

[8] *Id.* at 124.

[9] *Id.*

[10] *Id.*

[11] *Id.* at 125.

Recognizing how lawyers transform client stories is necessary before we can construct an effective model for legal interviewing and counseling. This power to transform the clients story puts a great deal of responsibility in the lawyer's hands. Unless lawyers are aware of this process, they may allow their own interests or the system's interests to take precedence over their clients. For example, a classic study of criminal defense lawyers found that they often urged their clients to accept plea bargains that were more in the system's interests than the clients.[12] Although other studies of the criminal defense bar present a more nuanced view,[13] they nevertheless support the view that most criminal defendants are not given the opportunity to participate in their defense.[14]

§ 2-3. CONTROLLING THE CONVERSATION

A second way that lawyers control the representation is by controlling the conversation with the client. Lawyers, particularly those unaware of their own cognitive tendencies and cultural biases, may transform the client's case by channeling the conversation into areas of the law that are more familiar to and more comfortable for the lawyer. When lawyers control the conversation, clients are unable to resist this transformation.

Gary Neustadter observed several consumer bankruptcy lawyers as they conducted initial client interviews.[15] Most of the attorneys controlled the content, sequence, and structure of the interview. Some attorneys controlled the content because they were predisposed to one form of bankruptcy and did not even discuss other forms. One attorney explained to Neustadter why he did not discuss a Chapter 13 plan:

> Clients who come to see me screen themselves. When they get here they know they want bankruptcy. They've read the brochure, filled out the questionnaire, and thought about it. I will sometimes spot problems and have them consider chapter 13.[16]

The lawyers in the Neustadter study also controlled the sequence of the interviews. One lawyer who predominantly handles Chapter 13 bankruptcies uses a videotape to explain the difference between Chapter 7 and 13. The

---

[12] Abraham S. Blumberg, *The Practice of Law as a Confidence Game: Organizational Cooptation of a Profession*, 1 LAW & SOC'Y REV. 28 (1967).

[13] *Compare* ANTHONY E. BOTTOMS & J. D. MCCLEAN, DEFENDANTS IN THE CRIMINAL PROCESS (1976) (participation in the case varies among criminal defendants) *with* Jack Katz, *Legality and Equality: Plea Bargaining in the Prosecution of White-Collar and Common Crimes*, 13 L. & SOC'Y REV. 447 (1979) (participation in case may vary according to type of crime).

[14] Rodney J. Uphoff & Peter B. Wood, *The Allocation of Decisionmaking Between Defense Counsel and Defendant: An Empirical Study of Attorney-Client Decisionmaking*, 47 U. KAN. L. REV. 1, 6 (1998) (finding that a majority of criminal defense lawyers in the study adopted a lawyer-centered approach to decision-making).

[15] Gary Neustadter, *When Law and Client Meet: Observations of Interviewing and Counseling Behavior in the Consumer Bankruptcy Law Office*, 35 BUFF. L. REV. 177 (1986).

[16] *Id.* at 207.

videotape skews the client toward Chapter 13 by presenting it first and in greater depth.[17] After the videotape and during the interview, she asks clients if they understand the difference and if they have any questions. Yet, this is followed by a consideration of Chapter 13 first, often with the introduction, "Let's see what a chapter 13 looks like."[18] Although the lawyer will handle a Chapter 7, it is only given a "passing mention" unless it is "clearly indicated" by the client's circumstances. The lawyer openly prefers Chapter 13 and structures her presentations in ways that dispose the client to favor them as well.

Last, the lawyers in the Neustadter study controlled the structure of the interviews by using forms to gather information. Every lawyer used forms to varying degrees. One office employed an elaborate form system and clearly structured the interview process around the forms. The sometimes lengthy forms solicited the same information in several different ways. Almost all of the lawyers used the information from the forms as the basis for the interview by looking at the information and then asking a series of "narrow questions " to provide more precise information if the client decided to file a bankruptcy.[19]

When it came to exploring alternatives with the client, only one attorney did so as a matter of course. However, even these alternatives were limited to the different bankruptcies available, and the lawyer rarely explored other options that could also solve the client's financial problems.[20]

Carl Hosticka studied the interactions between lawyers and their clients in a legal services office.[21] Hosticka saw the initial interview revolving around defining the clients' problems and prescribing what needed to be done.[22] He found that the lawyers asserted their power by controlling the topics of conversation and who talked about them.

The lawyers exercised floor control by indicating who should speak, by speaking in the absence of permission by the client, and by interrupting the client.[23] Topic control included introducing new topics into the conversation and continuing or terminating topics initiated by the client.[24]

---

[17] The first version of the videotape also analogized Chapter 7 to "amputations." *Id.* at 225 n.108.

[18] At this point, the lawyer uses a calculator on her desk to work out an estimated payment plan. *Id.* at 227. When one of us first read this vignette, we were reminded of the car salesman who works out the monthly payments on his calculator and then displays the results. This technique may effectively end any discussion of other matters, such as price, value of the trade-in, or alternative sources of financing. Although we do not believe the lawyer in this example used the calculator for that purpose, it effectively ended the discussion of alternative solutions as if that had been the purpose.

[19] *Id.* at 232 ("Through the use of these forms, interviewers control the structure, sequence, content, and length of the interview and generate information that supports standard solutions.")

[20] Other options may include making more money, fewer expenses, or debt consolidation.

[21] Carl J. Hosticka, *We Don't Care What Happened, We Only Care About What is Going to Happen,* 26 Soc. Probs 599 (1979).

[22] *Id.* at 599.

[23] *Id.* at 600.

[24] *Id.*

Hosticka found evidence of both of these in the ways that the lawyers asked and answered questions, changed topics introduced by clients or continued topics introduced by the lawyers, and gave explanations and instructions.

Clients would be invited to tell their story, but they would quickly be interrupted by the lawyer, who then channeled the case into a legal pigeonhole. The lawyers took over developing the information by asking the clients a series of questions, many of them leading.[25] Essentially, these lawyers cross-examined their own clients during the initial inter- view. Without asking the client what he wanted to do, the lawyer then told the client what kind of case he had and what would be done about it. The lawyers maintained control of the floor by interrupting the client once every three minutes. Clients interrupted the lawyers only once every ten minutes.[26]

Over 90% of the lawyers' statements were instances of topic control with a full 25% of these statements being leading questions.[27] Often the lawyer and the client fought for control of the conversation in these exchanges. Many times the client's answer introduced a new topic to the conversation. The lawyer would retain control by interrupting and asking another question.[28]

The result was to stereotype client problems and funnel them into areas more familiar to the lawyer.[29] This stereotyping had two consequences. First, it erased the differences among cases so that they could be handled routinely. The offices' large caseloads put a premium on efficiency. Cases that fit within the conventional molds could be routinized, while cases that fell outside of the ordinary would be looked at more carefully.

Stereotyping the cases affected the lawyer's perceptions of the facts and the law. Channeling the case into a familiar category framed the case and allowed the lawyer to discern "relevant" facts from "irrelevant" facts. This was self-fulfilling. The irrelevancy of the facts was determined by the quick, impressionistic judgment of the lawyer. These facts were further marginalized by the lawyer's cross-examination, like questioning of the client since only facts likely to support the initial judgment came out under this method of questioning.

Second, taking control of the client interview robbed the client's auton- omy. It denied to clients the very decisions that the ethical rules reserve to them: the right to determine the goals of the representation. When the lawyer announces what will be done, the client has no chance to define the goals of the representation. Indeed, this method makes interviewing simple and counseling non-existent. The interview consists of the lawyer

---

[25] *Id.* at 603-04.

[26] *Id.* at 605.

[27] *Id.*

[28] *Id.* at 606.

[29] *Id.* at 607.

asking enough questions to figure out in which category the client's case fits. If counseling is understood as involving the client in a discussion of the available options and the relative merits, then no counseling exists under this approach. The lawyer has already determined the options and merits of the case when he fits the case into its category.

Neustadter's and Hosticka's studies show how lawyers control the conversation with the client and thereby transform the case into something familiar to the lawyer. This technique denies to clients what the conventional view of the legal system promises: a champion who takes on the client's unique case and uses the law and the legal system to the client's best advantage. Although the clients may have needed the legal help they eventually received and the lawyers may have competently performed their duties in this regard, this came at the expense of the client's autonomy and, perhaps, at the expense of a better solution to the client's problems.[30]

Standardizing the lawyer's response forces the client to accept the lawyer's definition of what is at stake. Because the lawyer does not know what matters most to the individual client, he substitutes what his experience with the legal process tells him clients ought to consider important. Yet, the client may be motivated by a unique combination of values and interests that will be silenced by the standardization. Discerning these unique combinations would ensure that whatever solution the client eventually chooses will match the case and the client as much as possible.

§ 2-4.   INSIDER STATUS FOR SALE

As we saw in the previous section, lawyers can transform the case by controlling the content, sequence, and structure of the conversation with the client. Lawyers steer the conversation toward their status as legal system insiders. Rather than discuss how legal rules affect their clients' cases, lawyers discuss how their inside knowledge of the legal system and its participants will decide the case. In short, lawyers do not sell their legal knowledge; they sell their insider status.

A study of divorce lawyers suggests that lawyers do not discuss the law with their clients.[31] Austin Sarat and William Felstiner observed and recorded 115 client conferences over a period of 33 months. They followed one of the parties in each of 40 different divorce cases involving 20 different lawyers in two states, California and Massachusetts.[32] The authors attempted to track a case from the initial client-interview until the final order.

---

[30] Hosticka's lawyers rated the more persistent clients as more hostile. Interestingly enough, however, the lawyers worked more on their cases. *Id.* at 607. This echoes Rosenthal's findings that the more active clients may have achieved better results because their persistence forced their lawyers to do more work on their cases. It also suggests that these lawyers saw themselves as in charge of the case and viewed any input from the client as diluting their power.

[31] Austin Sarat & William L. F. Felstiner, *Lawyers and Legal Consciousness: Law Talk in the Divorce Lawyers Office,* 98 YALE L.J. 1663 (1989).

[32] *Id.* at 1669.

Although almost all cases started off with a discussion of the legal rules, the content of the conversation changed as the case progressed.[33] The conversations increasingly turned to the nature, operation, and efficacy of legal institutions, as well as the characteristics, motivation, and competence of legal actors.[34] These conversations happened in connection with significant events in the litigation. Although they were frequently initiated by the client, their content and structure remained consistent from lawyer to lawyer.

Sarat and Felstiner noticed that lawyers tended to talk to their clients the way they talked to other lawyers.[35] They focused on the personalities of the people involved in the legal system and highlighted the importance of local norms as opposed to legal rules. Among themselves and to their clients, lawyers tended to denigrate legal rules as hyper-technical on one hand and weak guidelines on the other.[36]

Lawyers subjected the people within the legal system to a withering critique.[37] Both judges and lawyers come off as stupid and incompetent. Judges were portrayed as lacking competence, integrity, motivation, sensitivity and concern.[38] Other lawyers were described as without integrity, ethics, and professionalism.[39]

Nor did the legal system escape this attack. Lawyers told their clients about an overloaded legal system in which clients are victimized and money and status get results.[40] Lawyers emphasized the randomness of judicial actions and their ability to trade on insider knowledge and status. These characterizations described the legal system as "idiosyncratic and personalistic, and in so doing, they endow lawyers with a mystique of insider knowledge that is unavailable to even well-educated, well read clients."[41] Lawyers can rest their professional power and control on both their technical expertise and insider status.[42]

Lawyers in this study went "to great lengths to impress their clients with their range of contacts and importance on the local legal scene."[43] What mattered most was the lawyer's reputation "in this court."[44] The legal system appeared as "localized, governed by peculiar and specific practices rather than universal norms."[45] Familiarity with local norms, as opposed to technical expertise, gets the best results.

---

[33] *Id.* at 1670.

[34] *Id.*

[35] *Id.* at 1672.

[36] *Id.* at 1674-1675.

[37] *Id.* at 1676-1682.

[38] *Id.* at 1678-79.

[39] *Id.* at 1681.

[40] *Id.* at 1682.

[41] *Id.* at 1679.

[42] *Id.* at 1684-1685.

[43] *Id.* at 1686.

[44] *Id.*

[45] *Id.*

Felstiner and Sarat believe that this kind of "law talk" may be responsible for the dissatisfaction clients feel after using the legal process, no matter how favorable the result.[46] Law talk tells clients that law routinely fails to live up to the expectations people have about it. It portrays a system in which no one, except the lawyer with insider status, has control. It requires clients to trust lawyers who, by their very inside manipulation of the legal system, appear unworthy of trust. Finally, it trivializes the law's moral concerns. What could morality have to offer in a system that, at best, operates randomly and, at worst, operates corruptly.

§ 2-5. STRUGGLING FOR POWER

The studies of lawyers and clients found that they regard each other with suspicion. Clients worry about whether or not their lawyers are committed to their cases and whether or not they can control what their lawyers do.[47] Lawyers worry about clients' emotional stability and unrealistic expectations about what the legal system can provide.[48] These concerns lead to mutual misunderstandings:

> Lawyers worried about the emotional instability of their clients often appear hyper-rational, detached, disloyal, and callous. Clients, put off and alienated by such appearances, appear even more unstable and unpredictable to their lawyers. Lawyers worry about distortions introduced by client accounts and attempt to test client stories without expressing overt skepticism.[49]

This mutual dependence and suspicion illustrates how the traditional model of lawyer dominance and client passivity is oversimplified. Indeed, lawyers and their clients feel both powerful and powerless during the course of the representation. Each attempts to control the power dynamics in the areas where he or she feels most comfortable. For lawyers, those areas are often the law and information about the legal system. For clients, those areas are often the "facts" and the time they have available to consult with the lawyer.

If lawyers and clients collaborated with each other they might construct a case that takes advantage of the lawyer's knowledge of the legal world and the client's knowledge of the social world. If they do not collaborate, they may engage in a struggle to assert their exclusive version of reality.[50]

In the divorce cases studied by Felstiner and Sarat, lawyers and clients did not collaborate effectively. Instead, they struggled for power as they defined the goals of their cases and how they would accomplish them. Lawyers and

---

[46] *Id.* at 1687.

[47] William L. F. Felstiner & Austin Sarat, *Enactments of Power: Negotiating Reality and Responsibility in Lawyer-Client Interactions,* 77 CORNELL L. REV. 1447, 1455 (1992).

[48] *Id.* at 1456.

[49] *Id.*

[50] *Id.* at 1460.

clients mirrored each other's tactics. Both used "procrastination, vacillation, disapproval, withdrawal, repression, and information problems that delay, distort, and jeopardize what they are trying to accomplish."[51]

This was rarely done overtly. Rather, lawyers used their knowledge of the law, the legal system, and its participants in an attempt to control the client's view of what was "realistic." Clients, on the other hand, used their superior knowledge of the "facts," that is, the social world from which their case sprang to try to control the lawyer's actions. Clients silently fought for control by changing their minds, putting off decisions, or withholding information. If they were not successful, they at times simply disappeared.[52] Lawyers controlled access by returning or not returning phone calls, sending or not sending letters, and procrastinating about client demands.

§ 2-6.   TRANSLATING THE CLIENT'S STORY

These studies suggest that lawyers will always transform their clients' stories.[53] This is necessary in order to frame the matter in a way that the legal system understands and accepts. At the same time, these studies show that lawyers who dominate their clients harm the clients' and the legal system's interests.

We need a new perspective on the lawyer-client relationship if we want to avoid the problems that these studies have identified. We need a perspective that maximizes the advantages of legal representation but mitigates its harmful effects. Clark Cunningham offers the metaphor of the lawyer as translator "as a way of both understanding and altering the ways lawyers change the meanings of their clients' stories."[54] Cunningham explains that translations always change the original story because translations are never perfect.[55] At the same time, translations give a voice to people who could not otherwise be understood. As Cunningham says,

> The good translator does not alter the speaker's meaning without the speaker's consent, and may even collaborate with the speaker

---

[51] *Id.* at 1467.

[52] *Id.* at 1497.

[53] Lawyers, particularly those who are not aware of their own cognitive styles and biases are likely to translate clients' stories into problems they can solve using their strengths. For example, when lawyers prefer thinking judgment, they are likely to look at a client's story for the logical analysis of the story and attend to those elements of the story that lend themselves to their knowledge of legal remedies. The values, feelings, and personal interests that might be picked up by a lawyer who prefers feeling judgment may be extraneous facts to a lawyer who sees his job as solving a legal problem with classic logic. Knowledge of psychological type preferences can help lawyers identify their own biases in hearing and understanding clients' stories as well as helping them listen with ears sensitized to values, feelings, and other personal perspectives. Chapter 12 provides more information on psychological type theory and its applications to interviewing and counseling.

[54] Clark D. Cunningham, *The Lawyer as Translator, Representation as Text: Towards an Ethnography of Legal Discourse*, 77 CORNELL. L. REV. 1298, 1299 (1992).

[55] *Id.*

to produce a statement in the foreign language that is more meaningful than a speaker's original utterance. Thus, translation offers both an image of the constraints upon a lawyer's ability to represent fully his client's story and a model for recognizing and managing the inevitable changes in meaning in a way that may empower rather than subjugate the client.[56]

Cunningham suggests that by becoming a better translator of client stories, lawyers can represent their clients better. If all lawyering translates the client's story into a new language and, in the process, changes its meaning, then the story is no longer the client's alone. It becomes a joint project of the lawyer and the client that is subject to revision as the representation moves along. Lawyers and client must effectively collaborate as they translate the client's story.

Cunningham uses his own experience as an example of how this translation occurs. He shows that being a good translator requires that lawyers listen carefully to the client's story and remain faithful to its original meaning. Otherwise, all the problems of lawyer dominance recur. Cunningham and his legal clinic students were appointed to represent M. Dujon Johnson in a misdemeanor case.[57] Johnson, an African-American man, was stopped by the police for allegedly running a stop sign. He was subjected to a brief search, and he was eventually charged with disorderly conduct for statements made to the police after they stopped him. The police claimed that Johnson refused to submit to a "pat-down" search while Johnson claimed that the police only stopped him because he was black.

Cunningham categorized the matter as a "stop and frisk" case. This categorization dictated the approach Cunningham took: attack the reasons for the search and exclude the evidence that resulted from it. Cunningham focused on the reasons for the "frisk." The law requires "particularized suspicion" that the suspect has a weapon. The police report did not indicate any particular facts that would lead to this suspicion. Cunningham theorized that the police simply frisked Johnson as a matter of course. Finding nothing, they fabricated a violation of the law to justify the search under another rule that allowed searches of persons who have been arrested.

If successful, Cunningham would exclude everything that Johnson said to the police officers after his stop. There could be no disorderly conduct without any evidence of what Johnson said. Even if Cunningham could not get the charge dismissed before trial, this tactic would allow him to cross-examine the police officers to hear what they had to say and introduce the judge to the theory, which could be revived at trial.

The judge denied the motion to exclude the evidence. Although this was not unexpected, what the judge next said stunned Cunningham. In denying

---

[56] *Id.* at 1300.

[57] *Id.* at 1304. Cunningham handled the case as a clinical supervisor in a law school clinical program. Students enrolled in the program worked with him on the case.

the motion the judge advanced a shocking approval of the officer's conduct saying that "this is definitely an attitude arrest and had the person never exhibited that attitude he exhibited he never would have been arrested. I think that's pretty obvious and I don't think there is anything wrong with that."[58]

Cunningham realized that victory at trial would take more than a conventional Fourth Amendment approach. During a pre-trial conference, they decided to have Johnson cross-examine the arresting officer. This would dramatically bring the racial dynamics of the case to the forefront and give Johnson an opportunity to reclaim his dignity. The prosecution, however, dismissed the case on the morning of the trial. The prosecutors could not justify the expense of trying what the judge called a "fifty dollar attitude ticket."[59]

Instead of being jubilant, Johnson was outraged. He was upset at Cunningham, as well as the prosecution. Johnson told Cunningham and his students that during the representation, he often felt like a child because the lawyers took on so much responsibility for the case. Having to ask for a court appointed lawyer, "means that I am in the back-seat. Even today during court this morning, I'm in the back seat. Always the secondary person."[60] They made him feel "indigent mentally as well as physically." By reminding him of certain routine matters, like the importance of attending court hearings, they implied that he was lazy and nonchalant:

> Do you guys actually think I'm stupid, lazy, and slow? Most black people have that stereotype, of being that way. You don't know that? . . . The way you guys talk to me and approach me — it's a little like the way [the trooper] approached me.[61]

Johnson said of Cunningham:

> You're the kind of person who usually does the most harm. You have a guardian mentality, assume that you know the answer. You presume you know the needs and answers. Oversensitivity. Patronizing. All the power is vested in you. I think you may go too far, assuming that you would know the answer.[62]

In Cunningham's terms, he mistranslated his client's case. When Cunningham categorized the case as a "stop and frisk" case, he used a language that focused on the police conduct and he lost a language that focused on the client's conduct. The trial focused on what the *police did* rather than on what *Johnson did not do*. The officer's testimony during the suppression focused the attention on the officer's fear for their safety and

---

[58] *Id.* at 1320.

[59] *Id.* at 1329.

[60] *Id.* at 1330.

[61] *Id.*

[62] *Id.*

their need to be cautious in every case, even if that meant a "minor" violation of Johnson's Fourth Amendment rights. The narrative's force made the officers seem reasonable when they acted to protect their safety and Johnson seem unreasonable when he did not cooperate with them.

The search and seizure strategy had a more insidious consequence, however. The stop and frisk argument assumed that the police had a good reason to stop Johnson, thus treating as true the claim that Johnson had run a stop sign. This fact was central to Johnson's story, the story that could not be told when Cunningham focused on the subsequent search. Johnson's story was about racial harassment. Its narrative focused on the events that led to the search. Left out "were the images of the police car 'whipping in' to block Johnson's car, the swaggering [officer] pulling on his black gloves as he stepped toward Johnson, and [the other officer] peering into Johnson's car with a flashlight."[63] The stop and frisk version left out facts that showed that Johnson was stopped because of his race.

Running the stop sign was the key to this story. Johnson explained his actions at the light in some detail during his initial interview. In fact, he undeniably came to a complete stop at the intersection. He could only shift gears by stopping the car, turning it off, shifting gears, and then restarting the car. He performed that operation at the intersection where the officers claimed he ran the stop sign.

If Johnson had not run the stop sign, the racial nature of the stop would have become prominent. Other facts also supported Johnson's version of the offense — that he was stopped because he was black. Johnson drove a sporty car at 4:40 a.m. in a predominately wealthy, white part of town and the troopers never told him at the time that they stopped him for running a stop sign. However, these facts were never developed.

Even though Cunningham understood that the case involved race, his legal strategy failed to offer a coherent translation of Johnson's situation. Indeed, the strategy failed to translate the most crucial words of the entire encounter, which occurred when Johnson told the police that he "was stopped because he was black."[64] These were the words that required "translation." Translating these words required a legal strategy that highlighted them and the reality they pointed to. It required a strategy that allowed Johnson to have some control over his fate, a control denied him by the officer's decision to charge him with disorderly conduct when he insisted that they follow the Constitution.

However, Cunningham's presentation of the case never raised the racial issue.[65] Rather, it was the judge who first raised the racial question by claiming that the police "didn't just see a black guy and arrest him." By

---

[63] *Id.* at 1367.

[64] *Id.* at 1370-71.

[65] *Id.* at 1385. Johnson told Cunningham that he "knew from the very beginning that [the arrest] was racially motivated. I would have confided this, but who would have believed me anyway?"

focusing on the search, Cunningham "presented a very distorted and rather unsympathetic picture of [his] client. What the judge 'saw' were two state troopers just trying to do their jobs, whose patience was exhausted by a guy who was 'too smart for his own good.'"[66]

Cunningham's story illustrates how even well-intentioned, well-trained lawyers transform their client's story. Cunningham and his students used client-centered techniques. They allowed Johnson to relate his story to them and, in fact, received from him an explanation of the events leading up to his arrest. This was not an example of poorly trained interviewers who failed to develop the facts. Nevertheless, they took over their client's case and channeled it into an area more familiar to them.

Cunningham and his students viewed the facts as neutral and without meaning until they assigned them meaning. The only facts that had meaning were the facts connected to the legal category that they assigned the case. Any facts that did not fit with the lawyers' legal theory were inconsequential, no matter how important they were to the client and the client's story.

The control this gave them was not much different than the control exercised by lawyers under the authoritarian approach described by Rosenthal. The lawyers were deceived into thinking they were sharing control, but the client really had no control at all. Johnson understood his powerlessness and his invisibility. In fact, he later insisted that Cunningham use his real name in the article that Cunningham wrote about the incident because "[i]f my name is not used I would be a non-person again. [During the case] I was talked over, I was talked through. [If my real name is not used] I still don't exist. I want to be identified. This anonymity has to end somewhere; I was anonymous in the courtroom."[67]

Effective legal interviewers understand the responsibility they have when they translate their client's story. They know that their perceptions of the client and the legal theories they choose frame the information they receive about the case. They also know that the way they take in information and process it will filter what they hear from their clients and what they consider important. These elements influence the questions they ask and the facts they pursue. Effective legal interviewers recognize that they will transform their client's story, but they take seriously the translator's job of hearing, understanding, and remaining faithful to the client's original meaning.

In the end, lawyers and their clients struggle for control over their lives, their cases, and their professions. Lawyers and clients interact in "a process of story-telling and interrogation in which the lawyer and the client seek to produce for each other a satisfying rendition of her distinctive world."[68] Effective legal interviewers treat this as a "joint

---

[66] *Id.* at 1375.

[67] *Id.* at 1383-1384.

[68] *See* Felstiner & Sarat, *supra* note 47, at 1454-55.

project . . . essential to construct a mutually tolerable story persuasive to judge or opponent."[69]

Cunningham described what Johnson believed effective attorneys had to do:

> He urged us to admit that we were different from him and there-
> fore were necessarily going to treat him differently. He asked that
> we be sensitive to the differences and adjust what we said and did
> accordingly. What he said was something very close to the follow-
> ing words: What's wrong with realizing that different people have
> different needs? . . . If both parties are making an effort, there
> eventually will be a consensus about how to deal with the solution,
> about how to communicate.[70]

§ 2-7. CRAFTING THE LAWYER-CLIENT RELATIONSHIP THROUGH COLLABORATIVE NEGOTIATION

Crafting an effective lawyer-client relationship takes work. The first step is for lawyers to recognize their obligation to be faithful translators of their client's stories. But that is not enough. Mr. Johnson's story shows that lawyers must open up their representation if they want to truly collaborate with their clients. If this kind of collaboration is to happen, lawyers and clients must form partnerships in which they share information, plan strategy, and exercise authority. As true collaborators, lawyers and clients must negotiate relationships that fit their needs.

Professor Alex Hurder describes what a negotiated approach might entail and how it might have changed Mr. Johnson's case.[71] Hurder suggests that "all decisions about the terms of the lawyer client relationship be made jointly by the lawyer and the client. Such decisions include select-ing mutual goals, choosing the means of pursuing mutual goals, dividing responsibility between the lawyer and the client, and establishing rules governing the relationship between lawyer and client."[72] Hurder proposes that the lawyer and client engage in collaborative negotiation, not adver-sarial negotiation. Lawyer and client share the same goals — effective client representation. In this context, collaborative negotiation is a matter of the lawyer and client together identifying what would be the most effec-tive representation.

If the lawyer and client are to act collaboratively within the lawyer-client relationship, the lawyer must equalize the power within the relationship.

---

[69] *Id.* at 1455.

[70] Cunningham, *supra* note 54, at 1382.

[71] Alex J. Hurder, *Negotiating the Lawyer-Client Relationship: A Search for Equality and Collaboration,* 44 BUFF. L. REV. 71 (1996).

[72] *Id.* at 79.

At times, the power is primarily in the hands of the lawyer; but in corporate settings it is likely to be in the hands of the client. In the end, flexibility is warranted. Some clients will be experienced enough to make such decisions but others will not. We suggest means that the lawyer might use to equalize the lawyer-client relationship in Chapter 3 (Communication) and Chapter 9 (Moral Choices in the Law Office). Because of the inherent power imbalance in many lawyer-client relationships, lawyers should proceed cautiously when trying to negotiate their relationship with a client.

§ 2-8. CONCLUSION

This chapter concludes the following:

- A client's story will inevitably be transformed by the lawyer.

- Lawyers in many situations dominate their clients, with corporate representation being the general exception.

- Lawyers tend to control the content, sequence, and topics of lawyer-client conversations.

- Lawyers tend to transform their clients' stories into ones with which lawyers feel more comfortable or more familiar.

- Thinking about lawyering as translation guards against lawyer domination.

- Translating the client's story suggests that the lawyer remain as faithful as possible to the client's original meaning.

- Even the best-intentioned lawyers can mistranslate their client's story.

- This mistranslation occurs when the lawyer places the client's story into a legal category that minimizes important aspects of the client's story.

- Lawyers and clients should collaboratively work out all aspects of the lawyer-client relationship.

- These aspects include selecting mutual goals, ways to achieve those goals, the division of responsibility, and the amount of client participation in the representation.

In this chapter, we have reviewed aspects of the lawyer-client relationship. We believe that by being attentive and faithful translators lawyers will improve their relationships with their clients and the work they do for them. This means that lawyers and clients should approach each matter as a collaboration in which both contribute to its make-up and success. But collaborators must be free to share, exercise, and delegate responsibility. Thus, we believe that lawyers and clients should openly and fairly work out the important aspects of the lawyer-client relationship.

In the chapters that follow, we lay out the skills we believe are necessary for lawyers to effectively interview and counsel their clients, but these skills are never exercised in a vacuum. They must be applied against the background of translation and negotiation that we have discussed in this chapter. Truly collaborating with clients means that these skills will be used in contexts that are different for each client and for each case.

CHAPTER 3

COMMUNICATION SKILLS

§ 3-1. INTRODUCTION

Client interviewing and counseling require effective communication. Effective communication happens when lawyers "communicate questions accurately and precisely . . . , maximize the client's ability and willingness to answer . . . , listen actively to determine the significance of statements, [and] probe to increase the validity, clarity, and completeness" of the client's answers.[1] Nevertheless, lawyers continue to approach their clients with little thought to their own communication styles or skills much less the understanding that clients differ in their communication processes and that these differences influence both the giving and receiving of information. See chapter 12 for a complete description of these differences. This chapter examines some models and methods to increase accurate communication and sketches their implications for legal interviewing and counseling.

§ 3-2. LISTENING

§ 3-2(a). PAYING ATTENTION

Good listeners pay attention. Paying attention requires that: 1) The listener be *mentally* engaged to hear and understand what the speaker is saying, and 2) the listener signal this engagement *physically* to encourage the speaker to continue. Paying attention, especially in a professional context, cannot be successful without both elements.

§ 3-2(a)(1). Paying Attention Physically

The lawyer who refuses to make eye contact, who fiddles with other papers, or who answers the phone during an interview signals to the client that the client's story is not important. Not only does this inhibit the client from fully confiding in the lawyer, it also makes it difficult for the lawyer to hear the important parts of the client's story.

The acronym S-O-L-E-R represents an easy way to remember how to physically signal that you are listening to the client.[2]

---

[1] MARK K. SCHOENFIELD & BARBARA P. SCHOENFIELD, INTERVIEWING AND COUNSELING 2 (1981).

[2] This device and the following descriptions are adapted from GERARD EGAN, YOU & ME: THE SKILLS OF COMMUNICATING AND RELATING TO OTHERS 114-116 (1977).

S: Face the client SQUARELY.

Turn your body toward the client. By doing this you tell the client that you are listening and that you value what the client is saying. Arrange your office so that you can easily face the client during an interview.

O: Adopt an OPEN posture toward the client.

Crossing your arms or legs signals that you are not receptive to what the client is saying. These postures indicate to clients that you have already made up your mind about them or their situation. Physical objects can also interfere with the communication between you and the client. Interviewing a client across a desk littered with books, pens, and other objects sends a different message than an interviewing space that places no objects between lawyers and clients.

L: LEAN toward the client.

Leaning slightly toward your client signals your involvement in his story, whereas leaning back in your chair, putting your feet up on the desk, and placing your arms behind your head all signal a detachment from the client's story. At the same time, leaning in too close to the client intrudes into the client's privacy. A distance of between two and three feet seems to be optimal for most people in the United States. Any closer makes people uncomfortable and any farther away makes people feel ignored.

E: Make and keep good EYE contact.

Looking at the client's eyes shows your readiness and interest in the client's story. However, appropriate eye contact is not the same as an unblinking stare into the client's eyes. Rather, it requires a moderate focus on the client's eyes and includes shifting your gaze to other parts of the client's face. When appropriate, the lawyer may look away or look down at her paper to take notes. But the lawyer should always return to making eye contact. Once again, moderation is the key. Clients will become uncomfortable if the lawyer never takes her gaze away from the client's eyes. This is the functional equivalent of leaning too closely to the client. On the other hand, a client will feel neglected if the lawyer seldom looks up from an intake form or notepad.

R: Be RELAXED during the interview.

People look relaxed when they are comfortable in their environment and with the task they are performing. Acting naturally conveys a confidence in your abilities. It also helps put the client at ease. However, being relaxed is not the same as being casual. The balance you should seek is between the formal and the casual. Being unnaturally formal or casual equally affects the communication from the client. People feel freer to speak about difficult matters when they are comfortable with the person to whom they are speaking.

§ 3-2(a)(2). Paying Attention Mentally by Active Listening

People tend to speak at a rate of 125 words per minute in normal conversation. We can listen at approximately four times that rate, however.[3] As we listen our minds typically are attending to a variety of other things. Good communication uses this "excess capacity" to attend to those things that will make our legal interview successful. We call this "Active Listening."[4] In general,

> active listening requires a constant analysis of the conversation's contents to decide whether the information is important and accurate. Even if the information is not accurate, it may be a significant indication of the client's psychological position. . . . [The lawyer should pay attention to] what was said and what was left unsaid, silences, and body language.[5]

Active listening also requires attention to the emotional content of the client's story. Thomas Shaffer and James Elkins remind us that "feelings are facts."

> [While] counseling decisions are influenced by what is loosely called "legal thinking," they are not confined to it. . . . Law office decisions proceed as much from subjective emotional factors as from rules of law. This is also, often, the case with decisions by judges or legislators — but the subjective is more obvious [in counseling], because it is not hidden in procedure and rational explanation. Counseling decisions often clearly proceed from feelings. . . . [6]

§ 3-2(b). ACTIVELY LISTENING TO THE CLIENT'S NONVERBAL MESSAGES

Begin listening actively by paying attention to the client's nonverbal behavior as well as the client's actual words.[7] Nonverbal behavior can deny or affirm what the client is saying.

It is easier to understand nonverbal messages if we first isolate the different ways that people can communicate without speaking. People send nonverbal messages with their bodies, the characteristics of their voices, and the way they use the space they are in.[8]

---

[3] MICHAEL MELTSNER & PHILIP G. SCHRAG, PUBLIC INTEREST ADVOCACY: MATERIALS FOR CLINICAL LEGAL EDUCATION 126 (1974).

[4] Some texts define active listening to include what we call "Reflective Statements." By distinguishing the two, we want to emphasize that "active listening" involves listening to the client, whereas "reflective statements" involve speaking to the client. They each require different skills.

[5] SCHOENFIELD & SCHOENFIELD, supra note 1, at 2.

[6] THOMAS L. SHAFFER & JAMES R. ELKINS, LEGAL INTERVIEWING AND COUNSELING 8 (1997).

[7] EGAN, supra note 2, at 117.

[8] This description and the information that follows is adapted from WILLIAM H. CORMIER & L. SHERILYN CORMIER, INTERVIEWING STRATEGIES FOR HELPERS 66 (3d ed. 1991). Cormier and Cormier use the terms kinesics (body movement), paralinguistics (vocal quality), and proxemics (the use of space). They add two other categories: environment and time. These aspects are covered indirectly in Chapters 4 and 5 and are not included here.

§ 3-2(b)(1). Body Language

People send nonverbal messages primarily in the use of their mouths, faces, head, limbs, and arrangement of their total body. Someone who purses her lips or folds her arms may be signaling discomfort. We use our bodies to express a variety of messages, often very subtly.

§ 3-2(b)(2). Eyes

A person's eyes can be very expressive. He can send a number of messages using his eyes, eyebrows, etc. We must, however, be cautious how we interpret those messages. A lack of eye contact may indicate that the person is uncomfortable or embarrassed. However, in some cultures, lack of eye contact is a sign of respect or an affirmation of a difference in status or gender. It does not necessarily mean that the person is not truthful.[9] People may also avert their eyes when talking, but look up when they want a response to their statements.

Most people move their eyes away from the other person's face periodically. Shifting the gaze may mean the person is thinking about what to say, forming words, or trying to recall some event or information. Quickly shifting the gaze from the person to other objects can indicate agitation.

While lack of eye contact does not correlate with deception, excessive blinking may. Blinking more than normal indicates that the person is anxious.[10] Anxiety may result because a client is not telling the truth. At the same time, it could also be due to the circumstances in which the client finds himself, for example the anxiety of speaking to a lawyer. Remember, blood pressure tends to be higher when measured in the doctor's office than when measured at home.

In general, certain factors seem connected with more or less eye contact.[11] More eye contact results when the parties are farther apart physically, when the discussion concerns less personal subjects, when two people interact naturally, and when one is listening to another speak. There seems to be less eye contact when the two people are closer together physically or when they are discussing difficult, embarrassing, shameful, or personal topics.

§ 3-2(b)(3). Facial Expressions

The total facial expression — eyes, mouth, cheeks, eyebrows, head — accurately conveys our emotional state. However, parts of our faces specialize in certain emotions. The mouth and jaw generally communicate happiness, surprise, and disgust, whereas the eyes are better at communicating anger. Combinations of facial features communicate more complex emotional states.

---

[9] *Id.* at 71.

[10] *Id.* Blinking between 6-10 times per minute is considered normal for an adult.

[11] *Id.*

Facial expression tends to support other nonverbal emotional indicators. For example, clients who walk into lawyers' offices with slumped shoulders, pursed lips, and dull expressions are pretty clearly saying that they are not happy! Visiting a lawyer is a stressful event for many people that has often been prompted by another stressful event. These postures signal that stress.

§ 3-2(b)(4). Using Knowledge of Body Language

Lawyers should not use their knowledge of body language to become amateur psychologists. There may be no reason to confront clients with the fact that their body language indicates that they are uncomfortable. The important thing is to be able to recognize their discomfort. Knowing of a client's discomfort alerts the lawyer that the client finds a particular topic uncomfortable. Depending on the context, the lawyer may want to avoid the topic or approach it more delicately. Nonverbal signals may also signal that the client is uncomfortable with the attorney. Attorneys should remember that trust is built. They should not assume that clients trust them simply because of their status. It may be necessary to discuss the client's discomfort openly.

In addition, knowing how to read body language enhances the accuracy of communication between the lawyer and the client and also leads to better decisions. For example, suppose the lawyer and client are discussing whether or not to accept a particular settlement offer. Consider the phrase "Sure, I can accept their offer." If the client says those words without pausing and while looking directly into the lawyers eyes, the lawyer can be confident that the client wants to accept the offer. In contrast, suppose the client says the same words while shifting her gaze around the room and blinking rapidly: "Sure [pause] I . . . I . . . can [pause] accept their [pause] offer." Here, the lawyer should recognize the client's hesitation and explore the client's misgivings before moving forward with the settlement offer.

§ 3-2 (c). USING KNOWLEDGE OF PSYCHOLOGICAL TYPE

Some of the nonverbal and body language differences we see across clients may be related to psychological type differences. Chapter 12 gives an in depth explanation of this theory, but we want to alert you to some common differences you may observe. There are two ways of directing one's energy and processing information, externally by talking and internally by thinking and reflecting. We all use both processes even within one interview or counseling session, but we prefer to use one more often and have more energy when using one of these processes than when using the other. This preference influences clients' communication to lawyers and the ways clients receive information from their lawyers. Clients who prefer to extravert may be quite anxious to tell their story and jump right into an interview. These clients may use a lot of nonverbal communication, particularly through using their hands to accompany their speech. They are likely to have told this story many times before telling their lawyer and may benefit from questions that take them to the context of the conflict and to parts of a sequence they may not realize they have skipped. These clients may seem to tell you more than you want to know, but watch for parts of their stories that they may skip over as unimportant or that put them in an embarrassing position.

Clients who prefer to introvert may pause to reflect as they tell their story. Be patient and use encouraging statements like 'tell me more about . . .' to prompt their telling of the events. Be aware that they may tell you less than you want to know because they are more likely to censor what they say. They may be telling you parts of their story for the first time and the less you anticipate what they may say and the more you reflect their content and feelings, the more rapport you will build and the more accurate and complete your interview will be.

There are other influences of psychological type on interviewing and counseling. A very detailed, sequential accounting may indicate a sensing preference that signals a lawyer to ask practical and pragmatic questions. Focusing on direct experiences gains the most information. Clients with intuitive preferences may tell their stories differently, giving a general overview and then skipping from one topic to another as they build the components of the story, its context, and their future concerns. As they talk, one event or detail may remind them of another part of the story. As they jump from one part to another, it may be difficult for a lawyer to follow. However, if they can tell their story in their own way once, a lawyer may find it helpful to impose a time line to get a better idea of the sequencing of the events and this time line may actually spark more important memories of events. These clients appreciate a summary of what the lawyer has heard and any preliminary ideas the lawyer has of a theory of their case.

Psychological type theory gives insight not only into client tendencies, but also to ways that lawyers communicate to clients and others. Awareness of these tendencies can help lawyers increase the effectiveness of their communication with clients and clients' communication to them.

Good communicators do not focus excessively on one aspect of the client's message. Rather, they integrate all aspects of the communication while they listen. They pay attention to body language and the content of the communication. They pay attention to the client's emotional language and the quality of the information the client conveys. They neither read too much nor too little into the client's words and actions. They consider the context of the client's communication and the person of the client, that is, they understand both the immediate and long term context of the conversation. Suppose a client avoids eye contact with the attorney and discloses little information without prompting. These behaviors may mean something different when the client is a teenager who has never been to a lawyer before as compared to an adult businessman who is an experienced user of the legal system.

§ 3-3. BUILDING RAPPORT

Active listening helps build rapport with the client. Good rapport helps build a relationship of mutual trust typified by cooperation, understanding, and responsiveness. Good rapport arises when the lawyer and the client genuinely respect and trust one another.[12] The client trusts the lawyer's professional competence and sensitivity, and the lawyer trusts and respects the client's judgment and input. Good rapport is necessary to enable the client to fully confide in the lawyer and for the lawyer to more fully appreciate the client's story.

§ 3-3(a). MIRRORING

§ 3-3(a)(1). Mirroring the Client

People can learn how to build rapport. One simple technique is to mirror, to an appropriate degree, the client's posture, movement, and emotion. This does not mean the lawyer should imitate everything the client does. Lawyers should not mimic a nervous client. The key here is for the lawyer's posture, voice, etc., to remain congruent, not identical, with the client's. The more congruent the lawyer and the client are, the easier it becomes for the client and the lawyer to communicate effectively. The lawyer should not adopt a casual posture with a nervous client who sits rigidly in his chair. Similarly, the lawyer should avoid speaking in a booming voice to a soft-spoken client.

§ 3-3(a)(2). Mirroring the Client's Language

Mirroring the client's language when discussing the client's case also builds rapport. Accurately restating the important parts of the client's story in the client's own words tells the client that the lawyer is listening and that what the client says is important. A good listener will fill in the listening-speaking gap by mirroring client movements and by planning how to mirror the client's language later in the conversation.

However, mirroring means more than adopting the client's way of speaking. Successful mirroring involves using language that fits with the way the client understands the world. People have a characteristic way of perceiving the world. They may primarily understand the world visually, aurally, physically, emotionally, or cognitively. They convey this understanding in the words they use to describe themselves or events or by emphasizing certain aspects of their stories.

For example, the visually oriented client may relate everything he saw and use visual language to do so. This client focuses on what the participants looked like or what they were doing. He may leave out the actual

---

[12] ROBERT M. BASTRESS & JOSEPH D. HARBAUGH, INTERVIEWING, COUNSELING AND NEGOTIATING: SKILLS FOR EFFECTIVE REPRESENTATION 66-67 (1990).

words of the participants. On the other hand, the aurally oriented client may relate everything the participants said and use sound-related words to describe events. This client may leave out visual details.

The physically oriented client may explain what things looked, smelled, or felt like, but he will exclude aural and visual details. He may remember whether or not the room was cold, but not what people said or did. The emotionally oriented client may relate the emotional content of the event (whether or not it was tense, happy, etc.) or describe the relationships among the participants. This client may exclude the physical details of the setting. Last, the cognitively oriented person may process everything in objective, impersonal terms. He may remember the rules that were followed or broken and the principles at stake, but he may be unaware of the emotional context in which these activities happened.

People respond better when others communicate with them using their primary process. Thus, a client who primarily uses visual images to explain his story will respond better to the attorney who says, "Do you see what I mean?", rather than to the attorney who says, "Do you understand what I said?" The first example uses a visual metaphor to ask the question while the second uses an aural metaphor.

This can be particularly useful regardless of whether the lawyer is responding to the client or asking for information. For example, the lawyer might respond to the visually oriented client by saying, "I can *see* why that conversation with your boss upset you." When the time comes to explore the client's story further, the lawyer can say, "Let's go back to when you saw your boss on the elevator. *Paint me a picture of exactly what happened* during that elevator ride." The aurally oriented client may respond better if the lawyer says, "You were upset when your boss *said* those things to you. Later, the lawyer can say, "Let's go back to when you *talked* to your boss in the elevator. *Tell me everything you remember he said to you* during that elevator ride." Similarly, the emotionally oriented client may prefer the following approach: "You *felt unfairly singled out* when your boss said those things to you." And later, the lawyer could say, "Let's go back to when you and your boss met in the elevator. Tell me *how he acted toward you* during that elevator ride." The lawyer is more likely to get accurate and detailed information by using statements and asking questions that mirror the client's primary cognitive mode.

The following chart summarizes the above discussion. The chart contains the emphases of each process, words and phrases related to the different ways of perceiving the world, omissions, and ways that the lawyer can mirror the client's process.

Process	Emphasis	Key words and phrases	Omission	Response
Visual	Visual details: what the client saw.	It *seems* to me a . . . ; That was a *clear* breach of contract; *Look* at how they treated me; Do you *see* what my children mean to me?	What people said.	"Paint me a picture . . ."
Aural	Aural details: what people said and what the client heard.	It sounded like they wanted to fire me; *Listen* to what they *said* to me; Let me *tell* you what I *heard*.	What people looked like; what they did.	"Tell me what he said to you."
Physical	Sensory details: descriptions using one or more of the five senses.	I *sensed* they wanted to fire me; I *felt* that was breach of contract.	Verbal details; emotional content.	"Describe what it was like at the meeting."
Emotional	Relationship details or a focus on values: emotions the client or others felt.	I was *hurt* when they fired me; I was not treated *fairly*.	Other details, especially physical and cognitive ones.	"How did he act toward you?"
Cognitive	Focus on rules or principles involved: neutral, objective descriptions of events.	They broke the *rules*; This is what *happened*.	Emotional context, possibly physical details.	"What happened during the meeting?"

There may be some value to phrasing questions in modes that the client does not prefer. This may be helpful when the lawyer needs information that has not been disclosed through the client's primary process. For example, many cases require specific details concerning events that a client may not readily remember. The lawyer may jog the client's memory by phrasing a question in a way that taps a different process. We will discuss this and other issues in more detail in Chapters 5 and 6.

§ 3-4.   WHAT TO AVOID

§ 3-4(a).   PROFESSIONAL BLINDNESS

A lawyer may be sensitive to the client and capable of framing questions and statements, but the lawyer's overall orientation to the client and the client's case may render all of these skills ineffective.

As the authors of a classic legal interviewing text put it:

> The chief danger that confronts a professional, in law or in any other field, is that he will tend to fill the gap with related informational material from other similar situations in his experience. Or, he may leap ahead and begin to anticipate information that may or may not actually be involved in the situation that now confronts him.
>
> In short, the situation becomes clouded by what the attorney brings to it that the client has not imparted to it. Unless the attorney is extremely careful, in a very short time *he will have reduced a unique set of facts to a standard pattern.* This pattern inevitably will be at least somewhat different from the situation that the client is trying to convey. *The more experienced and intelligent the attorney, the greater the danger that the gap (between what is being said and what actually registers in the attorney's mind) will be a large and unbridgeable one.*[13]

This tendency to reduce "a unique set of facts to a standard pattern" shows itself in what we call "Hardening of the Categories."

§ 3-4(b).   HARDENING OF THE CATEGORIES

Hardening of the categories happens when the lawyer prematurely forces the client's case into a legal category. Professor Carrie Menkel-Meadow captures the essence of this process in the following description:

> [T]he grievant tells a story of felt or perceived wrong to a third party (a lawyer) and the lawyer transforms the dispute by imposing "categories" on "events and relationships" which redefine the subject matter of dispute in ways "which make it amenable to conventional management procedures." This process of "narrowing" disputes occurs at various stages in lawyer-client interactions. . . . First, the lawyer may begin to narrow the dispute in the initial client interview. By asking questions which derive from the lawyer's repertoire of what is likely to be legally relevant, the lawyer defines the situation from the very beginning. Rather than permitting the client to tell a story freely to define what the dispute consists of, the lawyer begins to categorize the case as a "tort," "contract," or "property" dispute so that questions may be asked for legal saliency.[14]

---

[13] MELVIN S. HELLER, ESTHER POLEN & SAMUEL POLSKY, AN INTRODUCTION TO LEGAL INTERVIEWING AND COUNSELING 11 (1960).

[14] Carrie Menkel-Meadow, *The Transformation of Disputes by Lawyers: What the Dispute Paradigm Does and Does Not Tell Us,* 1985 MO. J. DISP. RESOL. 25, 31.

Often, the lawyer has some advance knowledge about the reason for the client's visit. The lawyer may reach a "tentative" conclusion about possible remedies based on this preliminary information. This tentative conclusion may then color what the lawyer pays attention to during the client interview. The lawyer will hear those elements of the client's story that confirm his tentative conclusion and ignore any elements of the client's story that do not.[15]

Clients can also influence the lawyer toward hardening of the categories. Clients may express what they want in conclusory terms. When asked why the client wants to see the lawyer, the prospective client may respond in terms he or she believes the lawyer wants to hear. Instead of giving a functional description of his goals, the client will give a legal conclusion. For example, the client may respond that he wants to file bankruptcy instead of saying that he is having a problem paying his bills. The danger is that when the lawyer hears the word "bankruptcy," the lawyer will place the client's case into the bankruptcy category. Once this happens, the lawyer may be unable to "hear" the client talk anything except bankruptcy talk.

§ 3-5. VERBALLY RESPONDING TO THE CLIENT

Effective interviewers have a purpose for everything they say and do. Responding to the client with statements or questions is not a random activity. Rather, effective interviewers know what they want to accomplish and they use statements and questions to accomplish their goals. The following sections will explore different ways to respond to clients and will explain the strengths and weaknesses of these different responses. Chapters 4, 5, and 6 will show how to use these different responses in the course of a legal interview.

Gerard Egan says, "The ultimate proof of good listening is good responding."[16] Egan contrasts the good listener who is capable of responding intelligently with the "hollow listener:"

Often when people say "I am a good listener," what their statement means is that:

- they don't respond by evaluating or judging what others have to say;

- they pay attention to the person speaking and they look involved;

- they indicate their involvement by nodding their heads, by good physical attending, by saying such things as "uh-huh" or "yeah";

- they sometimes respond with such cliches as "I understand" or "I think I understand."[17]

---

[15] *See* Leonard L. Riskin, *Mediation And Lawyers,* 43 OHIO ST. L.J. 29, 43-48 (1982).

[16] EGAN, *supra* note 2, at 137.

[17] *Id.*

Communicating well entails more than the kind of hollow listening described above. When a lawyer responds to a client with intelligence, understanding, and sensitivity it helps to create a climate of trust.[18] Effective communication requires the lawyer to listen carefully to the client's entire message, to identify precisely the content (cognitive and affective) of that message, and to respond in a way that shows understanding.[19]

This section outlines basic communication tools that make it easier to communicate effectively with the client. The tools are divided into two types: responsive statements and questions. Both types of responses focus a lawyer on a client's story because the lawyer must respond with a summary or a reflection. These responses keep the lawyer focused on the client instead of on the next thing the lawyer wants to say.

Responsive statements use the client's statements as the basis for the lawyer's reply. They build on something the client has said or implied. They either clarify something the client has said, reflect feeling or content back to the client, or paraphrase something the client has said.

Questions ask for more information about a topic the client already discussed or for information about a subject the client has not discussed yet. They also explore what the client said by searching for more detail.

§ 3-5(a).   RESPONSIVE STATEMENTS

§ 3-5(a)(1).   Clarification Responses

The clarification response is straightforward. The lawyer simply asks the client to clarify or explain something the client said. Ideally, it takes the form of a short question by the lawyer followed by a repetition of what the client said. Here are some examples:

- Tell me more about the day you were fired.

- Do you mean that you were fired when you returned from pregnancy leave?

- What did your supervisor say to you on the elevator?

Using clarification responses benefits the lawyer in two ways. First, it promotes good listening. Framing effective clarification statements requires the lawyer to listen carefully to what the client said and focus the clarification request on a specific ambiguity in the client's statement. Notice how the above examples focus on specific events surrounding the client's job termination.

Second, clarification responses increase the lawyer's knowledge and understanding of the client's story. Effective clarification responses verify

---

[18] *Id.* at 135.

[19] *Id.* at 137.

the accuracy of the lawyer's understanding, ascertain the existence of certain facts, or make explicit something that the client implied. The lawyer should verify his understanding before moving on to other aspects of the interview. Not only is it more efficient to do so, it also builds better rapport with the client because the lawyer is letting the client know that the lawyer has been paying attention.

§ 3-5(a)(2).   Reflective Statements

While some authors refer to reflective statements as active listening, this book uses the term "reflective statements" narrowly. "Reflective statements" are comments a lawyer makes that reflect back to the client something the client said or felt. It also refers to lawyer summaries of the client's story.

This is an important communication skill for several reasons. First, it shows the client that the lawyer is really listening. When a lawyer accurately restates something the client said, it shows respect for the client, helps establish rapport, and encourages the client to speak freely and fully in the future. Second, it helps clarify factual information. Restating what the lawyer heard allows the lawyer to check the accuracy of the client's statements, and it allows the client to correct any misunderstandings. Third, reflecting the emotional content of the client's story helps the lawyer understand how important certain aspects of the case are to the client. This helps the lawyer mirror the client's language and values, thus enhancing rapport. In addition, it helps the lawyer frame alternatives and discuss their consequences in a way that will be meaningful to the client.

Reflective statements should be used to

- Clarify what the client said.
- Encourage the client to continue speaking.
- Comfort the client under stress.
- Help the client focus on key issues or events.
- Signal a shift to a different stage of the interview.

§ 3-5(b).   KINDS OF REFLECTIVE STATEMENTS

§ 3-5(b)(1).   Paraphrasing

An effective and accurate paraphrase is an essential component of most reflective statements. This is because most reflective statements paraphrase the client's thoughts or feelings. It is possible to use the client's own words as part of a reflective statement, but this can be counterproductive. Frequently using the client's own words to construct a reflective statement can undermine the rapport being established. For example, a non-lawyer friend was counseling a client. She kept using the client's own words to reflect the content of the conversation back to the client. She hoped that by doing so she was letting the client know that she was paying attention to what she was saying and that what she was saying had value. This went on for a period of time before the client finally declared, "Why are you just repeating what I say? Aren't you listening to me?"

A paraphrase is a restatement of what the client has said. It condenses the client's words and presents them in a slightly different way. Paraphrasing is neither a literal retelling nor a translation. That is, the lawyer should not put the client's story into legal language. For example, a lawyer should avoid responding to a story about the client's dismissal from state employment by saying, "So you think that your supervisor acted under color of state law to violate your civil rights." Instead, the lawyer could say, "You were the first African American in the office and your supervisor gave you the most difficult assignments."

The restatement must contain the essential point, meaning, feeling, or thought expressed by the client. Accuracy is crucial. Accurate paraphrases verify the lawyer's understanding, build rapport with the client, and encourage the client to continue talking. Compare the following statements:

CLIENT: I never got the same kind of challenging assignments that the white workers got.

PARAPHRASE 1:   You didn't get good assignments.

PARAPHRASE 2:   You weren't allowed to do challenging work.

PARAPHRASE 3:   They gave the best jobs to the white workers.

PARAPHRASE 4:   They didn't treat you like the other workers.

PARAPHRASE 5:   They treated you differently than the white workers.

Each of these paraphrases emphasizes a different aspect of the client's statement about job assignments. The first restates the client's statement but omits the possible racial bias in the job assignments. It is likely to be affirmed by the client but may not produce any additional information. The others repeat the essential point the client made and include the element of differential treatment based on race. Not only are these paraphrases more factually accurate, they are more legally and emotionally accurate because they capture more precisely the nature of the client's claim. As such, they are more likely to encourage the client to continue speaking in this vein.

Here is a checklist to follow in putting together an effective paraphrase:

- Remember exactly what the client said.

- Identify the essential content or feeling of what the client said.

- Compress and restate the essential content or feeling.

§ 3-5(b)(2). Reflecting Content Alone

These are relatively brief statements of what the client said to the lawyer. Using the client's own words is most effective when the lawyer reflects back a small bit of important information. On the other hand, paraphrasing is more effective when the lawyer wants to clarify the lawyer's understanding or to encourage the client to continue talking.

§ 3-5(b)(3).   Reflecting Emotion Alone

Like content reflections, emotion reflections are relatively brief but complete statements that reflect the emotional content of the client's conversation. In their simplest forms, they reflect the emotions actually expressed by the client. For example, if a client tells the lawyer that he is "really mad" at his next door neighbor, he has clearly identified a feeling associated with his case. The lawyer appropriately reflects that feeling by saying, "So this problem with your neighbor really gets you angry (or upset, mad, etc.)."

It is more difficult to reflect emotional content that is implicit in the communication or that is not clearly expressed. Here, the lawyer must pay attention to the posture, conduct, language, and demeanor of the client. A client who describes his dispute with neighbor in an agitated tone is likely to be angry. Thus, the lawyer could respond by saying, "You seem very upset by this problem."

§ 3-5(b)(4).   Reflecting Both Content and Emotion

This is a more developed response that requires the lawyer to connect the content of the client's conversation with the emotions associated with it and then to venture some conclusion about the two. For example, the lawyer might say to the client, "You must have felt betrayed when someone you considered a friend did that." If accurate, this kind of statement greatly enhances both rapport and the quality of the communication. If inaccurate, the lawyer runs the risk of harming both.

Lawyers whose psychological type preference is thinking judgment may have to focus harder to recognize and accurately reflect a client's feelings. The objective orientation of the typical lawyer may cause the lawyer to overlook and disregard emotions that may be seen as subjective and outside of reasonable consideration for decision making. Lawyers may consider feelings not as important as the "facts." As the complaint goes, lawyers are not social workers, and therefore lawyers should deal only with the law and facts. Emotions are for psychologists.

This is short sighted, however. A client's emotions influence everything about the case. They may be the primary motivation for seeking legal advice, they may have influenced what the client has done and what the client remembers, and they may determine what the client is willing to accept in settlement. In short, a lawyer who ignores emotions only learns about a part of the case.

Here is a checklist to follow in framing reflective feeling statements:

• *Listen for the emotional content of the client's statements.*

A client may state a feeling while talking to the lawyer. For example, the client may say, "I'm really angry at my supervisor." Stated emotions can fall into seven categories: anger, fear, uncertainty, sadness, happiness, strength, and weakness.[20] Picking out the correct emotion will be easier if the lawyer listens for words that fit into one of these categories.

Often the emotion is camouflaged by the content of the client's statement. The lawyer can pick it out by paying attention to the tone of the client's statement and the client's behavior. As discussed in § 3-2, the way a client delivers a message may be as meaningful as what the client says. Recall that facial expressions, tone of voice, and body placement can tell a great deal about what the client is feeling.

• *Find words that accurately state the client's feeling.*

Do not overstate or understate the feeling. If there is any doubt, it may help to mirror the client's words. If the lawyer chooses a different word, make sure it conveys the feeling in a way the client can understand and appreciate. For example, a lawyer might say to a young person, "You feel pretty dumb about that." That same statement will sound foolish to a sophisticated adult client. The lawyer should also choose a word that accurately conveys the intensity of the feeling. Is the client annoyed, angry, or outraged? Finally, the lawyer can introduce the reflective statement with a statement that mirrors the client's sensory process. The following list matches introductory phrases with the primary process:

Visual:

> It appears that . . .
>
> It looks like . . .
>
> It's clear that you . . .

Aural:

> It sounds like . . .
>
> What I heard you say was . . .

Cognitive:

> I think you are . . .
>
> I wonder if you . . .
>
> It seems that . . .

Emotional:

> You felt . . .

Physical:

> That must have hurt.

• *Put the feeling in context.*

Describe the feeling, but also connect it to the situation that prompted it. For example, suppose a client said with obvious emotion, "He made me

---

[20] *Id.* at 97.

look terrible in front of my co-workers. I stormed out of the room as soon as it happened." The lawyer could respond, "I see (visual) you are still angry (feeling) *about the way you were treated by your supervisor* (context)." The context statement, with few modifications, can be plugged into each of the introductory phrases above.

It may help to place a short qualifying phrase in front of your reflection, especially if you are paraphrasing the client's content or you are suggesting how the client feels. Put some distance between the comment and the lawyer with short phrases like, "It seems to me . . . ," or "If I were you I would have felt . . . ," or "If I understand you correctly. . . ." It then offers the client the opportunity to verify the reflection. Be careful not to use these phrases too often, however. Frequently using such phrases may make the lawyer sound artificial. The client may come to believe that the lawyer is following a script and does not really care about what is being said. Sounding too psychological is another danger of overusing these introductory phrases. The client expects the lawyer to conform to a broad definition of lawyerly conduct. Sounding as though the lawyer is becoming a psychiatrist goes beyond these bounds.

§ 3-5(c).   SUMMARIZING

The summarizing statement is longer and more fully developed than any the statements we have discussed so far. It reflects the main points or themes of the client's story and any significant emotions. It should be succinct, but also comprehensive. It can include combinations of any of the reflective statements discussed above.

Summarizing has several purposes. First, it identifies the themes of the client's case. This can be done either by isolating discrete statements or by tying together disparate strands of the client's story. This helps both the lawyer and the client see aspects of the client's story that may not have emerged otherwise. It puts the pieces of the story together in ways that may not have been obvious. For example, the lawyer might say

> You said that you went to work here because this firm seemed female-friendly, but then they made demands on your time that seemed both excessive and unfair. It got worse after you talked to your supervisor about it. It seemed as though they were giving you all of the bad assignments and making it difficult for you to do your work. Now, you are so disillusioned with them that you are considering filing a lawsuit.

Second, frequent summarizing allows the lawyer to verify manageable amounts of information. It also helps the client break down the story into identifiable bits. Summaries focus the client and the lawyer's attention on the parts of the story so far.

Third, effective summarizing moderates the pace of the interview. It imposes a momentary break in the client's narrative, which gives a breather to both the client and the lawyer. This "breather" may be important for both cognitive and emotional purposes. The client may need to take a break to recall important details or take a break before or after recalling emotionally significant information.

Summaries can indicate transition points in the client's story and signal the client to continue with his or her narrative. A summary for this purpose may sound this way: "You told me that the firm began to make what you considered unfair demands on your time and that these demands increased after you talked to your supervisor. Tell me more about what happened after you first talked with your supervisor."

Summaries are condensations of either the content or the feeling of the client's story. By condensing the story, the lawyer makes it richer in the same way that a chef condenses a liquid to concentrate its flavors. Elements of the story are highlighted and put in sharper relief with other aspects of the story. The summary may allow the lawyer and the client to see how important or unimportant certain matters are. A good summary signals the client to either continue with the rest of the story or that a shift in the interview is about to occur (e.g., that the lawyer may need to ask some clarifying questions, etc.). For example, the lawyer may summarize the client's story by saying: "What I understand so far is that you and Mr. Smith have been neighbors for 15 years and you have always gotten along well. When you came home from work last week, you found him building a wall along a line that you believe extends three feet onto your property. When you asked him about it, he cursed you and said that he was tired of all the noise from your kids. Is that right?"

Listen for matters that the client emphasizes either by repetition, intensity of feeling, or placement in the conversation. These are clues to what the client considers important. These are the themes of the client's story. Often the client will present the important theme of his or her case during the opening moments of the interview.[21] At other times, the client will highlight his or her themes by returning to a certain item again and again during the interview. Finally, the theme may emerge by virtue of the client's emotions that are attached to certain items.

An effective summary requires three steps:

• *Organize the elements of the client's story for presentation in the summary.*

Consider what elements to include in a summary and the order in which they will be presented. Frequently summarizing the client's story makes this task easier.

• *Choose an appropriate tone for the summary.*

A cold summary of the facts after the client has just given a heart-rending story will leave the client hurt and cold. Try to match the summary to the emotional tone of the client's story even if the summary is about facts.

---

[21] *See* Gay Gellhorn, *Law and Language: An Empirically Based Model for the Opening Moments of Client Interviews,* 4 CLINICAL L. REV. 321 (1998).

● *Select the appropriate time for the summary.*

Summaries run the risk of stopping the client's narrative and sidetracking the client from matters the client considers important.[22] Therefore, reserve summaries for moments when they can accomplish their purpose. Summarize after hearing a lot of cognitive or emotional information, or when the client seems to have reached the end of his or her narrative. Use a summary when it is time to move to a different stage of the interview,[23] and tie the summary into a short statement telling the client what will happen next. For example, the lawyer could conclude this kind of summary by saying: "Now let's go back and explore in more detail what happened after your first conversation with the supervisor. Tell me what kind of assignments he gave you and what he said when he gave them to you."[24]

§ 3-5(d). SILENCE

Silence can be an effective response. Lawyers sometimes feel that every blank space in a conversation must be filled with sound. They are afraid that the client will not consider them competent if they remain silent for any extended time. However, silence can be appropriate in many situations. For instance, silence may be the correct response while a client is divulging a difficult and emotionally traumatic event. It can be useful when the client simply pauses in her narrative to collect her thoughts before continuing. Finally, silence may be the right response when the lawyer wants the client to continue and wishes the client to choose the direction to take.

Like everything discussed in this book, the effective use of silence requires the exercise of sound professional judgment. Effective interviewers know when to use silence by assessing the context of the conversation, the client's emotional state, and the stage of the interview. Silences may be more effective later in the interview — after the client has had the opportunity to trust the lawyer and has begun to reveal important information. Silences may be less effective in the early stages of an interview — before the client understands the interview process or develops any rapport with the lawyer.

§ 3-6. ASKING QUESTIONS

Alfred Benjamin remarked that interviewers "apparently reason that since asking questions is good, the more they ask the better."[25] There is a danger that by asking a number of questions one after another, the client is "taught" that the lawyer is in control of the interview. Clients will simply sit back and wait for the lawyer to ask for information instead of actively volunteering it.

---

[22] *See* Chapter 4 on Beginning the Legal Interview.

[23] *See* Chapter 5 on Hearing the Client's Story.

[24] *See* Chapter 6 on Developing the Client's Story.

[25] Alfred Benjamin, The Helping Interview 71 (3d ed. 1981).

[The conversation] develops a rhythm of a question-answer, question-answer, question-answer, somewhat like a Ping-Pong match. Once this tempo has been established, it is usually difficult for either the interviewer or the client to break.[26]

Lawyers naturally gravitate toward asking questions. Law students are subjected to questions from the first day of law school. Popular culture celebrates the trial lawyer who asks the incisive series of questions designed to reveal the "Truth" *a la* Perry Mason. The problem is that asking too many questions undermines the twin purposes of legal interviews: gathering information and building rapport. The questions posed during the Socratic method and cross-examination have little relevance during the legal interview.

Since only clients know the facts and their importance, "such question-and-answer sessions usually stay at the superficial level and deal only with what is obvious. They are also often characterized by a certain sense of randomness and a 'hit-or-miss' flavor."[27]

Effective legal interviewers know when to ask a question and what kind of question to ask. This section explores the various forms of questions that can be asked, the kind and amount of information they are likely to obtain, and their advantages and disadvantages. In general, as to a topic of inquiry, it is best to ask questions in the reverse of the order in which we describe questions below; it is best to move from open questions to closed questions.

§ 3-6(a). CLOSED-ENDED QUESTIONS

Closed-ended questions are narrowly focused and seek specific information. Here are some examples:

What did Mr. Smith say to you?

Who else attended that meeting?

When did you first see this memo?

Where did this accident happen?

How fast were you going?

As you can see, these questions ask the client to relate specific facts. These are prototypical closed questions because they ask for who, what, where, when, and how. Closed-ended questions do not have to appear in this form, however. Any question that narrows the focus of the answer falls into this category.

The advantage of a closed-ended question is efficiency. Because it narrows the focus of the client's answer, the lawyer is likely to acquire the information the lawyer is looking for. Closed-ended questions also allow the lawyer to control the topic if necessary.

---

[26] ANTHONY G. ATHOS & JOHN J. GABARRO, INTERPERSONAL BEHAVIOR: COMMUNICATION AND UUNDERSTANDING IN RELATIONSHIPS 422 (1978).

[27] *Id.*

On the other hand, closed-ended questions have several disadvantages. Because of their narrow focus, they may cause the client to neglect other important details. Closed questions divert the client's attention from what the client considers important to what the lawyer considers important. They are necessarily framed from the lawyer's perspective because they ask for specific bits of information. Although there are times when this diversion may be necessary, effective counselors limit these times to a minimum.

Closed questions also run the risk of distorting the client's recall. This may happen for two reasons. First, the question may suggest the answer. Even if the question is not a leading question, the narrow focus of a closed question often suggests the scope of the answer. Second, the question may encourage the client to give the answer that the client believes the lawyer wants to hear. All of us want other people to think well of us. Thus, when a person in authority asks a question, the person responding may answer in a way that he thinks will cause the one in authority to think well of him. This is not deliberate deception. Rather, it is a natural response to another person. A client is likely to respond to narrow questions in the manner that he thinks the lawyer wants.

Finally, closed questions may also inhibit rapport. Continually subjecting the client to the equivalent of cross-examination and never letting the client control the flow of the conversation eventually takes its toll. If questions are asked aggressively, with hostility, or suspiciously, they will surely invite the client to respond defensively. Even when questions do not have these characteristics, continual questioning undermines the client's trust for the lawyer because it introduces an evaluative tone to the relationship.[28] Clients may think that something a lawyer does not ask a question about is not important. Clients in this situation may eventually assert their feelings of powerlessness and loss of control by withholding information, becoming indecisive, or refusing to cooperate with the lawyer.

The correct time for closed questions is when the lawyer needs to nail down precise details or confirm a specific fact. When in doubt, effective counselors opt for open questions over closed questions.

§ 3-6(b). OPEN-ENDED QUESTIONS

Open-ended questions broadly focus the client's answer. They give the client more control of the topics to be discussed, their sequence, and the amount of information revealed. Here are some examples:

How can I help you?

Tell me about your goals for the partnership.

How did you feel when that happened?

What happened at the meeting?

How will your children react if you get into a custody battle with your wife?

---

[28] *See id.*

Notice that even open questions limit the scope of the answer somewhat. In fact, it would be impossible to conduct an effective legal interview using open questions that do not narrow the focus of the answer. The difference between an open and a closed question is really one of degree. Although the open question may focus the client on a particular time, place, person, or event, it gives the client control over the answer. If a lawyer asks, "What happened at the meeting?", the client chooses how to respond — which topic to introduce first, the sequence of those topics in the client's narrative, and how much to say about each of them. In addition, it encourages the client to go beyond one word answers.

On the other hand, a closed question — e.g., "Who talked first at the meeting?" — gives the lawyer control of the topic and the sequence. In addition, it invites a limited response — "Karen spoke first." Further exploration of the subject will depend on additional questions by the lawyer.

The form of an open question leads to distinctive kinds of answers:

- "What" questions invite the client to respond with facts;

- "How" questions elicit sequences or emotions;

- "When" and "Where" questions reveal answers relating to time and place;

- "Who" questions invite answers about people; and

- "Why" questions solicit reasons for certain actions or events.[29]

Of course, there is no magic at work here. A question that begins with one of the above words can be open or closed depending on what follows that first word. Effective interviewers are aware of the information they need and phrase their questions appropriately.

§ 3-6(c). GENERAL GUIDELINES FOR USING OPEN AND CLOSED QUESTIONS

§ 3-6(c)(1). The Advantages and Disadvantages of Each Type of Question

Open questions produce more accurate information than closed questions. A study of police interview techniques revealed that the accuracy of information gathered in an interview declined as the number of questions increased.[30] Moreover, the amount of information recalled was optimized when the witness was not interrupted by frequent questions.[31]

Open questions build rapport by enhancing the client's role in the interview. Alfred Benjamin noted that interviewers can condition the client to a certain mode of participation:

---

[29] WILLIAM H. CORMIER & L. SHERILYN CORMIER, INTERVIEWING STRATEGIES FOR HELPERS 113 (3d ed. 1991).

[30] Ronald P. Fisher, *Interviewing Victims and Witnesses of Crimes,* 1 PSYCHOL. PUB. POL'Y & L. 732 (1995).

[31] *Id.*

> [I]f we begin the helping interview by asking questions and getting answers, asking more questions and getting more answers, we are setting up a pattern from which neither we nor surely the interviewee will be able to extricate himself. By offering him no alternative we shall be teaching him that in this situation it is up to us to ask the questions and up to him to answer them.[32]

Open questions are also more efficient because they produce a great deal of important information in a shorter period of time.[33]

One of the authors of a book on interviewing in business settings summarized the advantages of open questions this way:

> I have often sat through meetings in which the interviewer's questions actively prevented the other person from giving the relevant answers. This was because all the questions were from the "asker's" frame of reference, and the asker did not know enough about the other person's situation to ask relevant questions. In most of these situations, the questioner would have received his answers more quickly and with less frustration if he had just shut up and listened long enough to hear how the other person described his situation.[34]

An open question may be inappropriate if the lawyer needs only a specific bit of information. They may encourage laziness in the lawyer if the lawyer relies on client narrative for all of the information about the case. They may inhibit rapport if the client believes that the lawyer is not paying attention to his story.

§ 3-6(c)(2). Asking these Questions in Context

The advantages and disadvantages of both open and closed questions can not be assessed in a vacuum. The advantage of one form of question may be a disadvantage in a different context or at a different stage of the interview. Moreover, interviews will have varied purposes which may suggest the use of one kind of question over another.

§ 3-6(c)(3). Summary

Asking open-ended questions is useful in these situations:

- At the beginning of an interview (or during its early stages).

- When the lawyer does not know either the purpose of the client's visit or the nature of the legal problem.

- When the lawyer is undertaking a new line of inquiry in the course of the interview.

---

[32] ALFRED BENJAMIN, THE HELPING INTERVIEW 72 (3d ed. 1981).

[33] DAVID A. BINDER & SUSAN C. PRICE, LEGAL INTERVIEWING AND COUNSELING: A CLIENT-CENTERED APPROACH 74 (1977).

[34] ANTHONY G. ATHOS & JOHN J. GABARRO, INTERPERSONAL BEHAVIOR: COMMUNICATION AND UNDERSTANDING IN RELATIONSHIPS 422 (1977).

- When the lawyer is interviewing a new client.

- When time is not a factor.

Asking closed-ended questions is useful when the lawyer needs:

- To obtain specific information.

- To quickly clarify something the client said.

- To narrow the focus of the interview.

- To explore the applicability of alternative theories to the client's case.

- To focus on specific aspects of the client's story.

The following are guidelines for effective questioning:

- Ask questions based on what the client said or on the client's concerns and not on the lawyer's curiosity.

- Pause after asking a question to give the client time to respond.

- Ask questions clearly.

- Ask one question at a time.

- Use questions intentionally, i.e., to achieve a specific purpose, rather than randomly.

§ 3-6(d).   LEADING QUESTIONS

Leading questions present special problems. Although these are excellent for cross-examination, they are generally ineffective in legal interviewing. They exacerbate the disadvantages of closed questions. They greatly narrow the focus of the question by suggesting the answer. They rob the client of any control of the topic, the sequence, or the amount of information conveyed. Moreover, they pose the very real risk of distorting the recall of the client. By suggesting the answer, they may cause an otherwise truthful client to unconsciously alter his memory to conform to the suggested answer. The client already inclined to lie will not need much encouragement.

Consider the following sequence from an actual case:

Q: Did you make statements to the police?

A: Nope. They couldn't get anything from me.

Q: Good. And they took you back to this house in the police car?

A: Yeah.

Q: And that's when the two witnesses identified you?

A: (Nods affirmatively).

In fact, the client had made damaging admissions to the police during the ride to the house, and the identification at the house could have been challenged if the lawyer had been made aware of some additional facts.[35] The leading questions caused the lawyer to get a distorted version of the facts.

Nevertheless, leading questions have some usefulness in legal interviews. They may prompt a client to continue talking when the client is unsure if he or she should continue. They may also help to verify information that the client has already given. The suggested answer should involve a fact that is not crucial to the case or a fact that the lawyer is certain exists.

Here are some examples:

You felt angry when your husband left, didn't you?

You didn't say anything to the other driver, did you?

You quit your job the next day, right?

The car hit you as you were turning left?

Leading questions may also help clients discuss difficult material or talk about things they may not consider important. Consider the following excerpt from an interview where the lawyer suspected that the client was minimizing the seriousness of her injury:

CLIENT: It didn't hurt much — I was back at work in a few days.

ATTY: You weren't in a lot of pain?

CLIENT: Not really. It wasn't so bad.

ATTY: Didn't you have trouble sleeping?

CLIENT: Well . . . as a matter of fact, I did.

ATTY: Well, most people would have complained like hell if it had happened to them. Do you feel uneasy about being a complainer?

CLIENT: I guess I do. I've never found it very easy to admit I was hurt — or even to talk about it.

ATTY: I thought maybe that was it. Why don't you tell me exactly what pain you experienced in as much detail as you can.[36]

This example also illustrates the importance of using leading questions carefully. Context is crucial. If the lawyer is not correct in his assessment that the client is minimizing the seriousness of the injury, the same questions could lead the client to create facts. Leading questions may increase

---

[35] GARY BELLOW & BEA MOULTON, THE LAWYERING PROCESS: MATERIALS FOR CLINICAL INSTRUCTION IN ADVOCACY 211 (1978).

[36] Id. at 210.

the possibility of an answer. Clients may not want to reveal something that will cast them as immoral, etc. Clients may deny their behavior rather than admit something that is inconsistent with their public image or their public morality. Thus, a question that leads a client toward this admission is more likely to get an accurate answer than a neutral question. There is a danger that such a question will be seen by the client as accusatory. The lawyer's non-judgmental acceptance will limit the possibility that such questions will damage the rapport with the client.

Robert Gorden lists these pre-conditions to leading questions:

- The information is clear in the respondent's mind, free from fading memory, chronological confusion or inferential confusion.

- Neither the information to be reported nor the relationship between the interviewer and respondent constitute an ego threat.

- There is no significant power imbalance between the respondent and interviewer.[37]

He warns that if the interviewer does not know in advance if these conditions exist, the interviewer should not use leading questions

§ 3-7. FINAL WORDS

Be wary of prescriptions (even the ones in this book) about the "right" and "wrong" way to ask questions. Good questions depend on the personal dynamics of the questioner, the context in which they are asked, the purpose for which they are asked, and the stage of the interview in which they are asked. If you want to know the time because you may be late for class, a closed question ("What time is it?") works better than an open one ("Tell me about your watch."). Finally, even perfectly formed questions may be rendered ineffective by the personality of the lawyer or the limitations of the client.

Bellow and Moulton offer the following pragmatic advice:

> [The effectiveness of questioning] depend[s] on the personal strengths, vulnerabilities, and perceptions of the client, as well as on the skills of the interviewer. . . . Do all of these reservations mean that attending to question form is unimportant? Perhaps. It may be that those who reflect on [the conventional techniques] 'learn' no more than the value of (i) care in their use of language, (ii) controlling their own tendency to interrupt; (iii) expressing their confusion or doubts; and (iv) using questions to assist the client in clarifying what he or she is trying to express. But even if focusing on question form is only a roundabout way to develop these general, rather obvious orientations, if it does that much — for many of us — it has done a great deal.[38]

---

[37] RAYMOND L. GORDEN, INTERVIEWING: STRATEGY, TECHNIQUES, AND TACTICS 216 (1969).

[38] BELLOW & MOULTON, *supra* note 35, at 211-212.

CHAPTER 4
BEGINNING THE LEGAL INTERVIEW

§ 4-1. INTRODUCTION

At the end of the initial interview, lawyers should

- Understand the goal(s) the client hopes to achieve.

- Understand how the client believes the lawyer can help achieve those goal(s).

- Understand enough about the matter to make an initial assessment of the client's goals and the possibility of achieving them.

- Have an adequate level of trust with the client.

At the end of the initial interview, clients should:

- Have had the opportunity to state or clarify their goals in the matter.

- Have had the opportunity to tell their story in sufficient detail.

- Understand how this lawyer can help them achieve their goals.

- Trust the lawyer enough to allow the lawyer to proceed with the case.

- Have a general idea of what will happen next and who will be responsible for it.

In the pages that follow, we present a model of interviewing that provides an opportunity for the interviewer to exercise flexibility. Many different styles and approaches can be and are successful. The legal interviewer should employ a range of appropriate techniques depending on the goals and circumstances of the interview.[1]

§ 4-2. EFFECTIVE LEGAL INTERVIEWING: BUILDING RAPPORT AND GATHERING INFORMATION

The goals of effective legal interviewing are to

- Establish rapport with the client, and

- Gather information necessary for the lawyer to represent the client.

---

[1] *Cf.* RAYMOND L. GORDEN, INTERVIEWING: STRATEGY, TECHNIQUES, AND TACTICS (1969).

Rapport building and information gathering never really end. They are not commodities that can be obtained and then preserved without effort. Legal representation is a dynamic process. New developments may require the lawyer to gather additional information from the client. The continuing interaction of the lawyer and the client may undermine the rapport established initially. When the case shifts to decision making (the counseling phase), rapport and fact-gathering interact as the client and the lawyer evaluate potential courses of action.

These goals structure legal interviews. A practical interviewer asks, "What is the best way to establish, build, and maintain rapport with my client and at the same time gather sufficient information to provide competent legal advice." The authoritarian model makes information-gathering predominant by putting the lawyer in control of the content, structure, and sequence of the interview. However, when the lawyer dominates the conversation with the client by asking questions, the lawyer may get information at the expense of rapport. Other lawyers may put rapport first. Yet, when the lawyer attends predominantly to the client's emotional needs, the lawyer may not discover enough facts to represent the client properly.

Maximizing both rapport and information-gathering is important for effective representation. Failure to do one frustrates the other. Clients who do not trust their lawyers may engage in tactics that frustrate the progress of the case. They may withhold important information, they may delay making important decisions, or they may change their minds about decisions already reached.[2] This greatly increases the cost and difficulty of representing the client. Ironically, the lack of rapport can sabotage the information sought in the first interview.

Building rapport makes legal interviewers more efficient by making them less likely to have to backtrack to acquire important information. Lawyers who do not get sufficient information in the initial interview may have to repeatedly contact their clients for the missing information. Moreover, the lack of sufficient information may cause the lawyer to ignore important aspects of the client's case. Either the lawyer must waste time by going back to the client or risk committing malpractice by missing an important claim. Frequently going back to the client for information also may undermine the rapport established in the first interview. The time spent building rapport is a worthwhile investment for the lawyer.

§ 4-3. THE GENERAL ELEMENTS OF AN EFFECTIVE LEGAL INTERVIEW

Stephen Feldman and Kent Wilson studied lawyer-client interactions to determine the value of interpersonal skills.[3] They wanted to see if a

---

[2] *See generally* William L. F. Felstiner & Austin Sarat, *Enactments of Power: Negotiating Reality and Responsibility in Lawyer-Client Interactions,* 77 CORNELL L. REV. 1447 (1992).

[3] Stephen Feldman & Kent Wilson, *The Value of Interpersonal Skills in Lawyering,* 5 LAW & HUM. BEHAV. 311 (1981).

lawyer's interpersonal skills played a role in determining how expert the client perceived the lawyer to be, how satisfied the client was with the lawyer's performance, and whether or not the client would recommend the lawyer in the future. They found that lawyers with high levels of interpersonal skills combined with high levels of legal competence were rated at the top of all of these measures. Moreover, they discovered that the lawyers' relational skills had more of an effect on the clients' perceptions than the attorney's legal competence.

The clients in the study consistently ranked attorneys with good interpersonal skills more expert, more capable of satisfying their goals for the case, and more likely to do as well for other people than equally competent but "relationally impaired" attorneys. Some clients may not have the knowledge or sophistication to determine whether or not the lawyer knows the law, but they can tell whether or not the lawyer is "paying attention" to them.

It is also important that lawyers learn how to gather sufficient data and analyze it properly. They cannot count on clients to police their information-gathering skills, however. The Feldman and Wilson study found that lawyers with high relational skills and low competence were rated higher than lawyers with low skills. Thus, it becomes necessary for the lawyer to police her competence. In the context of the initial interview, this means gathering sufficient information to allow the lawyer to make competent judgments about the law. In short, the lawyer must be relationally competent because that is how clients measure competence and satisfaction. The lawyer must also be legally competent because that is the *sine qua non* of legal representation.

Saying that lawyers must be relationally competent and legally competent begs the question: what does it mean to be competent in these areas? What specific behaviors must a lawyer engage in to display either or both of these skills? Here is the second area where Feldman and Wilson's study helps us. After studying the social science literature, they established a list of characteristics of those who exhibited high relational competence and high legal competence.

High relational skills consisted of

- Introducing the lawyer by using the lawyer's first name;
- Shaking hands;
- Making small talk;
- Letting the client talk without undue interruption;
- Leaning forward;
- Looking at the client;
- Reflecting the client's content and feelings; and
- Appearing warm, reactive, and animated.

High legal competence skills consisted of

- Obtaining sufficient factual data to determine the client's specific legal issue;

- Explaining court jurisdiction and procedure;

- Giving practical advice;

- Providing appropriate forms for gathering further information from the client; and

- Explaining relevant law.

Effective interviewers structure the interview to allow them to do the things that Feldman and Wilson describe as high relational and high competence behaviors. For example, introducing yourself to a new client is important but subsequent meetings shouldn't require repeated introductions. Similarly, gathering sufficient facts is crucial in the initial interview but may fade in importance as the case progresses. Giving practical advice may not be possible until the lawyer has gathered sufficient information about the matter. This may not be possible before the lawyer hears the client's story.

What follows is a suggested structure for an initial client interview. This structure allows the lawyer to use her own style to accomplish the twin goals of legal interviewing. This suggested structure should be used as a model. You should not think that you must follow this as you might a recipe in a cook book — from the beginning, with precise attention to the details, and only once. Rather, an effective interviewer may need to rearrange the sequence of the stages, start at a point in the middle, or repeat the entire sequence a number of times in the course of an interview.

Our structure breaks the interview down into several parts with each part linked by a framing question. The parts are described functionally; i.e., they try to describe the process in terms of what should happen in each section rather than what skills the lawyer must use.

§ 4-4. THE STRUCTURE OF AN EFFECTIVE LEGAL INTERVIEW

§ 4-4(a). OVERALL GOALS

The goals of an initial interview are as follows:

1. Establish rapport with the client. This involves

- Establishing a level of trust between the client and the attorney;

- Making the client feel comfortable confiding in the attorney; and

- Establishing appropriate roles for attorney and client.

2. Acquire facts necessary to understand the client's legal situation. This requires

- Establishing the goals of the representation; and

- Exploring the client's story in sufficient depth to ascertain its legal contours.

§ 4-4(b). STRUCTURE

In order to achieve those goals, we suggest the following structure:

1. Greeting and meeting the client (Chapter 4)

- Introductions

- Ice Breaking

- Explanations of time constraints, purpose of the interview, and confidentiality and fees

- Framing question: open question designed to elicit client narrative

2. Hearing the client's story (Chapter 5).

- Getting the client's story or narrative

- Initial clarification of general points

- Summary

- Framing question: summary of client story followed by request for specific details

3. Exploration and clarification of crucial elements of client's story (Chapter 6)

- Clarify descriptions or conclusions

- Explore major points

- Exploration of importance

- Framing question: statement of understanding

4. Ending the interview (Chapter 6)

- Define the role of the attorney

- Repeat highlights of the story

- Provide tentative diagnosis, if appropriate

5. Planning what to do next (Chapter 6)

- Explain next steps

- Finalize fee discussion

§ 4-5. THE OPENING STAGE OF THE CLIENT INTERVIEW

The opening stage of the initial interview is the lawyer's opportunity to lay a sound foundation for the rest of the lawyer-client relationship. This opening stage includes a number of different components. Each has its own purposes. Before we explore the individual components, we will discuss some general guidelines.

§ 4-5(a). PHYSICAL SURROUNDINGS

First impressions play a significant role in our perceptions. If lawyers want to successfully build rapport and convey competence, they must be particularly careful about their first impressions on clients.

How clients are greeted — whether they are greeted by a receptionist or the lawyer or whether the reception area or waiting room is comfortable — affect their perception of their lawyers. For example, one of us worked in a legal services office that bought an old house and adapted it to create large and comfortable offices for the lawyers and paralegals. The clients entered the building through the back door by climbing narrow metal steps. The door opened into a narrow, rectangular room in what used to be the back porch of the house. Chairs lined the long sides of the rectangle. When people sat on chairs opposite each other, their knees almost touched. Two people could not pass down the remaining space at the same time.

Imagine clients confronted with these surroundings. They may not have felt valued because they had to enter the back door. They may not have felt important because they were made to wait in uncomfortable surroundings. They might have felt powerless because the lawyer's space was so much more comfortable. Imagine the effect this might have had on rapport and information gathering. Clients who feel disempowered will engage in their own assertions of power with what they do control: access to information and their own availability. An office so designed might have a lot of clients who scheduled appointments but fail to show, a lot of "difficult" clients, and a lot of indecisive clients. In fact, this office was afflicted with all of these things.

§ 4-5(a)(1). The Office Building

Whatever the level of practice and the kind of clientele, the lawyer should make every effort to organize his physical surroundings so that they are comfortable and inviting yet "professional." At the very least, the lawyer should carefully arrange the first place the client sees when entering the office. If it does not help to establish rapport, it should be changed. Even something as simple as a fresh coat of paint can improve the quality of the surroundings.

§ 4-5(a)(2). The Lawyer's Office[4]

A pleasant physical setting helps build rapport. An office that includes cushioned chairs, soft lighting, rugs, and pictures on the wall helps place a client at ease. Offices with wooden furniture, fluorescent lighting, and bare floors and walls convey a colder image.[5] Cultural sensitivity also is important. Images or items that might offend clients should be avoided, and items that might make clients feel welcome should be included. At bottom, however, the furnishings should be genuine. Decorating an office with the "correct" items cannot substitute for a caring, competent lawyer.

The positioning of the lawyer and client is important. The lawyer should try to create an arrangement that puts a moderate distance between the lawyer and the client and allows them to at least partially face each other without obstructions. The lawyer should be neither too close to the client nor too far away. The farther a counselor sits from a client, the less effectively the counselor establishes rapport.[6] A distance of around 2-3 feet seems to work best in contemporary western culture. There are significant variations among subcultures, however. Lawyers should be careful to understand and respect these variations. We discuss some of these variations in Chapter 11.

§ 4-5(b). OPENING THE INTERVIEW

§ 4-5(b)(1). General Guidelines

In addition to the physical setting and the placement of the lawyer and the client, other general factors that contribute to an effective interview include:

- Leaning forward toward the client

- Making and keeping eye contact throughout the interview

- Smiling

- Nodding your head up and down

- Keeping your arms unfolded

- Using your hands for gesturing during conversation

- Speaking in a clear, audible voice without undue hesitations

All of these things help create an environment in which the client will feel comfortable and therefore more likely to give the lawyer more complete information. Of course, if the lawyer does not genuinely care about the client or the client's case, no external features will make the client feel

---

[4] The material in this section is drawn from IRVING L. JANIS, SHORT-TERM COUNSELING (1983).

[5] *Id.* at 90-91.

[6] *Id.* at 90.

comfortable. Being genuine "means being oneself without being phony or playing a role."[7] The lawyer's actions and environment must match the lawyer's feelings. This is not always easy to do. Effective counselors may be able to do this because they are able to identify with their clients without losing their own identities, they will wait for the resolution of the client's problem without prematurely imposing their own solution, and they are not likely to be provoked by the client.

§ 4-5(b)(2).   Building Rapport: Conveying Acceptance[8]

The twin goals of establishing rapport and acquiring facts are interdependent to a considerable degree and mutually reinforce each other. Clients may disclose facts that make them feel uncomfortable when they have developed a strong relationship with their lawyer. If these initial disclosures are met with acceptance by the counselor and not criticism or blame, the client is likely to trust the counselor. That is not to suggest that there will not be a time in the representation for the lawyer to raise moral issues with a client and express judgment as to matters relevant to the case, but it is best to raise such matters after the lawyer and client have developed a relationship. We discuss the matter of moral counsel in Chapter 9.

When a counselor listens without quickly judging what the client says, it sends a powerful message of acceptance to the client. The client is motivated to provide the lawyer with even more information. When the lawyer prematurely criticizes the client, the bond of trust is not developed and the client lacks motivation for further disclosures. For example, suppose a person seeking a divorce must disclose painful and embarrassing facts about himself. If the lawyer brushes off the client's embarrassment and comments negatively about the situation, the client may not be willing to make further disclosures. At the same time, if the lawyer remains affable and considerate, gives approval when otherwise appropriate, and does not reject the client as a person, the client and the lawyer may build an effective relationship.

The experience of representing a wide variety of people helps to prepare a lawyer for the variety of ways clients communicate their stories and evaluate their choices reflecting differences in psychological type, cultural values, and stress levels. Understanding these variations and anticipating individual differences helps the lawyer build a relationship with a client and at the same time retain the detachment that enables him to engage in wise deliberation with the client. As Mary Ann Glendon has said,

> Representing other people, in both friendly and adversarial situations, promotes in lawyers an ability to enter empathically into another person's way of seeing things while retaining a certain

---

[7] *Id.* at 91.

[8] The material in this section is drawn from IRVING L. JANIS, SHORT-TERM COUNSELING (1983).

detachment. That cast of mind in turn fosters a sturdier form of tolerance than that produced by mere relativism or pacts of nonaggression. Strong tolerance can be attentive, protective, and respectful to the other person without being "nonjudgemental."[9]

These techniques are designed to build trust in the client and understanding in the lawyer to overcome the natural protective barriers people erect when they must make decisions under pressure or in crisis. These barriers may harm instead of protecting clients by interfering with their ability to process information and evaluate alternatives.[10] They may also inhibit clients from making full disclosures to their counselors who especially need to know embarrassing information in order to anticipate problems and better protect clients' interests. Learning these techniques allows lawyers to better represent their clients. There is nothing about these relationship-building techniques that are inherently manipulative unless the lawyer is insincere. If the lawyer is not genuine, the client is likely to see through the lawyer's insincerity and deprive her of the referent power a more sincere and genuine lawyer would acquire.

§ 4-5(c). OPENING THE INTERVIEW: MEETING AND GREETING THE CLIENT

§ 4-5(c)(1). Introductions

Effective lawyers introduce themselves to their clients using their first names. While this seems a matter of common courtesy, it is also an important factor in establishing rapport with the client. The introduction need not be elaborate. The simple statement, "Hello, my name is Karen Smith" suffices. The introduction should also extend to anyone else who is going to participate in the interview.[11]

If the client continues to refer to the lawyer in formal terms (e.g., Mr. or Ms.) we believe that generally the lawyer should refer to the client in the same manner. This conveys the equality that we think is important in the client-lawyer relationship.

§ 4-5(c)(2). Ice Breaking

Ice breaking measures are a part of the "small talk" that Feldman and Wilson found to be important for the attorney establishing a good relationship with a client. Small talk such as asking the client "How are you?" or "Did you have any trouble finding us?" help relax both lawyer and client. They seem to provide a kind of psychic breathing space in which the

---

[9] MARY ANN GLENDON, A NATION UNDER LAWYERS 106 (1994).

[10] *See* IRVING L. JANIS, DECISION MAKING (1977).

[11] These may include associates who will be working on the case, secretaries, or paralegals. The presence of unnecessary third parties compromises the attorney-client privilege. This has been a major obstacle to the study of lawyer-client interactions. *See* Brenda Danet et al., *Obstacles to the Study of Lawyer-Client Interaction: The Biography of a Failure,* 14 LAW & SOC'Y REV. 905 (1980).

client makes the transition from the outside world with its rules and mores to the legal interviewer's world with its potentially different rules.

If used authentically, these ice breakers help establish rapport. They also allow the lawyer to identify areas where the lawyer and the client may share attitudes, activities, beliefs, or values. Clients can perceive if lawyers are simply following a script or if they are genuinely concerned with their welfare. Thus, when a client replies to the how are you question with, "I'm terrible. My car was stolen last night, my kids are in jail, and I was mugged on the way to this appointment," the lawyer had better say something other than, "That's nice. Do you want some coffee?"

Making small talk is important the first time you meet a client, but it is also important at subsequent meetings. In fact, it may even become more important because it is one of the few ways to reestablish rapport once introductions are out of the way. Similarly, it may be important to reestablish rapport with a former client who comes to you with a new case. Making small talk about the client's life enables the lawyer to reestablish a personal connection. It may be especially helpful for reestablishing rapport if the lawyer asks about aspects of the client's life that he learned about during the prior representation.

The ice breaking stage is not emotionally neutral. Being the first moment in which the lawyer and the client interact, it will have a powerful impact on the perceptions formed by the client about the lawyer. Warmth and personal interest in the client are highly valued by clients.

The ice breaking stage is not substantively neutral either. Clients are satisfied by lawyers who are both interpersonally effective *and* legally competent. Every communication from a client gives the lawyer the chance to display both. Moreover, the first words by clients, even those spoken during ice breaking, may contain "embedded messages" that are clues to both the emotional world of the client and the substantive nature of the legal claim.[12] Listen to how the client in this excerpt indicates his discomfort at having to seek disability payments.

Gay Gellhorn, *Law and Language: An Empirically Based Model for the Opening Moments of Client Interviews*, 4 CLINICAL L. REV. 321, 331-332 (1998)[13]

Mr. L. was a voluble, fifty-nine year old, illiterate African-American man who, in less than half an hour, spoke with grace and eloquence about his moral values. Mr. L. had worked for thirty-two years bussing dishes and mopping up at a restaurant, working twelve-hour days, starting at 75 cents an hour, and missing only one day. He had not had much formal education. As he explained, "I had eight sisters and all of them little bitty

---

[12] Gay Gellhorn, *Law and Language: An Empirically Based Model for the Opening Moments of Client Interviews*, 4 CLINICAL L. REV. 321 (1998).

[13] Copyright © 1998 by THE CLINICAL LAW REVIEW. Reprinted with permission.

and I had to drop out and, uh, you know, uh, work and feed, keep them in the house." A combination of health problems made it impossible for him to continue working, but he had been denied Social Security disability. He sought legal assistance to appeal that denial. Mr. L.'s first words invited the young white women interviewers to hear and understand the context of his reality as an active, hard-working, self-sufficient man.

L1:   This is P. [introducing student] [This is Mr. L.] [introducing client]

L2:   [Nice to meet you.]

C: How're you doing?

L1:   P's gonna listen in today.

C: Alright.

L1:   Have any trouble finding us?

C: No, no, uh-uhn, cause . . . mmm. . I usually, I used to work right across the street there.

L1:   [Oh, I think I know where that is.]

C: [in that school building.]

L1:   Oh, okay.

Mr. L.'s reference to working was critical information which the legal inter-viewer should not have ignored, even though it was communicated during initial ice-breaking moments ("How're you doing?" "Have any trouble finding us?") which legal interviewing texts seem to consider as content-free. As the interview and subsequent contacts with Mr. L. made clear, he was now struggling with the role of being cared for, a role thrust upon him by his disability and total lack of income, so that he could not so much as buy a soda or go to a medical appointment without reliance on others. For example, of his eleven siblings, "all of us livin'," he speaks over and over of his sister ("that's my heart") who has to pay his rent now and take him where he needs to go. His request for "the income, that's all I need," repeated eleven times in the twenty-eight minute interview, has meaning within this context of his difficulty in shifting roles from the helper to the helped, and in coming to terms with the fact that the only way to have some financial independence would be to be labeled "disabled." Mr. L. is similar to many other clients who express their sense of self as soon as they are given a chance to speak.

––––––––

In the above excerpt, the client expresses his pride in his work life by incorporating it into his answer to the seemingly neutral question about finding the office. Recognizing his pride and acknowledging it would give the client a chance to express his identity to the lawyer in his own words. If received warmly and incorporated into the handling of the case, it would help establish rapport and guide the lawyer and the client in the difficult decisions they have to make.

Gellhorn gives other examples of what happens when the client is first given the opportunity to speak. These examples illustrate how ignoring the concerns embedded in the client's statements may lead the lawyer to ignore the emotional reality of the client. In turn, this may lead the client to assert control over the representation by evading questions, withholding information, delaying decisions, and changing his or her mind. Lawyers might interpret these as the behaviors of a "problem or uncooperative client." How ironic that the lawyer may be the cause of these behaviors.

Sometimes the failure to pick up on these embedded concerns leads to substantive problems as well. Gellhorn compares the performance of two different sets of interviewers in a legal clinic. The first interviewer failed to identity his client's concern for her mental condition in the opening sequences of the initial interview. He repeatedly failed to understand that the client was telling him that she was seriously depressed when she kept "recycling" it in their follow-up conversations. This resulted in a denial of her disability claim because there was an insufficient record to support any claim of mental disability. The second group of interviewers, by seeing and acknowledging this concern, developed more complete medical evidence in support of her claim.[14]

In the following excerpt, Professor Gellhorn emphasizes the importance of attending to the client's first words during an interview. She extrapolates from the literature on medical interviewing to suggest some techniques that will better enable legal interviewers to effectively listen and respond to a client's embedded concerns when expressed early in the interview. Specifically, she suggests that lawyers:

- take almost verbatim notes of the client's first words,

- use responses and questions that encourage the client to continue talking, and

- avoid even moderately limiting responses and questions.

Gay Gellhorn, *Law and Language: An Empirically Based Model for the Opening Moments of Client Interviews,* 4 CLINICAL L. REV. 321, 345, 346, 347-348, 349-350 (1998)[15]

* * * *

[L]egal interviewers must be attentive at times and in ways they may not now be trained to be. My experience as an interviewer and as a supervisor

---

[14] We provide an extended discussion of this case study in Chapter 6.

[15] Copyright © 1998 by THE CLINICAL LAW REVIEW. Reprinted with permission.

is that minds wander, particularly during the "ice-breaking" stage, and new questions are formulated mentally without listening carefully to the clients' responses. "Attending" to clients is a paper in itself. David Berger, a psychotherapist, notes that "the basis of the empathic process is an evenly focused attention to the patient from within and from without (that is, as participant and observer)." The model emphasizes that legal interviewers must expect that the client's first words hold meaning and deserve exploration and encouragement. The words are so critical that they should be written down, as close to verbatim as possible. Even if the interview is taped and a transcription can be made at a later time, the discipline of capturing the clients' first words in writing will focus the interviewer's attention and ingrain a habit of listening well and with subtlety. . . .

The medical interviewing literature convincingly demonstrates the importance of not interrupting patients' statements of their concerns, although in practice physicians actually do interrupt most of their patients on average within eighteen seconds. Based on my anecdotal experience, it is unlikely that attorneys would make a better showing. . . .

Attentiveness to clients' first words does not preclude parallel attentiveness to nonverbal behaviors and cues. Nonverbal behaviors — posture, face, movement, tone, autonomic physiological responses (e.g. blushing, quickened breathing), physical characteristics, appearance — "leak" messages and "punctuate" what one is saying. Emotional expression — the eyes filling with tears, the hands sheltering a head hung low — are vital clues to a person's data base. These are part of the client's first words. . . .

In summary, legal interviewers should expect that clients' first words hold critical information or clues. Those words should be captured verbatim. Although the self-revelation will occur regardless of the interviewer's style, the better practice is to elicit a complete and uninterrupted statement of concerns at the outset of the interview. Interviewers can encourage completeness by limiting their linguistic techniques during the opening moments of the interview to continuers, non-judgemental straightforward statements, nonverbal facilitators/encouragers, and additional open-ended questions. Interviewers should avoid probes, elaborators, recompleters and closed-ended questions during the solicitation of the client's concerns or story telling. Use of this model will have a positive effect on the legal interviewer's ability to form a relationship with a client, to comprehend the full range of information the client needs to share, and to collaborate with the client to tell a story in legally and emotionally effective language.

———————

Gellhorn's work shows that the legal interview cannot be contained within rigid structural or theoretical boundaries. For example, the conventional view holds that during "ice breaking," the client will not reveal important information. After ice breaking, the client will tell her initial story and then the lawyer asks follow-up questions. Gellhorn shows us that effective legal interviewers must pay attention to what the client is actually saying and doing. If the client reveals embedded concerns early on, the lawyer should allow the client to continue even if the lawyer has not had the chance to finish the "Ice Breaking Followed by Opening Statement" script. As Gellhorn points out, client self-revelation will occur no matter what style the interviewers adopts. The question is whether or not the client will continue to reveal more information. Other research shows that clients whose initial self-revelations are ignored, ridiculed, or downplayed are less likely to continue to provide critical self-information.[16]

More broadly, this initial stage will color clients' perceptions of lawyers. The initial stage may determine whether or not lawyers will be perceived favorably and whether or not they will understand their client's case.

§ 4-5(c)(3).   Time Constraints and Purposes of the Interview

The lawyer should tell the client about any time constraints on the interview. This helps establish the boundaries of the interview and it enhances rapport. It is a matter of common courtesy as well as a way of framing the interview.

Similarly, the lawyer should advise the client of the purpose of the interview. Clients should be advised if the interview is exploratory, diagnostic, etc. A client may assume that the lawyer will "take his case" and be surprised when, at the end of the interview, the lawyer advises him that she will not handle the matter.

An initial statement might sound like:

> This interview is so that I can learn about your case and you can learn more about me. I need to know more about your situation before I know if you have a case I can handle. This interview will also give you the chance to learn more about me so you can decide if you want me to represent you. We have 45 minutes for this interview today. If we need more time, we can schedule another meeting.

§ 4-6.   EXPLANATIONS

§ 4-6(a).   CONFIDENTIALITY

It is important that the client understand the confidential nature of the conversations, their costs, if any, and what to expect during the interview. Many lawyers may be tempted to give the client a simple statement telling the client that everything they talk about will be "confidential." But consider the problems with this simple statement.

First, it is not literally true that everything is confidential. There are exceptions to the ethical rules that may prompt or even require the attorney to disclose parts of this conversation. In addition, the evidentiary

---

[16] *See* JANIS, *supra* note 4.

attorney-client privilege may also be waived under certain conditions, such as when the attorney and the client discuss a future crime. And, what does "confidential" mean? It may have a specific meaning to professionals but mean considerably less to nonprofessionals.

§ 4-6(a)(1). Discussing Confidentiality

Both the rules of professional conduct and the rules of evidence impose a duty of confidentiality on attorneys. These duties are frequently defended on the grounds that they encourage clients to be forthcoming with their attorneys and that they respect clients' dignity. Client decision making is enhanced because the lawyer is better able to assess the client's case and the client is able to make an informed, autonomous decision.

As a general proposition then, it would seem that most lawyers would want to give their clients a thorough explanation of the scope and nature of confidentiality. But a study showed that many lawyers rarely fully advise their clients of these rules and that many clients significantly misunderstand the confidentiality rules.[17] Lawyers owe it to the public to do a better job explaining confidentiality in light of the study's findings of widespread public misunderstanding. The best place to do this is where the lawyer meets the public, i.e., during the initial interview.

Because a proper client understanding of fees and confidentiality are important to establishing and maintaining trust and competence, we suggest that lawyers carefully plan how to explain them to their clients. It may be useful to distribute a written explanation of the rules on confidentiality and the lawyer's fee structure before the initial interview.

A written explanation of confidentiality allows the lawyer to cover both the ethical rule on confidentiality and the attorney-client privilege rule in that jurisdiction. This allows the lawyer to provide a full explanation to the client in a more efficient manner than a mini-lecture at the beginning of the interview, when the client may not be listening intently.

§ 4-6(a)(2). Talking About Confidentiality at the Initial Interview

The following are some guidelines for talking about client confidentiality.

1. Explain confidentiality early in the first interview:

We justify the rules about confidentiality by saying that clients will be more forthcoming. If clients do not know about these rules, however, there is no basis for them. Most clients do not know about either the ethical rule on confidentiality (Rule 1.6) or the attorney-client privilege.

2. Presume that all information is confidential:

The duty of confidentiality extends to preliminary conversations, even in cases where the lawyer eventually decides not to take the matter. The

---

[17] Fred C. Zacharias, *Rethinking Confidentiality,* 74 Iowa L. Rev. 351 (1989).

name of the person, the purpose for which the person sought advice (or even whether the person sought advice) should be considered confidential, regardless of whether you go on to represent this person in a matter.

3. Understand the difference between the privilege and the ethical rule:

Remember the ethical rule of confidentiality is broader than the evidentiary attorney-client privilege. The ethical rule applies at all times and protects all information "relating to the representation," even if it comes from a third party. The attorney-client privilege applies only when the lawyer is before a tribunal and protects only information given to you by the client and only when given under certain circumstances.

4. Train your staff to keep client information strictly confidential:

The rules require that lawyers ensure that everyone in the firm complies with the lawyer's ethical obligations. Partners must make reasonable efforts to put measures in place to ensure reasonable compliance. Direct lawyer-supervisors must make reasonable efforts to ensure compliance. Even if the lawyer could not be disciplined for breakdowns, the lawyer and the law firm may be liable in a malpractice action.

5. Prevent clients from seeing other clients' information:

Don't leave confidential information exposed on your desk so that other clients may see it. Keep a clean desk or find another place away from your desk to conduct interviews.

§ 4-6(b). FEES

§ 4-6(b)(1). Talking About Fees

Model Rule of Professional Conduct 1.5(b) states that "[w]hen a lawyer has not regularly represented the client, the basis or rate of the fee shall be communicated to the client, *preferably in writing, before or within a reasonable time after commencing the representation.*"[18] Handing out a fee schedule or an explanation of typical fees completely satisfies the rule. The client can review the fee information and make an informed choice about whether or not to continue the representation. In addition, clients can take the written statement home and review it at their leisure. The written statement can be used later in the representation when the client may have some questions. It may even head off fee disputes.[19]

---

[18] MODEL RULES OF PROFESSIONAL CONDUCT Rule 1.5(b) (1994).

[19] Fee disputes are among the most common form of complaints to disciplinary bodies. Most of these cases do not result in disciplinary action either because they fall outside of the jurisdiction of the agency or they are not founded. Frequently, they result from a misunderstanding between the attorney and the client about the amount or the nature of the fee. It stands to reason then that if the opportunities for misunderstanding can be decreased, the number of complaints can also be decreased. That is why we suggest that you give your client a written explanation of your fee structure early in the representation, i.e., in the waiting room, and that you go over it with the client near the end of the initial interview.

§ 4-6(b)(2). Talking About Fees at the Initial Interview

Here are some guidelines that summarize how to approach discussing fees with clients.

1. Tell a new client the basis or the rate of the fee:

This could be merely a reference to a copy of your fee schedule if that information is sufficient to let the client know how you will bill.

2. Tell the client about fees as early as possible:

Handing out your fee schedule when new clients come in but before they speak to you is a good idea. Because you begin to represent them as soon as you begin talking to them (at least for the purpose of deciding if you will take their case further) you should have a fee discussion as early as possible. Do not put it off. Clients generally appreciate candor about fees.

3. The basis or rate of the fee should be in writing:

Most fee agreements do not have to be in writing. If you charge by the hour or at a fixed fee, you need only communicate the fee orally. But contingent fees must be in writing and must include the information specified in the Model Rules.[20] Prudence dictates that all fees be in writing. A written fee agreement minimizes the possibility of misunderstandings. Remember, fee disputes are the most common source of complaints about lawyers to disciplinary authorities. Don't take chances. Talk about your fee early and put the agreement in writing.

4. Advise the client if you will be splitting the fee with another lawyer:

This applies to splitting fees with lawyers outside of your firm. Model Rule 1.5(e) requires a written agreement with the client if the lawyers will not split the fee in proportion to the work each lawyer performs.[21] In any event, the client must be "advised" of each lawyer's participation and must not "object" to his or her participation.

§ 4-7. SAMPLE DIALOGUE TO OPEN A CLIENT INTERVIEW

We have included a lot of guidelines and suggestions in this chapter. Here is a sample dialogue that integrates these guidelines that you can use to open an interview with a client:

> Before we get started, let me talk about those papers you received in the waiting room. One paper describes what lawyers call the rules on confidentiality. That generally means that I cannot tell anyone what we talk about unless you give me permission, but that paper explains some of the exceptions to the rule. The other paper explains what I charge in most cases. Now, I will not charge you for the time we spend today. If you decide that you

---

[20] *See* MODEL RULES OF PROFESSIONAL CONDUCT Rule 1.5(c) (1994).

[21] *See* MODEL RULES OF PROFESSIONAL CONDUCT Rule 1.5(e) (1994).

want me to represent you, I will explain my fees at that time. Do
you have any questions about confidentiality or fees?

Ok, I've set aside 45 minutes for this conference. If we need more
time we can schedule another appointment at your convenience.

As always, the lawyer must adapt this sample to conform to her own
personality and circumstances. What is most important is that the basic
elements of this dialogue are covered.

§ 4-8.   CONCLUSION

The beginning of an interview is very important. That is why we have
devoted so much material to it. What happens at the beginning of the
interview often determines how successful the lawyer-client relationship
will be. Lawyers should approach their clients with dignity, cultural sensitivity, and respect. They should give the client as much control over the
representation as the client wants.

Especially in the early stages of the representation, lawyers should
focus on building rapport with their clients.

- Building rapport at this stage pays dividends later.

- Clients who trust their lawyers are more likely to disclose important information than clients who do not trust their lawyers.

- Attending to the client's emotional and legal needs shows respect
  for the client.

Lawyers should put their clients at ease by:

- Having comfortable and inviting offices;

- Greeting clients warmly and personally; and

- Engaging in appropriate ice-breaking talk before the interview.

Lawyers must be aware that clients will reveal important emotional and
legal information even in the earliest stages of the relationship. Lawyers
should not be constrained to interview "by the book." Rather, they should
pay attention to the client and respond flexibly.

In the next chapter, we discuss how lawyers go beyond these initial
stages to listen to the client's story.

CHAPTER 5
HEARING THE CLIENT'S STORY

After the attorney begins the interview by making the client feel comfortable and explaining confidentiality and the attorney's fee structure, the interview moves into a new phase. Now the attorney hears the client's story in the client's own words. This chapter sets out a structure and some techniques that will help accomplish that goal.

§ 5-1.   THE FRAMING STATEMENT

We suggest that you use framing statements at the beginning of each section of the interview. These statements serve as transitions from one section of the interview to the next. They let the client know that the purpose of the conversation has changed. They also help organize the client's memory and the lawyer's perceptions.

"Frames" are ways that people organize their conversations and their perceptions into coherent themes. We tend to present information that is appropriate to the frame we perceive, and perceive information in light of that frame. Frames structure conversations by telling the speaker and the listener what to pay attention to. For example, students listen more intently and consider the information more important when the professor remarks that the subject will be on the exam. By the same token, the professor will make certain to be as accurate as possible because the students will be listening closely.

A framing statement begins a new section of the interview. By using a framing statement, the lawyer signals the client that the focus of the discussion will change. Making the frame broad or narrow helps focus the client's answers. The framing statement imposes a structure around the section of the interview it precedes.

A framing statement also allows the client to be a partner in the conversation. By framing the next section of the interview, the lawyer opens up the interview process for the client to see. Without a framing question, the client must respond to the lawyer's questions in a vacuum and without the context of the question's purpose or its range.[1]

The content of the framing statement will vary with each section of the interview. Generally, the interview will proceed from a general focus to a more narrow focus. The interviewer should phrase the framing statement in light of the purpose of that section of the interview. However, the

---

[1] *See* Gay Gellhorn, *Law and Language: An Empirically-Based Model for the Opening Moments of Client Interviews,* 4 CLINICAL L. REV. 321, 345 (1998).

statement should contain a summary of what the client has said up to that point, and then a statement explaining the purpose of the next phase of the interview.

§ 5-2. GETTING THE CLIENT'S STORY

Once all of the tasks appropriate to the beginning of the interview have been completed, the effective legal interviewer wants to acquire as much information about the client's situation as possible. To do this, we suggest that you use a framing statement that is as open and unfocused as possible.

§ 5-2(a). OPENING QUESTIONS

Broad, open questions get better answers than narrow, focused questions. People can accurately recall a great deal of information when simply asked to tell their story. In fact, both the accuracy and amount of information that a person recalls is adversely affected when an interviewer intervenes frequently by interrupting or asking specific questions.[2] Because effective interviews generate most of their useful information from the client's opening narrative,[3] the lawyer should primarily seek to gather as much information as possible at this stage of the interview. Asking a broadly focused opening question is the best way to do that. Later in the interview, it may become necessary to ask more narrow and precise questions in order to focus on specific areas of the client's story. Many inexperienced interviewers find it difficult to frame unfocused, opening questions and to refrain from immediately narrowing the question's focus. The following excerpt suggests ways to avoid this problem.

RAYMOND L. GORDEN, INTERVIEWING: STRATEGIES, TECHNIQUES, AND TACTICS 204-206 (1969)[4]

* * * *

It is important for an interviewer to become aware of this dimension, called "scope," since most people have an unconscious habit, developed in social conversation, of being unnecessarily restrictive in the scope of their questions. Perhaps it is a way of saving time or of restricting the other person's remarks so that we may express our point of view sooner. Or perhaps the efficient businessman, the incisive lawyer, or the police detective who "get to the point" in mass media portrayals influence our conversational

---

[2] Ronald Fisher, *Interviewing Victims and Witnesses of Crimes,* 1 PSYCHOL. PUB. POL'Y & L. 732, 741 (1995).

[3] *Id.* at 735.

[4] Copyright © 1969 by Dorsey Press, Homewood, Ill.

patterns. Regardless of the source, in training interviewers the writer has found that it is usually more difficult for them to ask broad questions than to ask each specific point separately. Frequently, the neophyte interviewer behaved as if his motto were "never use a general question if several specific questions can be used instead." By developing a sensitivity to how apparently small differences in the wording of a question make vast differences in its scope, the interviewer may guide his own behavior in accordance with the objectives of the interview, rather than be guided by unconscious habit.

To illustrate this different scope, let us compare three opening questions used by different interviewers in an interview with teenagers to discover some of the educational values of the county fair for city children.

    a) Tell me what happened at the Greene County Fair when you were there last Saturday.

    b) Tell me what you did at the Green County Fair when you were there last Saturday.

    c) Did you like the horse show at the county fair?

Regardless of which question is the best opener for this type of interview, the vast difference in scope is clear. The first question, by using the term "what happened," leaves the topic open for the respondent to report what he did, what others did, what he saw, what others saw, what he felt or thought about what he did or saw, and what he felt or thought about what others did or saw.

The second question logically restricts the area of discussion as much as 90 percent by asking only what the respondent did. This unnecessary restriction of the topic might constitute an ego threat in this case, because the respondent probably was mainly a spectator and could more spontaneously report what he saw than what he did. Also, the impersonality of "what happened" versus "what did you see, do, or think" often makes the respondent less self-conscious.

The third question restricts the conversation to some fraction of 1 percent of the respondent's impressions of the fair. It also inhibits the spontaneous flow of information, because it prevents the respondent from talking about what, for him, were the most memorable aspects of the fair. It also implies that a simple "yes" or "no" answer is required.

Dimensions of scope. Rather than examining scores of illustrations of differences in scope and discussing their possible effects on the flow of relevant information, we have devised a scheme to show some of the important abstract dimensions of scope. This allows the reader to generate his own examples. The chart below delineates four dimensions of scope, represented by the column headings, which apply to all questions. The columns are arranged in the order each dimension usually appears in the sentence structure of a question.

	Question	Actor	Action	Scene
A	What?	Unspecified actor	Happened	General topic of interview
B	Why or how?	You	Do (overt)	Restricted area of time
C	Where or when?	Others (in general)	See, feel, or think (covert)	Restricted location
D	How much? How many?	You (or specific others)	Specific verb	Specific event or situation
E	Did . . . ?	You (or specific others)	Specific verb	Specific object or characteristics of an object in a specified situation

Whenever possible, within each column the categories are arranged with the broader ones at the top and the narrower ones at the bottom. With some imagination, the reader can construct questions for a hypothetical interview using all possible combinations of the four dimensions.

To illustrate some possible combinations of these four dimensions, we will resume the interview on the educational effects of the county fair. The type of question being illustrated will be designated by giving four letters, for example AABB, representing the rows selected from each successive column.

Type AAAA: Tell me what happened at the county fair.

Type ABBD: What did you do at the fair last Saturday?

Type ADBD: What did your father say to you when you were at the fair with him last Saturday?

Type BDBD: Why did your father go to the fair last Saturday?

Type EBCE: Did you see the draft horses at the fair last Saturday?

Not all logical combinations of the four columns would make sense. Also, the number of categories is different in each of the four dimensions and in some cases may be arbitrary depending on how finely the distinctions are made. In spite of the lack of refinement, this scheme can help sensitize the reader to the fact that the scope of a question can be expanded or contracted by gradual degrees and that the answer to several of the narrower questions could be logically included in the answer to one of the broader questions.

———

This excerpt suggests a way to structure your opening question. The opening question should be stated broadly in all dimensions. It should ask what happened generally without referring to any specific person, information, or time frame. For example, the attorney could begin by saying any of the following:

Type AAAA: What can I do for you today?

Type AAAA: How can I help you?

Type AAAA: Tell me what brought you here today.

These statements give the client the maximum freedom to relate his story, beginning wherever the client chooses and relating whatever information the client chooses.

By asking broad and unfocused questions, the lawyer concedes control of the floor, the topics, and their sequence to the client. Clients can then talk about what is on their mind and, assuming a genuine interest on the lawyer's part, feel that they are being listened to. Being able to tell their story and be heard by their attorney greatly influence how clients feel about their lawyer.

Avoid words that pre-judge the matter or that frame the conversation too narrowly. For example, suppose you ask the client to tell you about his "legal problem." This tells the client that you have made a judgment that a legal problem (and perhaps a legal solution) exists. In addition, it tells the client to limit his conversation to the "legally relevant" things. Neither of these are desirable. It may either interfere with rapport or create a false rapport. In the first instance, the client may believe that he is in trouble and may fear further self-revelation to the attorney. In the second instance, the client may falsely believe that you have decided he has a "good" case and be disappointed when you later tell him that his claim is without merit.

It is helpful for the initial framing statement to give the client an overview of the interview. Consider the following:

We're ready to begin. I want you to begin by telling me what brought you to the office today. I want to hear what you have to say so I am going to do most of the listening and you should be doing most of the talking. When you've told me everything you need to, I may have some questions for you to help me understand something you've said or to get more information so I can figure how I can help you. Why don't you start wherever you like and tell me what brought you here today.

Sometimes short directions help. Look at the following example which a lawyer might use with a reserved client:

I am interested in helping you. It makes my job easier if I have as much information as possible. If you are not sure that something matters, go ahead and tell me. I would rather have too much information than too little.

This frame encourages the client to speak broadly. Clients may not know the ground rules of legal interviews and may not know what is important. They may be inclined to self-censor the information because they may not believe it to be "legally relevant." Moreover, people are not likely to divulge self-critical information unless they trust the other person. By explaining to the client that you are willing to hear what the client has to say, you are maximizing your chances of acquiring information and building trust.

§ 5-2(b). AVOIDING NARROW FRAMES

Sometimes the lawyer will have some preliminary information indicating the nature of the client's case. Legal services clients will have undergone a pre-screening for both income and case eligibility. Many private firms will also get some preliminary information before the initial interview.[5] This information can be helpful to the attorney because it frees her from collecting basic information, like name and address. In addition, it helps the attorney frame the client's story.

The dangers of this prior information are great, however. It may cause the attorney to prematurely categorize the client's case, causing her to ignore any contrary information or additional matters. We call this "hardening of the categories" because the lawyer may prematurely place the client's case in one category when, in fact, there may be other more creative ways of understanding the client and solving the matter.

For example, Gary Neustadter's study of bankruptcy attorneys, which we discussed previously, showed this process at work. Neustadter explains that there are generally several viable solutions for a client in financial distress.[6] However, with one possible exception, all of the attorneys channeled the client's case into a preconceived category. There was very little discussion of alternatives. Indeed, there was very little discussion of the alternative forms of bankruptcy. Two lawyers justified their narrow approach by claiming that the clients had already made up their minds. Because these attorneys were so thoroughly identified with particular forms of bankruptcy relief, they believed that the clients came to them to seek that kind of bankruptcy. One lawyer said, "Clients who come to see me screen themselves. When they get here they know they want bankruptcy. They've read the brochure, filled out the questionnaire, and thought about it. I will sometimes spot problems and have them consider Chapter 13."[7]

---

[5] *See* Gary Neustadter, *When Law and Client Meet: Observations of Interviewing and Counseling Behavior in the Consumer Bankruptcy Law Office,* 35 BUFF. L. REV. 177 (1986). All of the lawyers in the author's study used forms to gather information about their clients' financial situations.

[6] *Id.* at 194. They include 1) increasing family income or reducing monthly expenses to free up income to repay debts; 2) privately liquidating assets; 3) additional borrowing; 4) negotiating extensions or compositions with creditors; 5) resisting or defending against collection efforts; 6) filing a Chapter 13 bankruptcy in order to receive a court approved repayment plan; or 7) filing a Chapter 7 bankruptcy in order to liquidate all non-exempt property and to discharge most debts. An eighth possibility is to do nothing. Although it may not often be the best choice, there are times when no action satisfies the client's objectives better than anything that can be done, either by the client alone or by the legal system.

[7] *Id.* at 207.

The problem here is that the lawyer relies on the client's legal analysis — that bankruptcy (a particular kind of bankruptcy) is the correct remedy. In addition, it conceives of the problem from only one perspective — bankruptcy. It ignores the alternative legal remedies (there are two kinds of personal bankruptcies) and nonlegal alternatives. The other alternatives may better solve the client's problems.

For example, when one of us actively practiced law, the clients would respond to the perfectly formed open-ended question by saying, "I want to file bankruptcy." Most of the clients were eligible to file at least a Chapter 7 petition. After further conversation, the clients would reveal that they wanted to file bankruptcy because they had been receiving harassing letters from a collection agency or they were afraid that if their wages were garnished they would lose their job. Frequently, the client's problem could be resolved without resorting to bankruptcy. The lawyer may need to ask follow-up questions that will broaden the client's focus.

Framing the question narrowly may limit the information the client provides. The client may only provide information about the "legal issue." As we saw above, that is an untrained judgment and it may not serve the client's underlying interests. Clients may impose their own model of the law on the facts and filter out what they perceive to be legally immaterial facts. It would be as though a doctor asked a patient to discuss his pneumonia. The patient may understandably limit the conversation to his breathing problems and neglect to tell the doctor about the asbestos in his work place (indicating asbestosis) or the pains in his left arm (indicating heart problems).

Finally, a narrow frame may interfere with rapport by perpetuating a bureaucratic barrier between the lawyer and the client. The client may have a number of related concerns, some of which are legal and some of which are not. The intake worker or the receptionist may have placed the client in a box because that was required by office procedure. That box may not capture either the social, emotional, or legal reality of the client's case. When the lawyer simply reads the designation from the intake form, she fails to convey an interest in the real client before her.

As with every other suggestion in this book, the above advice cannot be applied to every situation. There may be times when narrowing is necessary. If the client is not motivated to speak freely about a subject, initially asking narrow questions that work toward a broader focus may help build enough rapport to enable the client to open up to the interviewer.[8]

§ 5-2(c). PROVIDING CONTEXT

Sometimes the client may need a context in which to answer the question. It may be helpful to tell the client the purpose of the interview, and

---

[8] *See* RAYMOND L. GORDEN, INTERVIEWING: STRATEGY, TECHNIQUES, AND TACTICS 269 (1969). Gorden refers to this sequence of narrow questions followed by broader ones as an "Inverted Funnel."

the subject(s), and the amount of time available. Professor Gellhorn provides a good example here. Notice how the interviewer constructs her
opening question. The question frames the interview by disclosing what
the interviewer already knows about the client's visit; it places the client
in the procedural framework of the case, and then invites the client to "tell
me everything." Note how the client lays out a powerful theory of the case
as well as stating his emotional discomfort when accused of receiving a
Social Security overpayment.

Gay Gellhorn, *Law and Language: An Empirically Based Model for the Opening Moments of Client Interviews*, 4 CLINICAL L. REV. 321, 330-331 (1998)[9]

* * * *

Jack (an assumed name the client asked to be called because the interview was being taped) was a mentally-limited white man in his early thirties who came to the interview with a social worker. Social Security was
seeking return of an overpayment made some years earlier when he
resided in an assisted-living facility (since closed down). The facility had
required Jack to sign over his disability check. While living at the facility,
Jack engaged in part time, sheltered work. Now, many years later, he had
received a notice from Social Security demanding that he pay back over-
payments made to him during the period he collected benefits and worked.
The interviewer was an African-American woman about his age, who spent
a minute or so with introductions, giving the client her card and so on.

> L: (1:58) I see you are here today for an SSI overpayment . . . for
> the time period October 1983 to July 1985. According to the
> Social Security Administration, you received a total — they —
> $4873.40 for that time period when you also worked. That's
> why they're claiming an overpayment. Now I just need for you
> to explain everything to me, from the beginning. . . . You have
> requested a hearing to appeal. . . . First you requested Social
> Security to waive your — the overpayment. It was denied, then
> you requested a hearing because you do not agree with this
> decision. Correct?
>
> C: That's correct.
>
> L: We just need for you, Jack, to explain everything in detail.
> Ummm. . . .
>
> C: Let me know when you are ready.

---

[9] Copyright © 1998 by THE CLINICAL LAW REVIEW. Reprinted with permission.

L: (2:30) Okay. I'm ready. (Putting aside her papers and turning her full attention to him.)

C: Okay. My name is Jack. I'm not the type of person who would have a job and steal from less fortunate who has more needs than myself. I enjoy being self-independent without any government assistant. Government assistant is only for emergencies and not for gains and misabuse. I'm not the type of person and I plead innocent to these charges. [The assisted living facility] is held responsible for these overpayment and I feel they should pay them back.(3:10)

In a few words, the client conveys the core of who he is, as well as a legal and factual theory of the case that respects his life-world.

§ 5-3.   HEARING THE CLIENT'S STORY

§ 5-3(a).   GETTING PAST FRAMING STATEMENTS

In the easy interview, the open framing statement leads the client to explain the story in complete and accurate detail. At that point the legal interviewer need only clarify a few details, like names, addresses, etc., to complete the story. Of course, not every client will respond to the open framing statement with a complete and detailed narrative. Many people will recite a short summary of their situation in response to the opening question. Think about what happens when a doctor asks a patient, "Tell me why you are here today." The patient may have memorized a script which recites, in conclusory form, why the patient came to the doctor. For example, the patient may say, "I haven't been feeling well," or "My back has been bothering me." Very rarely does a patient launch into a complete description of the entire course of his medical history, culminating in the most recent events that caused him to schedule an appointment.

So it is with many clients. They may have an idea why they came to see the lawyer ("I want to get a divorce"). They may also have some idea of the facts that are important to their case ("I was fired because I wouldn't work on the Sabbath"). But notice that these are summary statements inviting the attorney to make the next move in the conversation. This is natural for clients who may not be familiar with the way lawyers and clients interact. A brief statement of the "problem" does not indicate a lack of knowledge or that the client is "difficult." A brief initial statement is a reasonable conversational gambit in a situation where the client is unsure of the conversational rules.

We suggest that when this occurs lawyers should invite the client to continue with his narrative. Look at an example of this technique from a classic interviewing book.

ROBERT L. KAHN & CHARLES F. CANNELL, THE DYNAMICS OF INTERVIEWING: THEORY, TECHNIQUE, AND CASES 215-216 (1957)[10]

* * * *

[C]onsider the case of a lawyer who is attempting to obtain information from a witness to an automobile accident. This involves an effort to get relevant legal facts in an informal interview outside a courtroom.

> ATTORNEY: You mentioned that you saw an accident at the corner of Main Street and Third Avenue last Tuesday, I believe. Will you tell me what happened?
>
> RESPONDENT: Well, this car came around the corner and hit this man.

This terse response obviously leaves the attorney with any number of unanswered questions. Here are some of the supplementary questions he might be led to ask:

1. How fast was the car going?

2. Where was the man?

3. Whose fault was it?

4. I'd like to get as complete a picture as I can of just what you saw and heard. Why don't you take your time and tell me everything that you remember, just as it happened?

Consider the advantages and disadvantages of these supplementary questions. The first two questions have in common the problem that they direct the respondent's attention to a specific aspect of the accident, and they do so inappropriately early in the interview. It is, of course, entirely possible that at some later moment the attorney might find it necessary to direct the respondent's attention to some specific points. In this case, however, the attorney would be directing the respondent's attention to problems of speed and position before getting the general picture of what the witness saw.

The third question has the more obvious defect of asking the respondent to make a conjecture or draw a conclusion from facts that have not yet been ascertained. Again, this is a question that under different circumstances or perhaps later in the same interview might be entirely appropriate.

The fourth probe question has the advantage of instructing the respondent in a way that indicates clearly the lawyer's interest in getting a full

---

and complete response. Moreover, it tells the respondent that a literal statement of what was seen and heard, rather that any judgements or conclusions, is required in order to meet the interviewer's objectives. Within these limits the respondent is invited to speak from his own frame of reference and in his own terms.

———

Once the client is talking, effective legal interviewers encourage the client to continue talking by making appropriate responses that do not foreclose the continued story by the client. These are called minimal encouragers and include nodding the interviewer's head, saying "uh, huh," "ok," etc. They all indicate to the client that the interviewer has heard what was said and is interested in hearing more. Clients who may be unsure of the protocol will look for this encouragement to determine if they are relating the correct information and if they should proceed. Other ways to encourage the client to continue talking but that do not assert control of the floor include:

- *Reflective statements:* Reflect either content or feeling.

- *Encouraging directions:* "Tell me more," "And then what happened," or "Go on."

- *Additional open questions:* "Is there anything else you want to tell me?" or "Is there anything else I should know?"

- *Nonverbal encouragement:* hand gestures, leaning forward in the chair, making appropriate eye contact, or silence.

All of these allow the client to control the ongoing discussion. They do not restrict the topics chosen by the client or the sequence in which they are introduced. They allow the client to recall information freely without direction from the lawyer.

The attorney should continue in this encouraging mode as long as possible and return as often as needed. Avoid the temptation to seize control of the conversation as soon as the client hesitates. Sometimes silence is the most appropriate response. Silence allows the client to collect his or her thoughts and continue at the client's pace. Lawyers who are socialized by the rapid give-and-take of the law school classroom find silence awkward. Avoid the temptation to fill every silence with your own voice. Silence may be especially appropriate when the client has revealed emotionally significant information and needs some time to recover. It may also be appropriate when the client stops in the middle of her narrative and searches her memory for additional information.

We believe that legal interviewers should avoid even moderately limiting responses at this stage. As Professor Gellhorn points out in the following excerpt, even asking the client, "Tell me more about your landlord," runs the risk of missing the important elements of the client's story and diverting the narrative into unproductive waters. Moreover, they should expect the client to give them both content and feeling and be prepared to respond to both.

Gay Gellhorn, *Law and Language: An Empirically Based Model for the Opening Moments of the Client Interview*, 4 CLINICAL L. REV. 321, 346-347, 348-349 (1998)[11]

* * * *

The model urges legal interviewers to restrict themselves to linguistic strategies that encourage complete client response, such as:

- Silence

- Continuers ("Mm-hmm" "Yes?" "Uh-huh" "Go on")

- Non-judgemental straightforward statements ("You seem uncomfortable.")

- Non-verbal facilitators (hand gestures to continue, facial expressions, e.g., nodding, leaning forward, eye contact if culturally appropriate)

- Additional open-ended question: ("Are there other concerns on your mind?" "You've focused on X (e.g. needing your Medicaid). How does that problem fit with the rest of what's going on in your life?" "Can you tell me a bit more?")

As important as it is to use the linguistic strategies identified above, it is equally important to avoid some linguistic strategies that research has shown inhibit the expression of subsequent concerns. These techniques have their place in later phases of the interviewing process, but they do damage in the opening moments because they cut off expression of new concerns and prematurely define the focus of the dialogue.

- Avoid probes or elaborators (encouraging the client to continue talking on a particular topic or aspect, e.g., Client: I've had a lot of trouble with my landlord. Lawyer: Tell me more about your landlord.)

- Avoid recompleters (restating content of previous statement, e.g., in the previous example, lawyer responds "You've been having trouble with your landlord.")

- Avoid closed-ended questions ("Is your landlord refusing to make repairs?")

. . . If legal interviewers follow the model outlined above, it is predictable that some of the concerns and life-world context that clients reveal will be

---

[11] Copyright © 1998 by THE CLINICAL LAW REVIEW. Reprinted with permission.

emotionally charged. My guidance to students is that they should expect and be prepared to see, hear and accept emotion. Judging from the medical interviewing literature, doctors (like lawyers) need to be reassured that feelings addressed openly are not harmful, and that patients (and clients) will control how far they go in expressing those feelings. Because emotion is so predictable, and yet so unsettling to most listeners, there is every reason to practice responding in positive ways. The literature suggests a number of successful linguistic strategies that help build a relationship with a client who expresses emotion. A critical piece is to recognize and explicitly and accurately acknowledge emotional content, not attempt to ignore and avoid it, for example by taking back control of the floor and changing the topic. Acknowledgment can be fairly simple: "Your eyes are tearing up, that seems sad for you." A second piece is to offer empathic responses. I borrow the term "generative empathy" from the psychiatric literature and find it useful because it focuses on the interviewer's "specific intent of broadening the patient's understanding and ability to cope." I, too, want my clients to be better able to control or respond effectively to the factors in their lives that are involved in legal issues, and to do so long after their limited encounter with their legal representation has ended. I do not want to employ empathy simply as a technique, and a potentially manipulative one at that. Empathy is a process. Nevertheless, responding empathically can be taught and learned.

The model also draws on psychoanalytic theory to suggest that lawyers will do better at drawing their clients out and hearing and understanding their clients' problems and their context if lawyers are more excited about their client encounters and in particular the opening moments. [A leading author] endorses an attitude of interest and fascination. Interviewers should use all of their senses to be drawn into the other person's world. Communicating that interest to clients encourages them to talk, just as an actor is influenced by the audience.

The model draws on the medical interviewing literature to caution us to verify that clients have completed their statements of concern before we move on. Linguistic forms that accomplish this can be straightforward: "Is there anything else on your mind?" "I can hear you're concerned about that, but before we discuss it, is there anything else you'd like me to know about it?" Legal interviewers also can periodically resolicit a topic, particularly if a client appears to be recycling a topic, an indication that the topic is freighted in some way that the interviewer does not yet understand and has not yet acknowledged.

§ 5-3(b). IDENTIFYING THE CLIENT'S GOALS AND INTERESTS

Lawyers should try to get a coherent picture of the client's situation. This includes getting not only the facts of the client's "case," but also understanding the goals the client has for his situation. The client has already made a decision to seek legal advice. In some ways, the client has decided that she has a "legal" problem. But there may be a variety of goals that a client hopes to achieve. Indeed, the client may believe that some goals are unreachable because she has a "legal problem."

At this point, the lawyer should clarify the major points of the client's story only to the extent necessary to understand the broad problem and its context. The lawyer should then summarize what she has heard. The key word here is "summarize." It should not be verbatim playback of what the client said. Rather, the lawyer should paraphrase the story, using the client's own words as much as possible. This verifies the accuracy of what the lawyer has heard and enhances rapport with the client. It also signals that the interview will move to another stage.

However, lawyers interview clients in the real world where things do not always go as planned. Trying to fit each interview into a prescribed model may interfere with client recall and rapport. A lawyer can interfere with the client's story by excessive interruptions, narrow framing, inattentiveness, and distorting questions. The client can distort his story, on the other hand, by poor recall, automatic mental processing procedures, biases, or duplicity.

§ 5-4. LAWYER DISTORTIONS

§ 5-4(a). INTERRUPTIONS

Studies of doctor-patient interviews show that although medical schools train doctors to allow patients to complete an initial statement, most doctors fail to do so. Doctors interrupted their patients within 18 seconds of an invitation to "Tell me what brought you to the clinic today."[12] Once the patients began talking, the doctors tended to take control of the conversation.[13] The patients almost never got to finish a complete initial statement.

Lawyers do not fare much better. One study found that lawyers interrupted their clients more often than people interrupt one another in ordinary conversation.[14] Other studies showed that lawyers used these interruptions to wrest control of the conversation and channel it into areas of lawyer interest.[15] These lawyers then followed up their interruptions with narrow or leading questions resulting in missed legal issues and misdiagnosis of the client's case.[16]

A more recent study of clinical law students showed that some students are changing from this traditional model. Although students interrupted their clients, their interruptions were most often "cooperative." That is, the interruptions served to enhance rapport or encourage disclosure or both. Cooperative interruptions do not wrest control of the topics or their sequence.

---

[12] *See* Gellhorn, *supra* note 1, at 346.

[13] *Id.* at 29.

[14] Israel Bryna Bogoch & Brenda Danet, *Challenge and Control in Lawyer-Client Interaction: A Case Study in an Israeli Legal Aid Office,* 4 TEXT 249 (1984).

[15] Carl J. Hosticka, *We Don't Care What Happened, We Only Care About What is Going to Happen,* 26 SOC. PROBS. 599 (1979).

[16] *Id.*

When used appropriately, they facilitate the twin goals of the legal interview — building rapport and gathering information. On the other hand, excessive interruptions, even when nominally cooperative, undermine both goals.

In the following excerpt, Professor Linda Smith discusses the results of interviews by three students — Reyes, Mike, and Mary Jane.

Linda F. Smith, *Interviewing Clients: A Lingustic Comparison of The "Traditional" Interview and the "Client-Centered" Interview*, 1 CLINICAL L. REV. 541, 557-561 (1995)[17]

* * * *

All three interviews contained interruptions by both attorneys and clients. Since . . . an interruption can show competition or cooperation, each interruption was analyzed with respect to this criterion. Interruptions in which the speaker repeated a factual statement, expressed empathy or reflected the client's emotion, or began to provide an answer to a question while the questioner was still speaking, were designated as "cooperative." . . . [I]nterruptions that occur at the end of utterances are usually of this cooperative variety. Competitive interruptions include those where the interrupter changes the topic or insists upon an answer to a question which the other might have been avoiding. Competitive interruptions also include instances where one speaker discounts or ignores what the other is saying. Competitive interruptions occur more typically in mid-utterance, indicating an attempt to control the conversation.

An analysis of the interruptions shows that the student lawyers interrupted relatively frequently. . . . [T]his amount of interrupting in a legal interview exceeds interruptions in ordinary speech. However, unlike the lawyers studied by Hosticka, the law students did not interrupt more than their clients; the client interrupted as much or more than the law student. But more importantly, the interviews differed from [earlier studies] in that most of the interruptions (by both lawyers and clients) were "cooperative" interruptions. These client-centered interviews were not struggles for control nor exercises in attorney domination.

Some examples of the lawyers' interruptions may prove instructive. Reyes' first interruption was typical for him:

> Client A: . . . somebody had thrown rocks and bricks through most of the windows in my house. It was so upsetting. Anyway//[18]
>
> Reyes: // That's too bad.
>
> Client A: It's after midnight.

---

[18] Backslashes indicate when the lawyer and the client were talking at the same time or when one interrupted the other.

Inserting such an empathic and genuine statement should not be considered competitive or controlling.

Reyes made eleven interruptions and only two were competitive. The first was to "clarify" the date (erroneously) when the client was at the beginning of her "story." Here is that competitive interruption by the attorney, followed by a cooperative client interruption:

> Reyes: OK. Ike Jones is the landlord or is he the manager?
>
> Client A: He is the manager
>
> Reyes: OK . . .
>
> Client A: of the things, and so anyway.//
>
> Reyes: //I see this occurred during Memorial Day, right?//
>
> Client A: //No it was damaged
>
> Reyes: //this damage to the house?
>
> Client A: No, it was the week before.

The student has asked a narrow, clarifying question (about who Ike Jones is); the client answers it and attempts to continue with her story. At that point the student interrupts with a leading question seeking to "clarify" the date the damage occurred (the student is wrong). This is viewed as a competitive interruption because it takes the floor away from the client and makes the client address the lawyer's confusion over dates before the client can go on with her story.

Mike [the second student in the study] similarly interrupted primarily (4 of 6) with cooperative statements, particularly of emotional reflection or empathy. The first of the two competitive interruptions did not change the topic; it was designed to clarify a fact and to move the story forward in an orderly way:

> Client B: . . . I called them again and did reach this Ike Jones character, and he's the managing guy. He's the guy who's — I've never met the owner, but he's the guy who manages the property//
>
> Mike: //That was a personal visit or just a phone call?
>
> Client B: Phone call. OK. I finally got through to someone. He said he'd get right on it.

It may have been that the student was frustrated with the amount of detail the client was providing about personal relations and sought to get the client back to the "action" of the story — making a complaint. The client provided the answer and then immediately moved on with the narrative of what happened after the contact. Mike's other competitive interruption occurred at the conclusion of the interview. As the client was answering a question about "other concerns" by musing "I don't think . . . No.//I don't think I do," Mike interrupted after the "no" and said: "OK. Let me get right on this." Although the client is being silenced while she is musing about "other concerns," the attorney is at least interrupting her to tell her he will get to work on her problem.

Mary Jane interrupted more (16) than the two male students, but also employed mostly (13) cooperative interruptions, often simply to reflect a fact or goal the client had just enunciated or to comment empathetically "I believe it" or "I can understand that." Of her three competitive interruptions, one was an attempt to (erroneously) clarify a fact, another to continue rephrasing a question when the client had begun to answer it, and the third to clarify a previously stated fact and to keep the client focused on relevant details in the story when the client seemed to stray to trivial commentary. The third interruption is as follows:

Client A: . . . and so then on Saturday, I got up about 8:00 in the morning and about 8:30 //

Mary Jane: // I'm sorry, so from Wednesday when you spoke to him, [uh-huh] I think this was Saturday, [uh-huh]// no response//.

Client A: //No response// [OK], Nothing was done. [OK] OK. So finally Saturday I go. . . .

The clients' interruptions of the lawyers also were predominantly noncompetitive. The typical interruption was to begin to answer a question while the attorney was still asking it. These women clients either did not interrupt the male attorney at all or only once in a competitive way. The female client did interrupt the female attorney (in what was more of an interruption-filled interview) a total of 21 times, and 8 of these were deemed "competitive" interruptions. By and large, these competitive interruptions occurred when the student was still asking or modifying a question, and the client seized the floor to assert her views:

Mary Jane: Well, it sounds like this is your home//

Client A: //Yes it is. I don't like moving . . .

Mary Jane: and you want to stay. And at the time you signed this [lease], had you read over everything//

Client A: //Well pretty much so, I've rented properties before and you know, you read them and you — no wonder. But I mean aren't. . . .

Mary Jane: //and understood it?

This study of "client-centered interviewing" did not find interruptions indicative of a struggle for control, as did researchers who studied "traditional" legal interviews. The image of an attorney interrupting the client to challenge or to avoid hearing the client's story . . . was not apparent here. Nor is the image one of an attorney interrupting to cut off the client's account of one topic in order to redirect the client's attention to a different subject. Rather, most interruptions by both attorney and client were cooperative. The few competitive interruptions were primarily for clarification of something the client had already said, and only rarely to change the topic from what the client wished to discuss.

The fact that the interviews studied here, like those in prior studies, contained more interruptions than an ordinary conversation may simply be a fact to accept. The legal interview is usually time-bound and important to both conversation partners. The client wishes to get out his or her story and requests. The attorney wishes to collect the information he or she deems crucial and to clarify what the client wants done. Thus, both partners to the conversation have significant goals and only so much time to accomplish them. I believe we should accept that this type of conversation between client and professional will contain more interruptions than do typical, informal conversations. However, given the fact of these interruptions, the lawyer should be particularly respectful of the client's need to participate in the conversation as an equal partner and to tell his or her story and to express his or her concerns and goals.

———

Note that many of the "competitive" student interruptions in the above excerpt were "clarifying" interruptions. Generally, it is best if these clarifying questions can be held until the end of the client's statement, but sometimes the lawyer will need to have the answer to the clarifying statement before she can understand the rest of the client's story. The lawyer must make a judgment whether it would be best to interrupt the client (risking breaking the client's train of thought) or to wait (risking misunderstanding the client's story). This will turn on factors such as the tendency of this client to become confused and the importance of the fact at issue.

§ 5-4(b). NARROW QUESTIONS AND PREMATURE DIAGNOSIS

In addition to interrupting, lawyers can block the flow of information and distort its content in other ways. Narrowly framing questions can affect both the amount of information and its quality. Asking the client to tell you about his legal problem suggests a frame of reference — legal — that may unnecessarily narrow the client's description. It asks the client to filter what is being said by the client's own notions of legal relevance. Even follow-up questions that limit the topic may cause the client to veer off course.

Lawyers can also distort the process by making a premature diagnosis of the client's problem and then filtering what the client says through that diagnosis. Gellhorn provided a detailed analysis of a case in which one clinical law student seemed to decide that the client's primary disability was physical.[19] The student then ignored the client's repeated attempts to signal that she was depressed. Only when a different team of students took over did the client's depression become the focus of her disability claim.

§ 5-4(c). CROSS-EXAMINATION

Lawyers may be tempted to cross-examine their clients even during the initial interview. Law students are taught by a version of the Socratic

---

[19] Her case study is discussed in some detail in Chapter 6, § 6-3.

method that highly values quick insight and prompt response to questions. They are socialized into the adversary system which, they are told, is the best system for "getting at the truth." It seems natural to get information by initiating a Socratic dialogue with clients.

Many studies have confirmed this image. Rosenthal found that authoritarian lawyers seek to control the case from the very beginning, including the information received from the client. Early studies found an almost courtroom-like cross-examination style in lawyers.[20] The influence of client-centered interviewing may have altered this practice somewhat. The bankruptcy lawyers studied by Neustadter showed a mixture of styles ranging from traditional controlling to client-centered. Yet even these lawyers tended to control the interview by asking questions shortly after a brief opening statement by the client.

§ 5-5. CLIENT DISTORTIONS

Clients may also distort the flow of information. Their memories may be faulty, they may have an improper frame around their narrative, or they may be hiding information. Thus, the lawyer cannot go on automatic pilot during the client's narrative. The lawyer must pay attention to what the client is saying with an eye toward later clarifying what is unclear and exploring what is left out.

As the lawyer hears the client's story, the lawyer must start placing it into its legal context. In the way that law students are asked to spot issues on exams, effective legal interviewers spot legal issues as clients talk. If the lawyer knows what the client hopes to accomplish, the lawyer can view these issues using those goals as the baseline. If the lawyer does not know the client's goals, the lawyer should frame these issues broadly.

The danger for the lawyer is to prematurely diagnose the client's matter. Once that is done, the lawyer imposes a narrow frame on the client's story and runs the risk of ignoring the client's real goals and unduly limiting the possible ways to achieve those goals.

Clients may feel that they cannot remember matters well and thus give only a very short summary of the facts. Before the lawyer resorts to more specific questioning, there are several ways to jump start the client's memory:

- Help the client relax.

- Encourage the client's recall.

- Remove the pressure for "correct answers."

For example, the lawyer could say, "Don't worry. We all have trouble remembering things sometimes. Just tell me whatever you remember even if it doesn't seem important to you."

---

[20] *See, e.g.,* Hosticka, *supra* note 15, at 609.

It is not necessary to have clients provide their stories in chronological order in every case. Many clients naturally will relay their stories chronologically. The only thing needed from them might be more detail. Other clients will use a different narrative structure because they have not stored these events chronologically. Insisting on a chronology from these clients may actually distort their recall. In these cases, it will be up to the lawyer to restate the case as a chronology and verify the details by patient follow-up questioning.

§ 5-6. SUMMARY

Getting the client's story may be the most important stage of the interview. Allowing the client to completely tell her story builds rapport and obtains information. Clients who are allowed to tell their story are likely to trust their lawyers and, thus, be more likely to disclose even embarrassing information. In addition, allowing the client to proceed with minimal interruptions is likely to produce more accurate information than any other technique.

The lawyer's approach and techniques may enhance or detract from building rapport and gathering sufficient information. The best approach to follow is one that allows the client to do most of the talking during this stage.

Lawyers should

- Use an unfocused framing statement to begin this section.

- Ask only broad, unfocused questions, if necessary.

- Allow the client to speak without interruption.

- Encourage the client to continue talking.

- Allow the client to control the conversation.

- Avoid cross-examining the client.

In the end, allowing the client to speak freely at this stage will enhance both client rapport and client information.

CHAPTER 6

DEVELOPING THE CLIENT'S STORY

After the client has told the lawyer his story, the lawyer has an opportunity:

- to clarify anything that remains unclear,

- to explore areas that have not been covered, and

- to develop information related to the client's claims, defenses, or transactions.

§ 6-1. FRAMING STATEMENT: REPEATING THE HIGH POINTS

Once the client has exhausted his narrative, the lawyer should employ another framing question. The statement should contain a restatement of the important points of the client narrative, an explanation of the next phase of the interview, and a request for specific details. Consider the following:

> L: As I understand what you told me, you were driving from your house to the grocery store on Kavanaugh. You stopped to make a right turn at the stop light at Kavanaugh and Beechwood when a car tried to pass you on the right. As this car went by you, it grazed the side of your car. It never stopped. It caused a lot of damage on the right side of your car. Is that correct?

> L: Ok, now I want to ask you some questions that will help me better understand what happened and give me a better handle on how I can help you?

The first part of this framing statement allows the client to verify his story and allows the lawyer to check to see if she heard it accurately. The second part signals to the client that one section of the interview is over and a new section is about to begin.

§ 6-2. CLARIFYING AND EXPLORING THE CLIENT'S STORY

The goal of this phase of the interview is to clarify and to explore the client's story. First, the lawyer wants to fully develop all the facts that matter to the client's case. Second, the lawyer wants to explore potential legal theories and any potential solutions applicable to the client's situation. In the first instance, the lawyer is expanding on what the client has already explained. In the second instance, the lawyer is testing other possibilities suggested by the client's story. In either case, the lawyer must develop the details of client stories.

All statements are essentially summaries. When we say that the weather is beautiful, we are summarizing a variety of sensory data and making an aesthetic judgment. If we describe something as cold or hot, we summarize the physical sensations that led us to that conclusion. Similarly, when a person says that he "pulled up to the intersection," he is providing a narrative summary of an larger process. Frequently, this summary is all that is necessary. To make sense of an process, we impose a structure on it. This structure takes the form of a story. This involves eliminating things that we judge unnecessary to the story and highlighting things that seem important to it. Thus, "pulling up to the intersection" is part of the story of driving and having an accident. The climax of the story is the accident: those parts of the story that make the accident comprehensible in the narrative are highlighted. We tell the story of the accident as though it had a beginning, a middle, and an end.

"Pulling up to the intersection" eliminates a lot of material that is not central to the narrator's understanding of the story. We may not know the weather conditions or the time of day. We don't know how crowded the intersection was or what it looked like. Neither do we know about the selection playing on the radio, the items the driver was going to pick up, the thoughts in his mind, the condition of his car, etc. In short, statements like "I pulled up to the intersection" are packages of details. Some of those details might be important to the client's case. Those details must be explored.

In the early portions of the interview, the lawyer should concede control of the conversation to the client. Now we suggest that the lawyer take over control of the topics and their sequence but not the kind of information the client provides. That is, the lawyer will now focus the conversation on those aspects of the client's case that need clarification or exploration. The lawyer should review his notes of the earlier portion of the interview and identify things that need clarification. The lawyer can then proceed through his notes until all of these items are cleared up. In addition, the lawyer should explore things that suggest or support legal theories applicable to the client's case. The lawyer should carefully explore all facets of the case that may relate to one or more elements of one or more legal theories.

§ 6-2(a).   FUNNEL SEQUENCES

The most effective technique to help explore these events is the funnel sequence.[1] It is so named because it mirrors a funnel — it is broad at the top and narrow at the bottom. Each successive question is narrower than the previous one. The sequence can be described as going from the general to the specific, broad to narrow, open to closed. No matter how it is

---

[1] *See generally*, RAYMOND L. GORDEN, INTERVIEWING: STRATEGY, TECHNIQUES, AND TACTICS 266-269 (1969).

described its purpose is to explore an area of the client's case and generate important details about that area. The lawyer should use a separate funnel sequence to explore each important area of the client's story.

Funnels are useful when the purpose of the sequence of questions is to get a detailed description of an event, a situation, a setting, or a person. Funnels also help clients recall details. The open question at the top of the funnel allows the client to recall information using his or her own methods of association. This is almost always better than peppering the client with cross-examination questions about the details. The narrower follow-up questions trace the client's associations and allow the client to explore his or her memory thoroughly and freely.

Using funnels also mitigates against imposing the interviewer's frame of reference on the client's answers. When the client is prompted to "Tell me more about your business" she can provide the information without the possible distorting frame of the lawyer's mental map.[2]

Here is how the funnel sequence works in legal interviews. First, the legal interviewer asks an open but focused question — e.g., "Tell me what happened when you pulled into the intersection." This question relies on the client's open and unprompted narrative but now the frame is adjusted to narrow the area to the intersection. As the client finishes responding to the question, the lawyer asks narrower and narrower questions until the question seeks specific information. These narrowing questions are still open; only the frame is narrowed. Raymond Gorden's model for analyzing the scope of questions as to question, action, actor, and scene, helps to show the progressive narrowing of the questions. The chart summarizing the components of a question under Gorden's model appears in Chapter 5. For example, the sequence could go like this:

> Type ABAC: Tell me what happened when you pulled into the intersection. (General on the question and the action, slightly more specific on the person, and moderately specific on the scene.)
>
> Type ABCD: You said you looked to the right, what did you see? (General on the question, slightly more specific on the person, moderately specific on the action, and specific on the scene.)
>
> Type: EEDD: Did you brake when you saw the car in your mirror? (Very specific on the question and the person, specific on the action and the scene.)
>
> Type EEEE: When you pushed down on your brake, did your car stop immediately? (Very specific on the question, person, action, and scene.)

This sequence could go on focusing more and more intently on the events at the intersection. Using funnel sequences requires that the lawyer have some idea of the details that may be involved in the narrated events as well as some idea of their importance. It would waste time to randomly pursue irrelevant details. Effective use of funnels also requires patience

---

2 *See* Leonard L. Riskin, *Mediation and Lawyers,* 43 OHIO ST. L.J. 29, 43-48 (1982).

and diligence. The effective interviewer will explore all the events until she is satisfied that she has enough information to proceed.

§ 6-2(b). HELPING CLIENTS EXPLORE THEIR MEMORIES

Clients may not have clear memories of specific details. Interviewers can help clients recall details, however. Memory studies show that people can accurately recall more details about an event when they are prompted to recall the context in which the event happened; when they are encouraged not to limit what they relate; when they are asked to recall the events in a different order; and when they are asked to try to see the event through other observers' eyes.[3] It will also be useful if the lawyer asks the client to recall the event using his or her typical sensory mode.

Here are some examples:

1. Context:

> "Try to recreate the context surrounding the accident. Think about what the day was like, what the car looked like, what you had on, what smells there were and anything else that will help you picture the accident. Think about how you were feeling and what your reactions were, both before and after the incident."

Context recreation relies on the brain's ability to store information under a variety of "headings." By recreating the context, including both the physical and the mental contexts, the client is given an opportunity to access the information in his memory using an alternative filing system.

2. Encouragement:

> "Some people hold back information because they are not sure about what they remember. Please don't edit anything out. Tell me everything that comes to your mind about that day, even if you're not sure it is important."

Encouragement takes advantage of two memory techniques. First, it seeks to relax the person by removing performance anxiety. Second, memory seems to be enhanced when people recall as many details about an event as possible. Memory about events is enhanced when people simply recall as much as they can without filtering out the unimportant. For example, we have all had the experience of forgetting something important that someone said to us only to have it come flooding back to memory by recalling what we were wearing at the time.

3. Different order:

> "It is natural to go through the accident from beginning to end and you should try to do that first. But you might find that you remember

---

[3] The material in this section is drawn from Ronald P. Fisher, *Interviewing Victims and Witnesses of Crime*, 1 PSYCHOL. PUB. POL'Y & L. 732 (1995).

> more if you go through the incident in reverse order; or you might start with what impressed you the most about it and go from there, both forward and backward in time."

This takes advantage of how memory is often recreated. Memories probably do not exist as videotapes. They are not waiting on the shelf waiting to be placed into the "Recall Machine" and played. Instead, memory consists of bits and pieces of information stored all over the brain under different and multiple headings. It is as though the movie we rented had to be reassembled by putting together splices of it from all the shelves in the store. By rearranging the order, we force the brain to deliberately search for the bits and pieces of the story, some of which may get left out if we only go from beginning to middle to end. This is another reason why we should not force chronologies from every client. It may be helpful to use chronological order as a memory aid but not to rely on it if that is not how the client organizes his memory.

4. Other perspectives:

> "Try to imagine what the intersection would have looked like to someone who was standing at the corner waiting to cross the street or a driver on the opposite side of the intersection."

This technique relies on the recreation phenomenon to prompt memory. It asks the client to recreate the scene visually.

Although these techniques work well in combination with open questions, memory is further enhanced when the interviewer follows these techniques with a series of focused questions. These questions are specific as to the question, the person, the action, and the scene.

In our example, after the client attempts to remember the information using one or more of these techniques, the legal interviewer might ask:

- What color was the other car?
- What did the witnesses look like?
- What were they wearing?
- What kind of car hit you?

§ 6-2(c). STATEMENTS OF UNDERSTANDING

Once the lawyer and the client have completely explored and clarified the client's situation, the lawyer should employ another framing statement. The lawyer should not only summarize the client's story but also include within it the lawyer's understanding of the client's goals. It is not necessary to repeat all of the details that the lawyer clarified or discovered in the preceding portion of the interview. The lawyer should use this as an opportunity to have the client verify the accuracy of the lawyer's understanding of the case. The question signals that the information gathering phase of the initial interview has come to an end.

For example, at this point the lawyer might say:

> Let me summarize what I heard you tell me so that I can be sure it is accurate. You left the house to go the grocery store. It was about 9:00 a.m. on a Saturday. The traffic was light. You stopped your car at the intersection of Kavanaugh and Beechwood to turn left into the Kroger's parking when a yellow car ran the stop sign on your right and hit the right front of your car. Your car spun around twice and hit the utility pole on the opposite side of the intersection. The yellow car then drove off on Kavanaugh away from you. You want to know what you can do to get that driver to pay for your medical and car repair expenses. Is this right?

§ 6-3.　AN EXAMPLE OF SUCCESSFULLY EXPLORING A CLIENT'S CASE

Technique and sensitivity must always be combined. In their desire to fully explore and clarify their clients' stories, lawyers must be careful not to impose their own structure on their clients' stories. Lawyers should listen attentively to what the client is saying. If not, the lawyer may not get the full picture and fail to develop important information. In the following excerpt, Professor Gay Gellhorn relates how a clinical law student missed the crucial issue in his client's case. Two other students took over the case and, by listening to the client and sensitively exploring what they heard, they developed information that proved crucial to winning the client's case. This excerpt is an excellent example of how effective interviewers explore and develop information while at the same time building and enhancing rapport with their client.

Gay Gellhorn, *Law and Language: An Empirically Based Model for the Opening Moments of Client Interviews,* 4 Clinical L. Rev. 321, 350-356 (1998)[4]

* * *

Ms. R. came to the Clinic after twice being denied SSI (Supplemental Security Income). She had applied on her own, claiming that she was disabled because she had very limited use of one hand, which had been severely damaged when she caught her hand in an ice dispensing machine at a welfare motel where she lived with her three children. The Clinic's work with Ms. R. spanned two semesters. As it happened, students who had received different training in interviewing and talking with clients interviewed Ms. R. at different points in her disability case. . . .

---

[4] Copyright © 1998 by The Clinical Law Review. Reprinted with permission.

The older white male interviewer who first saw Ms. R. said that his goal for the initial phase of the interview was to convey that he was prepared and ready to get down to work so she would feel confident in her representation. He chose a nonverbal strategy: After they were seated, he removed his coat and tie and rolled up his sleeves as he talked about all the work to be done and explained various forms. The client's first quasi-invitation to speak did not come until nine minutes of lawyer domination of the floor.

> L: If you have any questions at any time, don't hesitate to call me and we'll be in touch with you frequently. As we get closer to the hearing . . .

> C: [interrupting] Let me ask you question.

She said she has a number of doctor appointments, including a psychologist, Dr. M., providing the first clue that she has a psychosocial problem as well as a physical disability. . . . [T]he client revealed key information in her opening statement — information that was of enough importance to her that she literally burst into the conversation in an attempt to take control of the floor and the topic. She got no further with this first attempt to express her concerns because the interviewer cut her off with a series of closed-ended questions about names, addresses and dates of the appointments.

A second effort by the client to raise her psychiatric concerns was also unsuccessful. Thirty-five minutes into the interview, the legal interviewer questioned her about her work history. She described unsuccessful work attempts as a home health aide, and, in response to an appropriate (albeit somewhat challenging) open-ended question ("Any reasons why you stopped working?"), alluded to her inability to get along with patients or staff. Her demeanor was cheerful, almost coquettish, but suddenly her voice dropped:

> C: I'm going to tell you something. I started something I didn't finish. I have a very crazy mind, OK?

> L: Don't we all? [smiling and shrugging]

> C: No, I'm serious, I have a crazy mind. I had a whole lot of problems, so I went to see a psychiatrist. He gave me medication for depression. But I don't take it. Like, I want to work.

> L: Good!

> C: In my mind, I know I should. Cause, like Friday, I freaked out on my kids. I was angry. Like, I get up, I may be fine. I'm not fine, but I pretend to be fine.

> L: Let me ask you this. . . .

Rather than allowing the client to tell her story, the legal interviewer again interrupted with closed-ended questions requesting names and addresses of the psychiatrist, and then changed the topic to "go back" to their discussion of her work history. The linguistic message was that her attempt to discuss her "crazy" mind was merely an interruption, not a central event in her life and in her application for disability benefits.

The legal interviewer reinforced this when Ms. R. appeared on the verge of a third attempt to talk about her mental state fifty-one minutes into the interview. He began with an appropriate open-ended question ("Tell me what it's like when you wake up.") No sooner did she begin to answer, however, than he interrupted to say "Think in terms of [the inability to use] the hand." The client's shift of direction indicated her conflict: She wanted to follow the interviewer's directions, but she also had a compelling need to talk about her "mind." In her response, she said she had talked to a psychiatrist because she had "a lot of fear" that people were trying to come into her home at night to harm her and her children, and she could not protect herself, hit or lift with her useless hand. "It made me mad." But the legal interviewer again took control of the floor and the topic: "So, without medication, how do you sleep?" Although the interviewer said he wanted "to focus on what you can't do," he imposed his narrow hypothesis on her ("Do you have trouble with buttons?") rather than opening himself to her life-world.

In a fourth attempt to convey her mental distress (63:47 minutes into the interview), the legal interviewer asked: "So during the day your kids are gone. Do you watch T.V.?" Her response is a classic description of depression. "I go to sleep. I don't put clothes on, I don't answer the phone. I don't do my hair." Finally she broke through to him. For the first time, he acknowledged her: "Tell — what's going through your mind?" She talked about anger at the doctors and at what she could not do. His empathic response (the first in the 65:29 minutes) — "That hurts, that hurts" — overlapped her repetition "when I can't do what I want to do." Reviewing the videotape without sound conveys the impression that something significant to the client occurred at this point, because she sat back in her chair in a more relaxed posture. Her body language said "Finally, he's hearing me."

The client's last words would remind an attending listener (but not this interviewer) that her mental state was her primary concern. In response to the legal interviewer's reassurance, as they prepare to conclude the interview at 86:25 minutes ("I'll check in with you once, twice a week.") she said "That's good — the way my mind is." The last word is hers, were there someone to heed it.

Although the student dutifully wrote for copies of Ms. R's psychiatric records, he did not leave the interview with a feel for the facts. . . . [A]s the hearing approached, he focused exclusively on her physical injury and its effect on her ability to work, together with her education and work history. To the degree he included her mental state, he related it entirely to her "understandable" feelings of sadness because of her physical limitations following her injury. . . .

Immediately prior to her hearing, Ms. R came back for a moot hearing [during which, in response to open-ended questions and neutral prompts, she] revealed that she was, indeed, seriously depressed, and had thought recently of suicide and of harming others.

This new information totally changed the theory of Ms. R's case. We lacked sufficient evidence to document Ms. R's affective disorder, and we knew in any case that the Administrative Law Judge would not rule on any mental impairment without receiving a psychiatric review from the state Disability Determination Service (DDS). [With Ms. R's consent, the case was remanded to the DDS for further review.]

The DDS, however, again denied Ms. R's claim. . . . [She described herself] as "worse" and we once again requested a hearing. Now in a different semester, the new legal representatives on the case — a white woman and a Nigerian woman not much younger than their African-American client — reviewed the records, critiqued the tape of the initial interview and planned a different strategy. . . . They identified their goal as eliciting information about Ms. R's past and present mental state so that they could (1) serve as her advocates as they helped her complete the forms requesting a hearing; (2) discover new avenues for evidentiary development; and (3) facilitate her telling her story effectively at a hearing. They began with an invitation and verbal statement that they would cede floor and topic control:

> L1: All right, Ms. [R]. We've signed the consent form for the video. I've handed you [the prior legal interviewer's] letter, indicating that two students are going to be taking over the case. And, um, this whole interview is totally confidential, and it just stays only between us. And, um . . . we just want you to relax, and, you know, whatever comes to your mind — like you spoke out — out there — just tell us. And, um, we basically want this interview — we want you to talk, and not just us to run the show. And if we have any questions, you know, we'll ask you about something. Okay.

The other legal representative took over with an acknowledgment that they were aware of her depression, as well as her hand injury, from reading her file. She concluded by saying "So if you could tell us something about your depression." With an invitation to talk, and specific permission to talk about her depression, the client assumed floor control and within 2:15 minutes spoke of her suicidal ideation.

> C: Right now I'm going through a depression stage. That's why I don't look so happy right now. (Laughs nervously)

> L1: Mm-hmm.

> C: I talks with Dr. M. yesterday because I was — I don't know — I felt like I might commit suicide. So, today, um . . . I was supposed to get some calls from a psychiatrist.

> L1: Okay.

> C: And they could see if they got any — this depression, I needed something, some sort of medication to help me from being depressed.

The client wanted to talk about her mental state and the legal interviewers respected her overarching choice of topic. In marked contrast to the interview taped the previous semester, where the legal interviewer controlled the floor, there was a far more equal sharing. . . . [But the new student was not passive. She] used appropriate, open-ended probes and occasional focused, closed-ended questions ("One day we were talking about you have some good days and some bad days. Ummm . . . how does a bad day — what is a bad day usually ?" "So, on your good days, how do you interact with . . . the children's teachers when you go pick them up?" "How is your sleeping affected by all this? What are your sleep patterns?") to gather facts about manifestations of depression in the categories that the Social Security Administration requires to prove disability.

At the conclusion of the interview, they had learned in the client's own words about her behavior at home with her children ("I mean, if I wanted to kill [my children], what would make you think I be thinking about if I kill myself, what's gonna happen to them?") and in the world, where she experienced unpredictable anger and homicidal fantasies.

> C: Like, maybe a couple of months ago, or a month ago, I almost killed [my fiancee].
>
> L1: Hmm.
>
> C: And that's much better to try to stay away from him.
>
> L1: I see. Mm-hmm,
>
> C: . . . I had a picture on my head and knew exactly how I was gonna trick him.

She has given the legal interviewers a glimpse of her childhood experience and early psychiatric care, enabling them eventually to track down her old medical records to establish the severity and duration of her illness.

> C: My mother tried to take my oldest son away from me. I was married — I got married at 16 —
>
> L1: Mm-hmm.
>
> C: — to leave home, because she was beating me so bad for no reason. And in my mind then — and that's when it really started, that 'I'm gonna kill this woman if she hit me one more time. I'm gonna kill her.'
>
> L1: Mm-hmm. . . .
>
> C: At that time I had this lady friend that would talk to me . . . she was talking but I just found myself crying.
>
> L1: Mm-hmm.
>
> C: Was just — just crying, you know — like, I wanted to die. So I went and got help.

She has spoken repeatedly of suicide. She has shared deep feelings ("In my mind — everything in my mind — I don't even know my own — my self — my own mind, sometimes. And that's what frightens me. Because I don't even know my own self.") and she has received empathic responses. Interestingly, the interview took half the time of the less fruitful exchange from the preceding semester. In due course, the Clinic was able to translate all this information into a winning case and simultaneously present the client in her own voice.

––––––––

§ 6-4.   ENDING THE INITIAL INTERVIEW

§ 6-4(a).   DEFINING THE ROLE OF THE ATTORNEY

In a perfect world, the interview would come to an obvious conclusion. The client and the lawyer would have thoroughly developed all of the facts, the lawyer would know the law to be applied, and the client would be perfectly situated to make a decision. In this perfect world the lawyer would then counsel the client about the decision, either immediately or at a future appointment. Possessing perfect information, perfect clients and perfect lawyers would reach perfectly optimal decisions. But the world is not perfect. Lawyers, clients, and their cases vary greatly. The means of developing the client's story that we have suggested is like every other recommendation in this book. It artificially isolates segments of the lawyer-client relationship and posits general guidelines for those segments. These are only guidelines and must be adapted to the situation. Nevertheless, they can be useful in structuring the lawyer-client relationship.

Eventually an interview reaches its end. The lawyer may not need any further information or there may be nothing more that the client can provide. Perhaps the lawyer needs to consider what the law requires, or the client and the lawyer run out of time. If the lawyer and the client are ready to make a decision at the end of the interview, they can proceed to the "counseling" stage. If the lawyer and the client are not ready to make a decision, then the counseling session can be deferred until later.

§ 6-4(b).   THINGS TO DO AT THE END OF EVERY INTERVIEW

The effective lawyer will take care of certain things at the end of the interview. The lawyer should:

1. Prepare and sign a representation agreement:

The decision to hire the lawyer should be formalized in a written agreement. The law does not require a written agreement but an agreement helps avoid later problems. Providing a written agreement that specifies what the lawyer will do for the client prevents later misunderstandings between the lawyer and the client. It may be perfectly clear to the lawyer that she will only take the case to the trial court and not to the appellate court, but the client can easily misunderstand the distinction.

2. Clarify the fee structure:

A written fee agreement also helps avoid misunderstanding. Fee disputes are one of the most common sources of complaints against lawyers.

Often these disputes arise because the lawyer did not clearly communicate the fee to the client. The client is later surprised by the size of a bill and, especially if the lawyer has not maintained a good relationship with the client, the client complains. Sometimes there is no choice but to put the fee agreement in writing. For example, the ethical rules require that contingent fees be in writing.

3. Explain what the lawyer will do next and when the lawyer will be done:

The lawyer should make sure the client understands the next things the lawyer will do. For example, the lawyer can say: "I will have to research the law to see if you can file a lawsuit or if you have other options. I should be finished with this research by next Friday." This not only keeps the client informed but also helps further build rapport by showing the lawyer's interest in the client's case.

4. Explain how and when the client can contact the lawyer:

The lawyer should also remind the client how to contact the lawyer. This reminder has several important benefits. It allows the client to keep in touch with the lawyer and makes it easier for the lawyer to discharge her obligation to keep the client informed about the case. It also makes it more likely that the client will follow through on the case. Research from other short-term counseling contexts shows that clients are more likely to listen to their counselor's advice and to comply with any course of treatment if they believe they can keep in touch with their counselor.

5. Explain the client's responsibilities:

Clients should also be reminded of their responsibilities. This serves several purposes. First, it involves clients in their cases. Rosenthal's study suggested that clients who participated in the resolution of their case received objectively better settlements and were subjectively more satisfied. Second, this involvement reinforces the relationship between the lawyer and the client. Clients receive mixed signals if the lawyer treats them as partners during the interview and then tells them at the end of the interview, at least implicitly: "Don't worry. I'll take it from here."

6. Prepare a written memorandum documenting the interview:

Lawyers should prepare a written memorandum outlining what they have learned during the interview. The memorandum should be prepared immediately after the interview. It should include all of the important facts relating to the client's situation as well as a clear statement of the client's goals. The memorandum should also include a description of the next steps, who will be responsible for them, and the date by which they should be taken.

§ 6-4(c). THINGS TO DO WHEN NO DECISION ABOUT THE CASE IS MADE AT THE END OF THE INITIAL INTERVIEW

When the lawyer and the client do not make a decision at the end of the initial interview, the lawyer can enhance the client's ability to make a decision later by doing one or more of the following things.

1. Ask client to reflect on goals:

Clients should be asked to think about what they hope to accomplish. Ideally, the decisions in a case will all facilitate the accomplishment of the client's goals. Clients should be reminded that their goals and not the lawyer's will determine the course of the representation. They should be asked to think about all of the possible goals they want to reach and to put them in some order. This will help later when the lawyer and the client weigh the advantages and disadvantages of various alternatives.

2. Ask client to brainstorm alternative means:

The client should be asked to identify as many alternative ways as possible to accomplish the client's goals. This encourages "vigilant information processing." It also keeps the client involved in her case. The client may believe that her ability to control the representation ends once she leaves the lawyer's office. Brainstorming alternatives mitigates this tendency by keeping the client involved in the case.[5]

§ 6-4(d). THINGS TO DO WHEN A DECISION ABOUT THE CASE IS MADE AT THE INITIAL INTERVIEW

If a decision about the case is made at the initial interview, the lawyer should:

1. Explain how it will be implemented, by whom, and when:

This prevents misunderstandings. For example, the lawyer and the client may agree that the lawyer will file for divorce but only after the client has moved out of the house. The lawyer should make it clear that she will not do anything on the case until the client takes that step. This avoids the problems that arise if lawyers and clients leave the initial interview with different ideas about how to proceed.

2. Assure the client of the lawyer's availability for follow-up counseling:

Being available for further consultation gives the client a chance to re-evaluate the decision in light of second thoughts or new information. Good decision-makers are able to reassess their decisions. Sometimes people do not believe they can or should change their minds after they make an initial decision. Unless there is some reason to act immediately, the client should be encouraged to re-think the decision. The client is more likely to do that if she knows that the lawyer is available for further counseling.

3. Provide a deadline for the client to change decision if needed:

Unlike some personal decisions, the law often imposes deadlines for actions. The statute of limitations may expire, the deadline for responding to a lawsuit may be approaching, or a business opportunity may only be available for a limited time. These factors should be explained clearly to the client. The lawyer should give the client a deadline in those cases in

---

[5] See Chapter 8 for a discussion on brainstorming.

which a deadline exists. The deadline should not be artificial. It should be based on the legal and factual reality of the individual client's case. The lawyer must balance the need to allow the client time to reevaluate the initial decision with the inflexible deadlines imposed by the law. Of course, in some cases, the lawyer will not need to set a deadline. For example, the client who has decided not to prepare or change a will can change that decision at any time.

§ 6-5.   CONCLUSION

Legal interviewers are not born, but neither can they be mass produced. Our natural styles will influence how we conduct interviews. We have set out in this chapter a structure to follow during an initial interview and we have suggested a number of specific techniques to use during the interview. With practice everyone can learn to use these techniques. But your personal style will make some of these techniques seem more natural and easier to learn than others. Effective legal interviewers do not reject techniques merely because they are difficult to learn immediately. Effective legal interviewers integrate these techniques into their personal styles yet remain flexible enough to change their approach in different situations.

CHAPTER 7

DECISION-MAKING

The next four chapters concern client counseling. Effective client counseling helps the client make wise decisions. In Chapter 8, we present a step-by-step method of client counseling. In this chapter, we take a more theoretical look at decision-making: What leads to good and bad decision-making, no matter who is doing the deciding. But first, we make a comparison between legal and therapeutic counseling.

§ 7-1. LEGAL AND THERAPEUTIC COUNSELING: SIMILARITIES AND DIFFERENCES

Rational choice is the law's predominate model.[1] The law believes that 1) clients are rational, and 2) they will act rationally by choosing the path that leads to maximum utility, and 3) lawyers act professionally when they base their professional behavior on these assumptions. Clients need the information that will allow them (or their lawyer) to calculate the costs and benefits of each decision. In essence, law transplants the assumptions of classical economics into the realm of lawyer/client decision making.[2]

Recent research casts doubt on the rational choice model of decision making. This research shows that not all people make decisions by carefully listing options and thoroughly discussing them.[3] Real people use

---

[1] *See, e.g.,* RICHARD A. POSNER, ECONOMIC ANALYSIS OF LAW 3 (5th ed. 1998); Russell B. Korobkin & Thomas S. Ulen, *Removing the Rationality Assumption from Law and Economics,* 88 CAL. L. REV. 1051, 1060 (2000). *See generally* Gary L. Blasi, *What Lawyers Know: Lawyering Expertise, Cognitive Science, and the Functions of Theory,* 45 J. LEG. EDUC. 313, 324 (1995):

> Our legal system is predicated on unstated and generally unstated assumptions about what lawyers do. For each of us, lawyers and law professors, the concept of "lawyer" draws upon a prototypical lawyer engaged in a prototypically lawyerly endeavor.

[2] *See, e.g.,* Mark C. Suchman, *On Beyond Interest: Rational, Normative and Cognitive Perspectives in the Social Scientific Study of Law,* 1997 WISC. L. REV. 475, 475 ("Much of the sociology of law (like much of social science in general) rests on certain implicit or explicit assumptions about how people make decisions. . . ." one of which is an economic or instrumental approach that assumes compliance with law is a calculated assessment of costs and benefits); Jeffrey J. Rachlinksi, *Gains, Losses, and the Psychology of Litigation,* 70 S. CAL. L. REV. 113, 114-115 (1996). Law and Economics as a movement is not concerned with the techniques of legal interviewing. Rather, it concerns itself with "how actors in and subject to the legal system respond to legal directives." Korobkin and Ulen, *supra* note 1, at 1055. Nevertheless, the idea that clients would make decisions based on a rational framework and that these decisions would be based on maximizing client self-interest have permeated the legal interviewing and counseling literature.

[3] *See generally,* IRVING JANIS & LEON MANN, DECISION MAKING: A PSYCHOLOGICAL ANALYSIS OF CONFLICT, CHOICE, AND COMMITMENT (1978). *See also,* Korobkin and Ulen, *supra* note 1, at 1057.

perceptual shortcuts, cognitive end runs, and "irrational" factors to make important and not so important decisions.[4] The rational choice model does not give an accurate picture of how actual clients make litigation decisions.[5] One commentator notes that "[c]urrent theories of litigation fail to account for the possibility that litigants' behavior under risk and uncertainty may not comport with rational theories of behavior, and they therefore fail to paint a complete picture of litigation."[6]

Incorporating these insights can improve legal counseling. Lawyers sometimes claim that they are not counselors, however. As the argument goes, lawyers are trained in the law. They tell clients what the law means, how it applies to their situation, and what to expect from the legal system. Clients do not come to lawyers for counseling. They come for legal advice. If clients ask whether or not they should file a lawsuit, they would be put off if the lawyer responded by saying, "And how do you feel about filing a lawsuit?" Lawyers are trained to handle facts not feelings and laws not longings. Thus, counseling is simply immaterial to what lawyers do or should do.

This criticism of the lawyer-as-counselor is based on an oversimplified and inaccurate view of lawyering. It ignores the similarities between lawyers and counselors. Counselors help people make decisions. People counsel people all the time. Psychologists, social workers, clergy, friends, parents, and lawyers all counsel other people. Suppose a person's long-time spouse dies. A member of the clergy helps make decisions about the funeral, a psychologist helps that person enter new relationships, a hospital social worker may help decide how to pay for medical expenses, a friend helps choose a new house, a parent offers advice about the children, and a lawyer may help decide whether or not to file a wrongful death lawsuit or whether to make a new will.

While there are important similarities among all types of counseling, there are important differences as well. One difference between legal counseling and therapeutic counseling is that the lawyer becomes the client's agent during the legal representation. This has legal and practical ramifications because, unlike a therapeutic counselor, the lawyer's words and actions will bind the client and can be taken as the client's own words

---

[4] Amos Tversky & Daniel Kahneman, *Judgement Under Uncertainty: Heuristics and Biases,* 185 SCIENCE 1124 (1974); RICHARD NISBETT & LEE ROSS, HUMAN INFERENCE: STRATEGIES AND SHORTCOMINGS OF SOCIAL JUDGEMENT (1980). *See also,* Chris Guthrie, Jeffrey J. Rachlinski & Andrew J. Wistrich, *Inside the Judicial Mind,* 86 CORNELL L. REV. 777 (2001) (empirical study showing that cognitive illusions had significant impact on judicial decision-making); W. Kip Viscusi, *Jurors, Judges, and the Mistreatment of Risk by the Courts,* 30 J. LEG. STUD. 107 (2001) (Study showing cognitive illusions influencing jurors' decisions); Jeffrey J. Rachlinski, *Heuristics and Biases in the Courts: Ignorance or Adaptation,* 79 OR. L. REV. 61 (2000) (showing a pattern of judicial ignorance of or adaptation to cognitive illusions.).

[5] Rachlinski, *supra* note 2, at 116.

[6] Rachlinski, *supra* note 2, at 114. *But see* Robert E. Scott, *Error and Rationality in Individual Decisionmaking: An Essay on the Relationship Between Cognitive Illusions and the Management of Choices,* 59 S. CAL. L. REV. 329, 330-331 (1986) (The difference that rational choice critics found is the difference between "the real and the ideal.").

and actions. Thus, when she acts for the client, the lawyer-counselor must step into the client's shoes.

Lawyers may also provide an additional service for their clients after counseling. Clients come to lawyers for advice, but that advice is often secondary to something else. The lawyer may be asked to file a lawsuit, draft a document, negotiate a settlement, or evaluate a proposal. The result of the counseling may be a decision that the lawyer provide legal services. This makes the lawyer an interested party in the counseling. The lawyer has monetary and professional interests in the outcome of the counseling. Indeed, the decision may be to shift the burden of dealing with the matter from the client to lawyer.

People go to therapeutic counselors to be cured. They perceive that something is wrong with them and the counselor can help fix it or cure it. Similarly, clients may see a lawyer if they have legal troubles that they believe the lawyer can fix. But clients also see lawyers because they need legal services. Clients need wills drafted, agreements reviewed, deals constructed, etc. These clients do not have any legal "disease" to cure. Rather, they are purchasing a service that they cannot perform on their own.

The most obvious difference between therapeutic counseling and legal counseling concerns the likely effect of the counseling on the client. Legal counseling is not designed to change the client (though change may come through legal representation). It is not intended to provide the client with any heightened awareness of or insight into his or her life. Legal counseling is intended to help the client reach a decision about a matter within the lawyer's legal competence. In addition, it is designed to provide the lawyer with instructions about what to do next for the client. While there may be some therapeutic benefit from the process, it is incidental and not fundamental. Fundamentally, the goal of legal counseling is to advance the clients legal interests in the particular representation.

This chapter is based on the premise that counseling is primarily helping someone make a good decision. The similarity among different types of counseling suggests that counselors could benefit from a study of each other's techniques. We should ask:

> [W]hen, how, and why counselors can be effective in just a few sessions with clients who seek help when they are making vital decisions concerning their health, career, marriage, or other aspects of their personal lives.[7]

Lawyers can improve their counseling skills by borrowing from the rich literature of the other helping professions. Effective legal counselors should be aware of their own and their client's cognitive obstacles to fully rational decision-making. Once aware, they should adjust their

---

[7] IRVING JANIS, COUNSELING ON PERSONAL DECISIONS 5 (1979).

approaches to counter these obstacles.[8] The following chapters draw from that literature, as well as decision-making theory, to create a model for the counselor-at-law.

§ 7-2.   APPROACHES TO LEGAL COUNSELING

§ 7-2(a).   THE CLIENT-CENTERED APPROACH

Most legal counseling books recommend a client-centered approach. This approach, which borrows its name and methods from Carl Rogers' school of psychotherapy, suggests a non-directive style of legal counseling.[9]

This approach is reflected in client-centered legal counseling, which "assumes that most clients are capable of thinking through the complexities of their problems[,]" and that clients should be responsible for "mak[ing] those decisions which are likely to have a substantial legal or non-legal impact."[10] Client-centered lawyers are careful not to tell their clients what to do. Instead they provide information about several possible courses of action and let the client choose among them.[11]

§ 7-2(b).   THE AUTHORITARIAN APPROACH

The client centered approach contrasts with the authoritarian-directive approach, which frequently characterizes the counseling given by large numbers of professionals, such as physicians, attorneys, and financial advisors. These counselors generally listen to each client's statement of the problem at the start of the first session and then use their expertise to decide on the best course of action. Before the first session is over, the client is usually told exactly what to do. If the client returns to discuss any complication that has arisen, the authoritative counselor once again tells the client, in the same directive manner, what to do about it.[12]

---

[8] *See* Richard W. Painter, *Irrationality and Cognitive Bias at a Closing in Arthur Solmssen's The Comfort Letter,* 69 FORDHAM L. REV. 1111 (2000); Richard Birke & Craig R. Fox, *Psychological Principles in Negotiating Civil Settlements,* 4 HARV. NEGOT. L. REV. 1 (1999); Russel Korobkin & Chris Guthrie, *Psychology, Economics, and Settlement: A New Look at the Role of the Lawyer,* 76 TEX. L. REV. 77 (1997). Information in this chapter is adapted from John M.A. DiPippa, *How Prospect Theory Can Improve Legal Counseling,* 24 U. ARK. LITTLE ROCK L. REV. 81 (2001).

[9] One author described Roger's "client-centered" psychotherapy as follows:

At each session conducted once or twice or a week over a period of several months, the counselor is non-directive. He or she listens attentively to what the client says about personal problems and consistently responds in an accepting and empathic manner, reflecting the emotional content of the client's statements. The counselor carefully abstains from offering any advice or specific recommendations as to what the client should do.

See JANIS, *supra* note 7, at 1.

[10] DAVID A. BINDER ET AL., LAWYERS AS COUNSELORS: A CLIENT-CENTERED APPROACH 17, 20 (1991).

[11] *Id.* at 259-260.

[12] IRVING JANIS, SHORT-TERM COUNSELING 8 (1983).

Under the authoritarian approach, the lawyer treats the case rather than the client, and the lawyer imposes what she sees as the best "legal" solution.[13] As we have previously noted, this is the approach many lawyers have traditionally taken to client counseling.

§ 7-2(c). THE DECISION-COUNSELOR APPROACH

Another approach views lawyers as "decision-counselors." Under this approach, lawyers resemble short-term decision counselors because lawyers are professionals who meet with clients in a few sessions when the client is making vital decisions concerning some aspect of their lives.[14]

These "decision-counselors" occupy a middle ground between the directive and the non-directive camps. This counseling

> involves the joint work of the counselor and the client in diagnosing and improving the latter's decision making efforts. . . . The counselor attempts to help the person resolve realistic conflicts that arise when he or she is facing a difficult choice. . . . This type of decision counseling is usually non-directive as to substantive issues involved in the decision: the counselor abstains from giving advice about which course of action the clients should choose and even avoids suggesting in any way that he or she regards certain choices as good or bad. Instead, the decision counselor tries to help clients make the fullest possible use of their own resources for arriving at the best possible decision in terms of their own value systems. Much of the counselor's work consists of making clients aware of the decision-making procedures that they are using and of alternative procedures that they are not using. The counselor may be somewhat directive, however, in suggesting where to go for pertinent information, how to take account of knowledge about alternative courses of action, how to find out if deadlines need to be taken at face value or can be negotiated, which risks might require preparing contingency plans, and the like.[15]

Clients who seek short-term counseling face specific problems in their lives that cannot be remedied without the help of a professional counselor. Although the problem may have discrete boundaries, it is one that could potentially have far-reaching consequences for the client. In these situations, the resolution of the client's problem does not necessarily lead to personal growth or happiness. People seek short term counseling for things they choose and want to do — buying a house, adopting a child, getting married, etc.

---

[13] *See* BINDER ET AL., *supra* note 10, at 17 ("Under the traditional conception, lawyers view client problems primarily in terms of existing doctrinal categories such as contracts, torts, or securities. Information is important principally to the extent the data affects the doctrinal pigeonhole into which the lawyer places the problem. . . . [L]awyers primarily seek the best 'legal' solutions to problems without fully exploring how those solutions meet clients' non-legal as well as legal concerns.").

[14] Irving Janis studied people seeking short-term marriage or career counseling and individuals seeking help with a lifestyle change, like quitting smoking or losing weight. *See, e.g.,* JANIS, *supra* note 12.

[15] *See* JANIS, *supra* note 7, at 6.

Many of the lawyer's clients have problems with the same features. The client who wants to adopt a child, the criminal defendant, the divorce client, and the defendant in a civil lawsuit have legal problems and they need the lawyer's help. The decisions they make will significantly affect their lives for years to come.

Even clients who are not required to hire a lawyer may see one for help with particular matters. For example, the client may want help in negotiating the purchase of a business or may need assistance in putting a deal together. The common factor in all of these cases is that the "problem" to be solved has certain definite contours and its resolution will have a real, practical effect on the client's life. The lawyer does not offer self-awareness, but instead offers a product (the lawyer's skill, time, or experience) that the client needs.

§ 7-2(d). COLLABORATIVE LEGAL COUNSELING

The most effective legal counselors adopt some of the techniques of both the client-centered and the short term counselor approaches. We have called this the "collaborative" approach to legal counseling. Like client-centered counselors, the collaborative legal counselor considers both the legal and non-legal consequences of the client's decisions. Like short-term decision counselors, a collaborative legal counselor recognizes that solving the client's problem is the goal of the representation. A collaborative legal counselor directs the client through a process designed to produce what is, given the client's objectives, the optimal solution. At times, when the need is clear, that includes directive methods.

§ 7-3. COMMON ELEMENTS OF EFFECTIVE LEGAL COUNSELING

Effective counselors have good relationships with the people they counsel and help them make wise and prudent decisions. What makes counseling effective has a great deal to do with specific actions that build good relationships and create good decision processes.

Specifically, effective counselors do the following:

- They give clients emotional and social support for making their decision.

- They provide clients pertinent information about the available alternatives.

- They clarify clients' personal objectives.

- They encourage clients to develop a way to organize information about the available choices.[16]

The following table shows how these practices enhance either the relationship or the decision process.

---

[16] *Id.*

RELATIONSHIP BUILDING	DECISION PROCESS
Provide support by:	*Structure decision by:*
■ Conveying benevolent options	■ Giving information on attitude
■ Providing uncontingent acceptance	■ Helping to clarify client's goals
■ Pointing out similar beliefs, attitudes, and values	■ Organizing the decision-making process
■ Giving appropriate praise	
■ Genuinely caring about client's welfare	

§ 7-3(a). RELATIONSHIP BUILDING PRACTICES

Relationship building practices are most important in the early stages of the relationship because they develop the critical elements of an effective helping relationship: empathy, acceptance, and genuineness.[17] As we noted in the interviewing chapters, relationship building is important for the interviewing process but it continues to be important in the counseling process.

These factors influence the relationship by helping the client develop a bond of trust in the counselor that is necessary if the client is to engage in a thorough decision-making process.[18] As partners in the final decision, the lawyer and the client will have influence on its shape. Counselors always have an influence in the outcome of the counseling no matter how open or non-directive they may be. Clients look to their lawyers for advice, guidance, and wisdom and effective lawyers give that to their clients. Effective legal counselors are aware of the kind of power that counselors typically possess and use only that power that enhances either their relationship with the client or the decision process.

Counselors typically draw on four sources of power:

- *Legitimate Power:* This power comes from the counselor's socially defined role. It is the power society gives to the counselor by virtue of their role.

- *Expert Power:* This power comes from the manner in which the counselor communicates her competence.

- *Referent Power:* This power comes from the relationship between the client and the counselor. It is strengthened by the counselor's attractiveness, friendliness, and similarity to the client.

---

[17] *See* WILLIAM H. CORMIER & L. SHERILYN CORMIER, INTERVIEWING STRATEGIES FOR HELPERS: FUNDAMENTAL SKILLS AND COGNITIVE BEHAVIORAL INTERVENTION 21 (3d ed. 1992). *See also* Carl R. Rogers, *The Necessary and Sufficient Conditions of Therapeutic Personality Change*, 21 J. CONSULTING PSYCH. 95 (1957).

[18] CORMIER & CORMIER, *supra* note 17.

- *Coercive Power:* This power comes from the ability of the counselor to force the client to do something. It is the crudest form of power.

The counselor uses these sources of power consciously and subconsciously to help the client choose an appropriate remedial strategy and successfully implement that strategy.[19] The more referent power counselors gain, the more likely their clients will listen to their counselors, be satisfied with the advice, and comply with the chosen course of action.[20]

Attorneys may draw from all three sources of power. For example, people go to see attorneys for help with their legal problems because attorneys are the only people allowed to practice law. This gives attorneys "legitimate power." Particular attorneys project an air of expertise. Their clients believe that they know the law. This is called "expert power." Finally, some attorneys have good interpersonal skills. Their clients will feel comfortable confiding in them. They have "referent power."

Attorneys most frequently use expert and legitimate power.[21] Lawyers enjoy a heightened status by virtue of their profession. They already have a degree of legitimate power when clients come to see them. They typically gain power by asserting their expert knowledge and subtly rewarding clients who follow their direction.

> [S]ome attorneys . . . concentrate narrowly on their professional tasks. They tell their clients what they ought to do without paying much attention to the clients' psychological resistance. A few are so businesslike they do not openly show any concern about the client's plight or future welfare. Such counselors, in effect, rely heavily on legitimate, expert, and reward power but neglect the potential increase in their ability to influence clients that would come from acquiring referent power as well.[22]

By ignoring relationship-building steps, however, the lawyer loses out on the opportunity to further enhance the lawyer-client relationship. This is not simply about gaining control over the client. Clients who lose trust in their lawyer will be less likely to fully disclose important material, less likely to follow through on necessary steps, and less likely to comply with any agreement the parties reach. Recall how clients who engage in power struggles with their lawyers withhold information, vacillate about a decision, and fail to comply with agreements.[23]

In one study, clients were more satisfied with lawyers who used referent power than with lawyers who used coercive power.[24] Using coercive

---

[19] *Id.*

[20] *See* JANIS, *supra* note 7, at 44-45.

[21] Marcia Amanda Hillary & Joel T. Johnson, *Social Power and Interactional Style in Divorce Attorney/Client Dyad,* 12 J. DIVORCE 89, 89-90 (1989).

[22] *See* JANIS, *supra* note 12, at 22.

[23] *See* William L. F. Felstiner & Austin Sarat, *Enactments of Power: Negotiating Reality and Responsibility in Lawyer-Client Interactions,* 77 CORNELL L. REV. 1447 (1992). *See also* Austin Sarat & William L. F. Felstiner, *Lawyers and Legal Consciousness: Law Talk in the Divorce Lawyer's Office,* 98 YALE L.J. 1663 (1989).

[24] *See* Hillary & Johnson, *supra* note 21, at 95.

power negatively affected the clients' satisfaction with the lawyer and their perception of the lawyer's competence, whereas using referent power positively affected client satisfaction.[25] Some lawyers adopted a style that emphasized the social distance between themselves and the client ("distancing"). Other lawyers focused on the legal task at hand ("task"). A third group centered on the client's needs ("client"). Clients were more satisfied with the lawyers who used the "client" style and believed these lawyers to be more competent.[26] On the other hand, clients were less satisfied with lawyers who used the "distancing" style and believed these lawyers to be less competent.[27] The following chart illustrates these relationships.

STYLE	SOURCE OF LAWYER'S POWER	CLIENT SATISFACTION	PERCEPTION OF LAWYER COMPETENCE
Distancing	coercive, legitimate, expert, reward	Negative	Negative
Task	legitimate, expert	Neutral	Neutral
Client	referent, legitimate	Positive	Positive

When it comes to building a relationship with clients, lawyers may have an advantage over other counselors. Lawyers and clients often identify in ways other counselors and their clients do not because the lawyer must step into the client's shoes. This may communicate the kind of acceptance and social support that enhances the relationship between the lawyer and the client. Putting on the client's shoes and articulating the client's cause is likely to appear to the client as an acceptance of the client.

Lawyers can gain referent power and enhance their relationships with clients by:

- Conveying a benevolent attitude toward clients

- Providing non-contingent acceptance of clients

- Identifying similar beliefs, values and attitudes

- Praising clients for accomplishments in line with the clients' goals

- Genuinely caring about the clients' welfare[28]

When a lawyer identifies similar beliefs, attitudes, and values, it breaks down the barriers created by the lawyer's expert status. A moderate level

---

[25] *Id.*

[26] *Id.* at 98.

[27] *Id. See also* Stephen Feldman & Kent Wilson, *The Value of Interpersonal Skills in Lawyering*, 5 Law & Hum. Behav. 311 (1981) (finding that high competence and high relational skills positively correlated to perceived satisfaction and competence).

[28] *See* Janis, *supra* note 12, at 20-25.

of self-disclosure puts clients at ease, makes it more likely that they will disclose important information, and enhances compliance with any decision.[29] Too much disclosure, however, works against rapport. Counselors who tell their clients too much about themselves cross over into self-indulgence. Clients see the counseling as having less to do with them and more to do with the counselor's ego.

Praising clients who make progress toward their goals with empathic, appreciative, and approving comments reinforces clients' resolve and solidifies the lawyer-client relationship.[30] Praise encourages the client to persist in a stressful course of action. Praise also shows that the lawyer views the client's actions as worthwhile. Be careful, however, because praise loses its impact if it is excessive and can weaken the relationship. Furthermore, clients doubt the counselor's sincerity unless the praise sounds genuine.[31]

§ 7-3(b).   DECISION PROCESS PRACTICES

Decision process practices include any action the lawyer takes to aid the client in effective decision-making. Effective decision-making requires the following:

- Thoroughly canvass a wide range of options;

- Understand the full range of goals to be fulfilled and the values implicated by each option;

- Carefully weigh the positive and negative consequences of each option;

- Search for new information relevant to further examination of each option;

- Take account of new information or expert judgments, even when they are inconsistent with the initial choice;

- Reexamine the positive and negative consequences of all options, including those originally deemed unacceptable; and

- Make plans to implement the chosen option, but also make contingency plans.[32]

The more diligently decision-makers follow these seven steps, the more confident they can be about their decisions. Effective legal counselors help

---

[29] *Id.* at 117-118.

[30] *Id.* at 108.

[31] *See id.* at 91-92 (stating that genuiness depends on truly accepting the client, honestly expressing acceptance, and professional norms to support acceptance). At the same time, the counselor's personality has a great deal to do with genuiness. Janis cites research that identifies three personality traits of effective counselors: a capacity to identify with their clients, a capacity to wait for each client to resolve his situation, and a capacity to refrain from retaliating when provoked. *Id.* at 92.

[32] IRVING T. JANIS & LEON MANN, DECISION MAKING: A PSYCHOLOGICAL ANALYSIS OF CONFLICT, CHOICE, AND COMMITMENT 11 (1978).

guide their clients through this process. The counseling process detailed in the next chapter is based on these factors.

People are not machines, however. They rarely follow all of these steps fully. Indeed, there are times when following all of these steps would be overkill. Whether or not you eat rice or corn cereal in the morning hardly warrants a complicated decision process. On the other hand, deciding whether or not to file for a divorce, to accept a settlement offer, or to invest a large sum of money demands more attention.

§ 7-4. FACTORS THAT INTERFERE WITH EFFECTIVE DECISION-MAKING

There is a gap between the way people ought to make decisions and the way they often do. Effective decision counselors are aware of this gap and structure their counseling sessions to encourage effective decision-making.

There are two approaches to studying decision-making:[33]

- Normative (The way it should be)

- Descriptive (The way it is)

The normative approach is the classic way to look at decision-making. It studies the process of decision-making to detect flaws that prevent people from making the best decision under the circumstances.[34] It makes several assumptions that parallel the assumptions of classical economics:

- Humans are rational.

- Humans act to maximize their interests.

- The best decision maximizes the decision maker's interests under the circumstances.[35]

These assumptions dictate a decision process of listing, evaluating, and choosing.[36] People are advised to make a list of the available options, to evaluate each option by measuring the gain and loss if that option is pursued, and to choose the option that results in the most gain or the least loss.[37] Most people are familiar with this process from the ordinary method of drawing a line down the middle of the page and listing the

---

[33] *See, e.g.*, MAX BAZERMAN, JUDGMENT IN MANAGERIAL DECISION MAKING 3-5 (1994).

[34] JANIS & MANN, *supra* note 32, at 11-12.

[35] Daniel Kahneman & Amos Tversky, *Prospect Theory: An Analysis of Decision Under Risk*, 47 ECONOMETRICA 263, 263 (1979).

[36] *See, e.g.*, BAZERMAN, *supra* note 33, at 3-4; JANIS & MANN, supra note 32, at 11.

[37] JANIS & MANN, *supra* note 32, at 11. They list the following components of optimal decision-making: Consider a large number of factors; the goal is to consider as many as possible. Generate as many alternatives as possible; delay decision in favor of more alternatives; test best alternatives repeatedly, arranging them in multiple ways to allow comparative judgments; take account of magnitude of all the pros and cons; look for tradeoffs between high values on some and low values on others. *Id.*

"pros" of the decision on one side and the "cons" of the decision on the other.[38]

Effective decision-making requires accurately describing the situation calling for a decision, discussing a wide range of alternative solutions, identifying, weighing, applying appropriate evaluative criteria, and systematically reaching a decision.[39]

These assumptions work well at general levels. For example, they seem to explain macro economic behavior, i.e, behavior on the largest scale. They allow economists to create models of the national economy on which to base large-scale economic policy.

Studies in the fields of social psychology and economics have called each of these assumptions into question.[40] These findings argue that the normative approach and classical economics fail to provide an accurate picture of how people actually make decisions. These theorists argue that a more effective approach would be to study and describe actual human decision making.[41]

People make decisions all the time but for most of these decisions they have neither the time nor the resources to engage in an optimal search and evaluation process.[42] Research shows that people have developed cognitive shortcuts to make ordinary decisions easier.[43] These cognitive shortcuts or schemas are essential to daily life.[44] People could not function efficiently if every decision required complete analysis, no matter how

---

[38] *See also* BINDER ET AL., *supra* note 10, at 307.

[39] *See, e.g.,* BAZERMAN, *supra* note 33, at 3-4.

[40] *See* Christine Jolls, Cass R. Sunstein & Richard Thaler, *A Behavioral Approach to Law and Economics*, 50 STAN. L. REV. 1471, 1478 (1998) ("[E]xpected utility theory is not a good description of actual decisionmaking"); Cass R Sunstein, *How Law Constructs Preferences*, 86 GEO. L.J. 2637 (1998) (Normative account of rational choice lacks "descriptive accuracy.")

[41] Jolls et al., *supra* note 40, at 1476 (Task of behavioral economics is to study actual human behavior and its implications for law.); Sunstein, *Preferences, supra* note 40, at 2637 (Although real people depart from rational choice model, their decision making is not "unpredictable, systematically irrational, random, rule-free, or elusive." Rather, their departures can be "described, used and sometimes even modeled.")

[42] JANIS & MANN, *supra* note 32, at 22; Jolls, et al., *supra* note 40, at 1471; Donald C. Langevoort, *Where Were the Lawyers? A Behavioral Inquiry into Lawyer's Responsibility for Clients' Fraud,* 46 VAND. L. REV. 75, 99 (1993) ("Attorneys are confronted with immense amounts of intellectual stimuli each day and must implicitly or explicitly make thousands of decisions and judgements through inductive reasoning.); Korobkin & Ulen, supra note 1, at 1077-78 (The decision to use a simple decision process "might be sensible given the marginal benefits and costs of making an optimal decision relative to a satisfactory one; in other words, the decision not to maximize utility when solving a single problem might in fact maximize the actor's overall utility.")

[43] NISBETT & ROSS, *supra* note 4, at 7.

[44] Langevoort, *Lawyers, supra* note 42, at 99 (Without cognitive shortcuts, "life would be unbearably chaotic."); Korobkin & Ulen, *supra* note 1, at 1076 (Without cognitive shortcuts, "the task of making even relatively simple decisions would become so complex that daily life would almost certainly grind to a halt.")

often they may have faced the same choice in the past or how inconsequential the decision may be.[45]

§ 7-4(a).   SATISFICING

Many people choose a course of action that is "just good enough." People tend to choose the first alternative that satisfies a minimal set of requirements. This is called *satisficing*.[46] The decision maker believes he has made a good decision because the choice represents an improvement over the status quo.

However, the notion that he has made a good decision may be illusory. The choice may not have been the best choice of all choices available. The decision-maker satisfices by comparing the alternative to the status quo rather than to other options available. Satisficing decision processes may seem complex. They may involve a diligent search for information. They may seem to cover a wide range of alternatives. In the end, however, choosing the "just good enough" alternative short-circuits the ideal decision process and often fails to identify the best option or combination of options. (Though the person using the "just good enough" method may stumble into the best option; even a blind hog finds an acorn once in a while.)

Satisficing may occur because people are not able to process the amount of information necessary to reach the best decision.[47] Our ability to handle information and to project future consequences from that information is limited. Decision theorists call this "bounded rationality."[48] At some point, a decision-maker will simplify the process. In satisficing, the decision-maker simplifies the process by using the "good enough" criteria and seizing upon the first alternative that satisfies this simplified criteria. When coupled with other psychological processes, people can make decisions that, in the long run, may not be in their best interest.

Satisficing is an especially common strategy when people make decisions under stress. This may explain the passivity that some lawyers see in their clients. People narrow their focus to rely on simple rules to make a decision:

---

[45] NISBETT & ROSS, *supra* note 4, at 7; Langevoort, *Lawyers, supra* note 42, at 99-100 (Cognitive shortcuts work well in everyday life because they are "curiously functional" and more precise mechanisms are not practical.)

[46] BAZERMAN, *supra* note 33, at 5 (*citing* J. G. MARCH & H.A. SIMON, ORGANIZATIONS (1958)).

[47] *Id. See also* NISBETT & ROSS, *supra* note 4, at 17-42. *See also*, Rachlinski, *Heuristics and Biases, supra* note 4. (Human brain has limited ability to process information and uses shortcuts that allow it to perform most tasks well.); Korobkin & Ulen, *supra* note 1, at 1076 (Bounded rationality the "unintentional consequence of an unconscious use of heuristics in judgement and decision-making tasks".).

[48] HERBERT A. SIMON, MODELS OF MAN (1957). Simon describes Bounded Rationality in this way: "The capacity of the human mind for formulating and solving complex problems is very small compared to with the size of the problems whose solution is required for objectively rational behavior in the real world — or even for a reasonable for a reasonable approximation to such objective rationality." *Id.* at 198. *See also* Jolls, et al., *supra* note 40, at 1477 (Bounded rationality describes the systematic ways that people try to cope with their "limited computational skills and seriously flawed memories.")

Men and women in serious trouble are likely to consult whichever physician or lawyer is recommended by a trusted friend and then to accept whatever course of action the advisor recommends, without spending the money or effort to get a second opinion. The sole decision rule in such cases is often simply "Tell a qualified expert about your problem and do whatever he says — that will be good enough.[49]

Satisficing is acceptable for many decisions. Using a "just good enough" criterion is fine when choosing a breakfast cereal, or buying socks, or renting a video. Yet people persist in satisficing even when making major decisions. Government officials often use satisficing when making major domestic or foreign policy decisions.[50]

A comparison between satisficing and optimal decision-making shows that they differ markedly:

	SATISFICING	OPTIMAL
Number of requirements to be met	Small number, maybe only one; ignores other factors	Large number of factors; goal is to consider as many as possible.
Number of alternatives generated	Sequentially tests alternative; chooses first one minimally satisfactory	Generates as many alternatives as possible; delays decision in favor of more alternatives
Ordering and retesting of alternatives	Tested once in haphazard fashion until minimally satisfactory one arises; search ends	Tests best alternatives repeatedly, arranging them in multiple ways to allow comparative judgments.
Type of testing model used	Sees if alternative meets minimal cutoff, each cutoff point equally important	Takes account of magnitude of all the pros and cons; looks for tradeoffs between high values on some and low values on others.

Satisficing can lead to hasty and ill-considered decisions. The criminal defendant who takes the first plea bargain offered may do so because it

---

[49] *See* JANIS & MANN, *supra* note 32, at 27.

[50] *Id.* at 105-133.

meets a single criteria — keeping him out of jail — even though the plea bargain may have serious long term consequences.[51]

§ 7-4(b).   ELIMINATION BY ASPECTS[52]

This is a variation of satisficing, but it is still not an entirely optimal way of making a decision. The "elimination by aspects" strategy involves narrowing down a list of alternatives by testing them against a sequence of criteria. If the alternative does not satisfy a criterion, the alternative is dropped. If the alternative meets a criterion, it is then tested against the next criterion on the list. The client chooses from the alternatives that remain when the list is finished. But there may not be any options left. Every option may fail to satisfy one of the acceptance criteria. The decision-maker may end up eliminating all of the options.

The problem is that each criterion receives equal weight. In most situations, however, the criteria will in fact have different values to the decision-maker. That is, one factor may be more important to the decision-maker than another. By weighting them equally, the decision-maker uses relatively minor criteria to eliminate options that, while not perfect, may accomplish most of that person's goals.

For example, suppose a client seeks advice from a lawyer concerning which of several business proposals to accept. The client may have multiple goals that might influence the decision. The client may want to reach a certain level of income, break into a certain field, make contact with important persons in this field, locate in a certain geographic area, and enjoy his or her colleagues. But not all of these are likely to be equally important to the client. Income may be more important than location, yet under the "elimination by aspects" method the client may eliminate a proposal failing the location test even though it offers more income. The proposal that the client ultimately accepts only minimally meet each criterion, whereas the rejected proposals may be unacceptable on only one criterion and well beyond the minimum on the others. The client may choose the mediocre proposal unless the criteria are weighted and the alternatives are compared against each other.

§ 7-4(c).   INFORMATION PROCESSING FLAWS: HEURISTICS AND BIASES[53]

§ 7-4(c)(1).   Heuristics

Heuristics are models that help people make decisions. The value of the decision depends on the extent to which the heuristic's factors are accurate,

---

[51] *But see* Richard Birke, *Reconciling Loss Aversions and Guilty Pleas*, 1999 UTAH L. REV. 205 (Prevalence of plea bargaining may be the result of bad lawyering, bad information, or both.)

[52] *See* JANIS & MANN, *supra* note 32, at 31-33.

[53] *See generally* NISBETT & ROSS, *supra* note 4; Tversky & Kahneman, *Heuristics and Biases, supra* note 4. *See also* Paul Brest & Linda Krieger, *On Teaching Professional Judgement*, 69 WASH. L. REV. 527 (1994).

complete, and objective. If heuristics are not used appropriately, they lead to weak, biased, or ineffective decisions.

Heuristics simplify decision-making and allow people to efficiently make ordinary decisions. They "produce vastly more correct or partially correct inferences than erroneous ones, and they do so with great speed and little effort."[54] Yet they also can lead to poor decisions by short-circuiting the decision-making process at crucial stages.

There are three kinds of heuristics:[55]

- *Availability:* People make judgments about events based on the availability of information in their memories. Readily available information provides the basis for judgments about the causes, frequency, and probability of past and future events. Recent and vivid events are more readily available in memory than old or bland events.

- *Representativeness:* People make decisions by relying on the similarity of their current situation to past situations. They assume that events will occur as they have in the past or people will act as people have acted in the past. The decision-maker may place the current situation into a category of similar past situations and then use the past to guide the present.

- *Anchoring and Adjustment:* People tend to anchor decisions to some initial reference point. That is, people need baselines against which they can evaluate their choices or from which they can make initial estimates. Thus, when people seek jobs, they want to know what the "going rate" is so they can decide whether or not the salary they want is reasonable and also whether or not the salary they are offered is reasonable. They then adapt revisions to their position in light of this reference point.

These heuristics indispensably aid decision-making. People could not function day-to-day unless they simplified decision-making processes. Though these heuristics do not yield decisions that are as good as a thorough analysis of options would yield, they are necessary in a world where there is a limited amount of time. These heuristics allow people to learn from their experience and to make consistent decisions. They also allow people to efficiently consider decisions. They save time and resources by preventing duplication of effort, by keeping recent decisions in the foreground, and by providing an objective reference point against which to measure decisions.

§7-4(c)(2). Biases

The key to effective use of heuristics is to avoid the typical biases that result from the inappropriate use of heuristics. These biases include

---

[54] *See* NISBETT & ROSS, *supra* note 4, at 18.

[55] *See* BAZERMAN, *supra* note 33, at 7-9.

availability biases, representative biases, and anchoring and adjustment biases.[56]

§ 7-4(c)(2)(i). Availability Biases

We will look at two biases that result from the tendency to use information that is readily available in a person's memory. They are:

- *Recalling recent or vivid events:* People tend to overestimate the significance of and the likelihood of recurrence of recent or vivid events. Because of this, plaintiffs may be more likely to want to file lawsuits after reading newspaper accounts of high verdicts, while defendants may be more risk averse after reading the same story.[57]

- *Connecting events based on our experience:* People often generalize their own experiences and observations. For example, compared with people who hold jobs, unemployed people overestimate the percentage of unemployed people.[58] We may believe that teenagers are bad drivers because a few teenagers we know are bad drivers. However, we would have to look at a large group of teenage drivers and compare their driving records to all other drivers before we could reach a reliable conclusion. Clients (and lawyers) fall into this trap when they make judgments about a person's motivation, the causes of current events, or the meaning of occurrences based on similarities to people, events, or occurrences in their own experience.

§ 7-4(c)(2)(ii). Representative Biases

There are biases that result from the tendency to use one event to represent or stand for another event. They are:

- *Ignoring base rates:* People often make predictions about people and events by relying on minimal information without considering the big picture.[59] For example, people starting businesses may fail to consider the failure rate of new ventures and people contemplating marriage may ignore the high rate of divorce. In both instances, they may predict success for themselves without appreciating the hard work necessary to achieve success in light of the overall rates of failure.[60] Lawyers commit this mistake by making abstract predictions about the success or failure of projected

---

[56] *See id.* at 12-47.

[57] Brest & Krieger, *supra* note 53, at 544-545.

[58] Nisbett & Ross, *supra* note 4, at 19-20

[59] Bazerman, *supra* note 33, at 21-22.

[60] *Id.* at 22.

courses of action without reference to any objective base rate. For example, a lawyer may predict that a lawsuit has a 75% chance of success without knowing the actual success rate of similar claims.

- *Ignoring sample size:* People predict future events based on what has happened in the past, but they often fail to consider whether or not these past events are drawn from a representative sample.[61] Small samples are more likely to generate inaccurate data. For example, a plaintiff's lawyer may predict a high jury verdict in his client's case because juries in two other cases of which the lawyer is aware did so. But the lawyer may not know about the several dozen cases where the jury did not return a large verdict.

- *Ignoring chance events:* Most people believe that an event that has happened recently is less likely to happen again. For example, people are likely to believe that after a coin comes up "heads" four times in a row, a fifth throw is likely to come up "tails." [62] But there is no connection between the four "heads" and the fifth flip. The chance of a tail is identical on every flip of the coin. People believe that events "even out" over time. Thus, a lawyer who believes that a jury is due to return a favorable verdict in the client's case because another jury recently returned an unfavorable verdict in a similar case falls into this trap.

By the same token, people also believe in the "hot hand."[63] This is typified by the belief that events happen in clusters. When something happens several times in a row, people believe that it will happen the next time.[64] Lawyers who believe that judges and juries are "on a roll" fall into this trap.

§ 7-4(c)(2)(iii).   Anchoring and Adjustment Biases

The biases that result from the tendency to use faulty anchors or baselines are:

- *Inaccurate or irrelevant anchors:* People's judgments can be affected by wrong or irrelevant information that they use as a baseline. For example, when asked to estimate a fictitious person's starting salary, people's estimates were affected by the

---

[61] *Id.* at 23.

[62] *Id.* at 25.

[63] *Id.*

[64] This belief is especially prevalent in athletics. But a study of two professional basketball teams showed that there was no correlation between a player scoring a basket and that same player making the next basket. Instead, chance or the player's overall probability of success determined the success of each successive shot. BAZERMAN, *supra* note 33, at 25.

estimates of others. Prior low estimates led to lower guesses while prior high estimates led to higher guesses.[65] Lawyers and clients can fall into this trap if they rely on subjective estimates and do not look for objective measurements of value.

- *Overconfidence:* Many people are unrealistically confident about their ability to predict events.[66] They are more confident when predicting unfamiliar matters than when predicting familiar matters. The danger is that overconfidence may cause faulty predictions in situation when people should be most cautious. For example, lawyers may overconfidently predict a settlement in a case and fail to accurately advise their clients. By the same token, clients may unrealistically estimate their willingness to pursue a case.

- *Looking for confirmation:* Most often, people seek information that confirms their tentative conclusions and do not look for information that refutes their conclusions.[67] Thus, lawyers and clients may only see the facts that support the client's case and fail to explore the facts against them. Similarly, clients may only report the facts that support their conclusion about their situation.

- *Professional blindness:* People's views are often distorted by their specialized knowledge. One study found that marketing experts are not as good as non-marketing experts at estimating consumer behavior.[68] Lawyers may fall into this trap when they try to predict the behavior of judges and juries. They may ignore signals that people from outside the legal system can see.

§ 7-5.   DEALING WITH UNCERTAINTY

§ 7-5(a).   RISK

Important decisions often must be made in uncertain conditions. Decision-makers do not have perfect knowledge of the future and cannot precisely predict future conditions. People try to reduce uncertainty in a number of ways. For example, people sometimes believe that predicting chance events requires an element of skill. Gamblers throw dice harder when they need certain combinations, and lottery ticket buyers create systems to choose a winning ticket.

Every decision requires an element of guesswork or intuition. In the absence of perfect knowledge, every decision requires the decision-maker

---

[65] NISBETT & ROSS, *supra* note 4, at 19-20.

[66] BAZERMAN, *supra* note 33, at 37-39.

[67] *Id.* at 40-41.

[68] *Id.* at 44.

to take a risk. Thus, the question is, "What is the appropriate level of risk for this decision?" This section sets out some of the pitfalls that arise when decision-makers consider risk.

§ 7-5(b).   FRAMING GAINS OR LOSSES

Prospect theory is a particular application of the anchoring and adjustment heuristic.[69] Prospect theory research shows that people will opt for a small certain gain instead of a riskier larger gain even when the net value of the "at risk" benefit is greater.[70] This is called "risk aversion." For example, suppose a speaker offered everyone who exited from the north door an envelope containing a $20 bill. The speaker offered everyone who left through the south door an envelope randomly pulled from a container, with one out of every four envelopes containing a $100 bill. Research suggests that most people would choose the $20 bill even though the transactional value ($25) of the second option is greater.[71]

At the same time, people will gamble to avoid sure losses even if the potential loss from the gamble will be significantly greater than the sure loss. This is called "loss aversion." For example, suppose that in the example above guests who chose the north door had to pay a $20 exit fee. Guest who chose the south door, however, drew envelopes from a container. Three out of every four envelopes contained a pass allowing the guest to exit for free. The remaining envelopes required the guest to pay $100. When given this kind of choice, most people choose to gamble on the south door, i.e. they try to leave for free and face the risk of paying $100 instead of opting to pay the certain $20 exit fee. In summary, people will not take as great a risk to obtain a possible future gain as they will to avoid the loss of what they already have — they are more "risk averse" than they are "loss averse."

Prospect theory research showed that response to losses is greater than the response to gains.[72] For example, people will charge more to part with an item than they will pay for it.[73] Defying the assumptions of conventional

---

[69] Korobkin & Ulen, *supra* note 1, at 1104. (Prospect theory incorporates empirical findings about decision making under uncertainty that contradict rational choice models.)

[70] *See* BAZERMAN, *supra* note 33, at 55-56.

[71] Each chance for $20 has the same value. Each chance for the $100 bill is worth $25 because there are four chances for the prize. *See* Robert H. Mnookin, *Why Negotiations Fail: An Exploration of Barriers to the Resolution of Conflict,* 8 OHIO ST. J. DISP. RESOL. 235 (1993).

[72] Amos Tversky & Daniel Kahneman, *Rational Choice and The Framing of Decisions,* 59 J. BUSINESS 251, 258 (1986). This effect is exaggerated even more by the different subjective value people assign to essentially the same loss. For example, the difference in value between a gain of $100 and $200 is perceived as greater than the difference between a gain of $1100 and $1200. *Id.* Even though the actual amount of the gain is the same in both instances, a person's subjective perception of the value is different. The same is true for losses. The difference between a $100 and a $200 loss is seen as greater than the difference between an $1100 and a $1200 *loss. Id. See* Sunstein, *Preferences, supra* note 40, at 2646 (People are roughly twice as displeased with losses.)

[73] Tversky & Kahneman, *Rational Choice, supra* note 72, at 258.

economic theory, selling an already paid-for item is perceived as a loss while purchasing a new item is seen as a gain.[74]

Whether or not a person perceives his choices as losses or gains influences or frames his willingness to take risks.[75] Tversky and Kahneman's experiments showed that decision-makers are risk averse in gain frames and risk seeking in loss frames.[76] That is, people are more likely to "play it safe" to retain a perceived "gain" but are more likely to take risks when they might suffer a perceived "loss."[77] Which frame a person uses depends on a number of contextual factors but the status quo is frequently the initial reference point and the frames are fluid and easily manipulated.[78]

These factors can be manipulated by the initial presentation of the problem. Decision-makers evaluate gains and losses from a fixed neutral reference point. When a problem is framed in terms of securing gains from the reference point, decision-makers become more risk averse. When a problem is framed in terms of avoiding losses from the reference point, decision-makers tend to be more loss averse. Thus, lawyers can influence the client's perception of the case by framing alternatives in terms of either gains or losses.

Consider the following example from a leading study.[79] A large car manufacturer is having economic problems. The company may have to close

---

[74] Sunstein, *Preferences, supra* note 40 , at 2646 ("Contrary to economic theory, people do not treat out-of-pocket costs and opportunity costs as if they were equivalent."); Korobkin & Ulen, *supra* note 1, at 1107-1108 (Rational choice theory predicts that "[w]hether [a person] owns the loaf of bread or the glass of wine, or neither should make no difference as to which item he would prefer . . . [but] individuals often place a higher monetary value on items they own than on those they do not own.")

[75] Tversky & Kahneman, *Rational Choice, supra note 72*, at 259: "[T]he effective carriers of values are gains and losses, or changes in wealth, rather than states of wealth as implied by the rational model." This may be due to our basic psychological makeup. "Our perceptual apparatus is attuned to the evaluation of changes or differences rather than to the evaluation of absolute magnitudes. When we respond to attribute of brightness, loudness or temperature, the past and present context of experience defines an adaptation level, or reference point, and stimuli are perceived in relation to this reference point. " Amos Tversky & Daniel Kahneman, *Prospect Theory: An Analysis of Decision Under Risk,* 47 ECONOMETRICA 263, 277 (1979).

[76] Tversky & Kahneman, *Rational Choice, supra* note 72, at 258.

[77] *See* Cass R. Sunstein, *Human Behavior and the Law of Work,* 87 VA. L. REV. 205 (2001) (critiquing current employment law rules as based on an inadequate sense of workers' actual values and behavior because, among other things, workers, like all people, are especially adverse to loss).

[78] Sunstein, *Preferences, supra* note 40, at 2647 ("Whether an event 'codes' as a loss or a gain depends on a range of contextual factors, including how the event is framed. The status quo is usually the reference point, so that losses are understood as such by reference to existing distributions and practices but it is possible to manipulate the frame so as to make a change code a loss rather than a gain, or vice-versa.").

[79] *See* Cass R. Sunstein, *Human Behavior and the Law of Work,* 87 VA. L. REV. 205 (2001) (critiquing current employment law rules as based on an inadequate sense of workers' actual values and behavior because, among other things, workers, like all people, are especially adverse to loss).

three plants and lay off 6,000 workers. The Vice President for production has come up with two alternative plans to deal with the problem. Without getting into the details, the plans will have the following results:

Plan A: Will save one of the three plants and 2,000 jobs.

Plan B: Has a 1/3 probability of saving all three plants.

Even though these plans offer the same objective outcome, most people choose Plan A. The plans are framed in terms of saving jobs and plants. The possibility of losing everything becomes the reference point and people become more risk averse. People want to secure whatever gains they can. Thus, saving jobs appears more attractive than betting on a one-in-three chance.

Now consider the following alternatives:

Plan A: Will result in the loss of two of the three plants and 4,000 jobs.

Plan B: Has a 2/3 probability of resulting in the loss of all three plants and all 6,000 jobs but has a 1/3 probability of losing no plants and no jobs.

Once again the plans offer the same outcome but most people choose Plan B. Here the plans are framed as avoiding losses and the status quo becomes the reference point. Now people become more loss averse and are willing to take a greater risk to avoid a certain loss. Thus, betting on a one-in three chance appears more attractive than losing two out of three plants and workers.

All four of these plans are functionally identical. They each carry the same risk of loss and the same chance of gain. Yet, the choice of one over the other was greatly influenced by the way the plans were framed.

Prospect theory shows that lawyers can influence a client's choices to sue or to settle by framing the options in one way or another. In fact, framing may be the most significant influence on settlement behavior.[80] As two leading scholars put it:

. . . [F]rames matter in legal dispute resolution. Disputants may reject a settlement offer economically sufficient to produce a negotiated settlement if they view it in relation to a reference point that suggests accepting the offer would mean accepting a net loss on the transaction. Conversely, an adverse party might perceive an offer framed in its best light as favorable, even if she would reject a frameless presentation of the same substance.[81]

---

[80] Russell Korobkin & Chris Guthrie, *Psychological Barriers to Litigation Settlement: An Experimental Approach,* 93 MICH. L. REV. 107 (1994). Russell Korobkin & Chris Guthrie, *Psychology, Economics, and Settlement: A New Look at the Role of the Lawyer,* 76 TEX. L. REV. 77, 121 (1997): "Cognitive heuristics may be more deeply ingrained in people's minds than socially-constructed desires such as the desire to be treated fairly or to have the validity of one's position acknowledged."

[81] Korobkin & Guthrie, *Barriers, supra* note 80, at 137.

Framing causes plaintiffs and defendants to view the same offer in different ways.[82]

Being a plaintiff or a defendant "influences the attractiveness of a settlement offer in a way that is consistent with framing theory. Plaintiffs prefer sure, riskless settlements more than defendants."[83]

The structure of litigation places defendants in loss frames and plaintiffs in gain frames. Far more of the loss frame defendants choose the riskier course of action than the gain frame defendants."[84] Thus, defendants are more likely to pursue risk seeking options — refusing early settlement or taking a chance at trial — while plaintiffs are more likely to pursue risk-averse choices — seeking settlement in lieu of trial or for less than the desirable amount.[85]

Framing also influences the eventual amount of a settlement.[86] Chris Guthrie and co-author Russel Korobkin found that negotiators who began with a moderate offer were less likely to reach settlement.[87] This is because "a litigant who opens a negotiation with a moderate settlement offer inadvertently erects psychological barriers — namely, anchoring and adjustment effects and dissonance avoidance — that reduce the likelihood that his adversary will accept a final settlement offer."[88]

Frames may also influence the decision to sue.[89] Risk-averse plaintiffs may avoid lawsuits while risk seeking plaintiffs may more eagerly pursue lawsuits. Many plaintiffs might be initially risk-seeking because plaintiffs will frame their situation as a loss. They have already suffered some "damage." Unless they file a lawsuit, they face the certainty of never recovering anything for that loss. Plaintiffs will not have the legal

---

[82] Rachlinksi, *Gains, supra* note 2, note at 119-120. He conducted three controlled studies in which he presented first-year law students a litigation scenario and then asked them whether or not they would accept a certain settlement offer. He told some of the students that they were defendants and he told other students that they were plaintiffs. He put the offers in gain and loss frames. In one case, the frame suggested that the choices all involved losses while the other frame suggested that the choices involved gains. His subjects typically made risk seeking choices in the loss frame and risk averse choices in the gain frame. Plaintiff-subjects consistently chose settlement while the defendant-subjects consistently chose trial.

[83] Rachlinski, *Gains, supra* note 2, at 140.

[84] *Id.* at 142. They were also willing to sacrifice ethics in the loss frame.

[85] Rachlinski does not doubt that people seek the best possible outcome. Rather, he argues that people may be hindered in their ability to identity the best outcome. Rachlinski, *Gains, supra* note 2, at 118. Cognitive factors influence their ability to accurately evaluate available information. *Id.* These are not character flaws. That is, this inability does not stem from a lack of effort or motivation. Rather, "the structure of many choices lures people into making decisions that are suboptimal, from the perspective of a rational model." *Id.*

[86] Russel Korobkin & Chris Guthrie, *Opening Offers and Out-of-court Settlement: A Little Moderation May not Go a Long Way,* 10 OHIO ST. J. ON DISP. RESOL. 1 (1994).

[87] *Id.* at 5.

[88] *Id.*

[89] Chris Guthrie, *Framing Frivolous Litigation: A Psychological Theory,* 67 U. CHI. L. REV. 163 (2000).

expertise to accurately evaluate a case. They may see a lawyer and decide to file a lawsuit because they believe that they have "nothing to lose" by filing a suit. Filing a lawsuit is like rolling dice. Unless the gambler rolls the dice, they have no chance to gain anything.

The nature of the legal system may encourage risk-seeking plaintiffs in the first place. Plaintiffs must go through a complicated and difficult psychological and social process even to seek legal advice.[90] It is possible that this process weeds out many risk-averse plaintiffs. They may become frustrated by the arduous process of finding a lawyer and deciding to sue. They may also believe that they will experience more losses in time, status, or money if they file a lawsuit. These plaintiffs may abandon any idea of a lawsuit. Thus, many plaintiffs may initially be risk-seeking because they may have framed the case as a loss and therefore be more willing to go through the difficult process of finding and consulting a lawyer.

Lawyers may mitigate or exaggerate framing's influence. Lawyers may mitigate the effects of framing because of the way lawyers resolve or are trained to resolve problems.[91] Lawyers in fact use a "rational" or objective approach more consistently than their clients do.[92] Lawyers are less likely than clients to be influenced by psychological factors.[93] Lawyers may be more likely to evaluate settlement decisions on the basis of the expected value of the various options without regard to the frame in which those options are presented.[94]

Personal factors may also play a role. Lawyers as a group may be made up of people who are more inclined toward a "hard" approach to problems rather than a "soft" approach. Considerable data over the years has highlighted some of the cognitive differences between lawyers and the rest of

---

[90] *See* William L. F. Felstiner, Richard L. Abel & Austin Sarat, *The Emergence and Transformation of Disputes: Naming, Blaming, and Claiming*, 15 LAW & SOC'Y REV. 631 (1980) (outlining how litigants must first perceive that they have been harmed, then decide that someone else is responsible for their harm, and then seek a remedy from the wrong doer and describing the process as subjective, unstable, reactive, complicated, and incomplete); Marilyn May & Daniel B. Stengel, *Who Sues Their Doctors?: How Patients Handle Medical Grievances*, 24 LAW & SOC'Y REV. 105 (1990) (describing how litigants maneuver through the "thickets of diversion" to file medical malpractice lawsuits); Phoebe A. Morgan, *Risking Relationships: Understanding the Litigation Choices of Sexually Harassed Women*, 33 LAW & SOC'Y REV. (1999) (showing how women who consider filing sexual harassment lawsuits take into account the risk to their maternal, marital, and familial relationships); Rosalie R. Young, *The Search for Counsel: Perceptions of Applicants For Subsidized Legal Assistance*, 36 BRANDEIS J. FAM. L. 551 (1997-1998) (because of institutional, professional, and social obstacles subjects brought lawsuits only when there seemed to be no other way to solve their problem).

[91] *See* Fernando Colon-Navarro, *Thinking Like a Lawyer: Expert-Novice Differences in Simulated Client Interviews*, 21 J. LEGAL PROF. 107 (1996) (Experience leads to more effective interviewing techniques).

[92] Russell Korobkin & Chris Guthrie, *Psychology, Economics, and Settlement: A New Look at the Role of the Lawyer*, 76 TEX. L. REV. 77, 82 (1997).

[93] *Id.* at 82.

[94] *Id.* at 121-122.

the population.[95] Professor Susan Daicoff has collected all of this data and concludes that lawyers do tend toward a more analytical, objective, and impersonal approach than other people.[96] Thus, they may encourage clients to evaluate options on the basis of their costs and benefits.

Lawyers may mitigate risk-seeking clients by persistently overstating the level of risk. Conventional wisdom holds that lawyers frequently overstate risk.[97] Psychological dynamics may dictate this practice.[98] Lawyers will be tempted to take the safe course and estimate just enough risk for the lawyer to manage.[99] Thus, overstating the risk may be a way to avoid the chance of failure present in accurately stating the risk. Lawyers are also faced with considerable uncertainty when initially asked for advice. Under these circumstances, they may develop "defensive pessimism": dwelling on the potential negative consequences of the possible choices.[100] Finally, a lawyer's overstatement of the risk may counter balance the unreasonable optimism to which some clients may fall prey.[101]

Because most choices can be framed in both a gain and a loss frame, the lawyer can avoid the most damaging effects of framing by offering alternative ways of viewing choices:

---

[95] *See, e.g.,* Don Peters, *Psychological Type Theory, the Myers-Briggs Type Indicator and Learning Negotiation,* 42 DRAKE L. REV. 1 (1993).

[96] Susan Daicoff, *Lawyer, Know Thyself: A Review of Empirical Research on Attorney Attributes Bearing on Professionalism,* 46 AM. U. L. REV. 1337 (1997). *See also,* Susan Daicoff, *Asking Leopards to Change Their Spots: Should Lawyers Change? A Critique of Solutions to Problems with Professionalism by Reference to Empirically Derived Attorney Personality Attributes,* 11 GEO. J. LEG. ETHICS 547 (1998). There is some disagreement as to whether or not these differences are gender-related. *Compare* RAND JACK & DANA CROWLEY JACK, MORAL VISION AND PROFESSIONAL DECISIONS: THE CHANGING VALUES OF WOMEN AND MEN LAWYERS (1989) *and* Bryna Bogoch, *Gendered Lawyering: Difference and Domination in Lawyer-Client Interactions,* 31 LAW AND SOC'Y 677 (1997).

[97] Donald C. Langevoort & Robert K. Rasmussen, *Skewing the Results: The Role of Lawyers in Transmitting Legal Rules,* 5. S. CAL INTERDISCIPLINARY L.J. 375 (1997). Overstating risk may be a way for lawyers to make more money. The more investigation the case needs, the more hours a lawyer can bill. *Id.* at 389-390 (showing how the per-hour fee arrangements create incentives toward overstatement of risk).

[98] Langevoort & Rasmussen, *supra* note 97, at 394-295. The lawyer may want to enhance his or his law firm's reputation with this and other clients. Leading a client astray into a risky venture can cause great reputational damage. At the same time, clients are not in the position to effectively evaluate a lawyer's advice. If the lawyer counsels against a course of action there is rarely a way to study the alternative course. On the other hand, if the lawyers counsels action that changes the status quo, the client has a way to evaluate the lawyer's advice. If the choice is successful, then the advice was essentially self-fulfilling. But if the choice does not lead to success, the client will immediately know that the lawyer's advice was faulty. In short, clients can only know the quality of the lawyer's advice after the fact.

[99] *Id.* at 394-295.

[100] *Id.* at 424 (*citing* Hillel J. Einhorn & Robin Hogarth, *Decision Making Under Ambiguity,* 59 J. BUS. 225 (1986)). *See also* ROBIN HOGARTH, JUDGEMENT AND CHOICE (2d ed. 1987).

[101] Langevoort & Rasmussen, *supra* note 97, at 422-423, listing the possible factors that might encourage underestimation of the risk.

An attorney may have some power to reframe a settlement offer, sparing the client the most costly aspects of framing . . . by pointing out the losses that the defendant is sure to face from continued litigation or by pointing out that a settlement offer is an improvement over previous offers. The attorney is in a position to wrestle the defendant out of the loss frame that would lead the defendant to make risk-seeking choices. The principle benefit that framing theory presents for attorneys lies in the attorney's perspective on the client's choices. Framing asserts, after all, that the clients are in a bad position to make decisions in their best interest. To the extent that an attorney is concerned with promoting the client's best interest, framing theory gives them a significant role."[102]

Both parties — client and lawyer — must be fully engaged in the decisions of the case but lawyers can mitigate the influence of "irrational" psychological factors in a client's decision if they take an active role in litigation decisions.[103] Lawyers should "sit down, face-to-face, and explain the psychological barrier to the client."[104] Even then, overcoming psychological barriers will be difficult and there is still the chance that lawyers will unnecessarily usurp the client's decision making authority.[105]

Guthrie and Korobkin recommend that lawyers take a "Cognitive Error" approach to counseling clients.[106] They describe their approach in this way:

We think it clearly self-evident that a lawyer who knows his client is embarking on a course with a lower expected utility than an alternative course has an ethical obligation to take preventive action. On the other hand, when the client's expressed litigation desires maximize his expected utility, the lawyer should avoid any action that might convince the client to abandon his position. . . . The cognitive error approach to counseling, then requires the lawyer to assess whether an observed difference between the lawyer's and the client's analysis of decision options is due to the client's cognitive error or is merely the manifestation of differences in utility functions. If the difference is due to cognitive error, the lawyer should attempt to change the client's outlook. If the difference is the result of different preference structures, the lawyer should scrupulously avoid any interference.[107]

---

[102] Rachlinski, *Gains, supra* note 2, at 171-72. *See also* Birke & Fox, *supra note* 8, at 19 (suggesting that negotiators use an objective system to add up value "across all issues" and thus avoid measuring gains and losses relative to an artificial reference point.)

[103] Korobkin & Guthrie, *New Look, supra* note 92, at 120:

[A]t least in some circumstances, a lawyer taking an active role in their client's litigation decisionmaking processes probably can affect the extent to which psychological factors, as opposed to the comparison of the expected financial values of alternative litigation options, motivate litigant's ultimate decisions.

[104] Korobkin & Guthrie, *Barriers, supra* note 80, at 163.

[105] *Id.*

[106] Korobkin & Guthrie, *New Look, supra* note 92, at 83.

[107] *Id.* at 130.

This is not to say that lawyers must become psychologists. Rather, the lawyer should "steer a middle course between indiscriminately attempting to influence settlement decisions and indiscriminately avoiding such a role."[108] They suggest that lawyers "engage the client in an interactive counseling process" that may eventually lead to the lawyer volunteering advice.[109] This advice should always be "accompanied by an explicit description of the considerations underlying the advice and an explanation of the considerations that suggest that the client might not want to alter" the decision.[110] This process tracks with the model we describe in Chapter 8.

§ 7- 5(c).   GUIDELINES FOR ACCURATELY FRAMING RISK

Knowing about these influences is only the first step. Lawyers can easily influence their clients' perceptions by framing offers of settlement either as gains or losses. Effective decision-makers deliberately set out to minimize the inappropriate influence of risk and loss aversion. Here are some ways to do that.[111]

- *Choose reference points carefully:* Because the options will be evaluated by the reference point, the lawyer should carefully and consciously choose how to express the risk. At times, it is best to express options in terms of both loss and gain, so as not to unjustifiably influence the client. This allows the client to choose the reference point. For example, option "A" in the example above could be explained as follows: "If we compare Option 'A' with the losses that the company is facing, it will save one plant and 2000 jobs; but if we compare it with the company's current position, it will still require you to close two plants and lose 4000 jobs." Option "B" could be explained as follows: "Option 'B' can be viewed as either creating a 1/3 chance that we will save all three factories and all 6000 jobs or as creating a 2/3 chance that we will lose all three factories and all 6000 jobs."

  However, if it is clear that if the company does not take one of the options, it will lose all of the factories and jobs, it is probably most realistic to use that as the reference point:

  "Plan A will save one of the three plants and 2,000 jobs; Plan B has a 1/3 probability of saving all three plants and all 6,000 jobs."

- *Avoid creating unreasonable expectations:* When people believe that something good may happen, they will be more likely to act to preserve that chance.[112] Clients who unjustifiably believe that

---

[108] *Id.* at 136.

[109] *Id.*

[110] *Id.*

[111] The following guidelines are adapted from BAZERMAN, *supra* note 33, at 55-76.

[112] BAZERMAN, *supra* note 33, at 62-63.

there is a strong chance for a favorable verdict at trial may resist reasonable settlement offers. Because of this, lawyers should avoid exaggerating the strength of the client's case or the ability of the lawyer to solve the client's problem.

- *Consider "paying premiums" versus "accepting losses":* Monetary losses are more acceptable if seen as insurance premiums.[113] That is, people are more willing to accept paying money to reduce the certainty of a larger loss. When a defendant settles a case by paying money to the plaintiff, it can be described as an insurance payment against the uncertainty of a trial. It can also be seen as diluting the bottom line. The former has a better chance of being accepted by the defendant than the latter. It is probably best to describe a settlement possibility in both ways to the client.

§ 7-6. CONCLUSION

This chapter identifies the theoretical framework for the model presented in the next chapter. Legal counseling closely resembles short-term decision counseling as opposed to therapeutic counseling. Because of this resemblance, we outline a number of factors in the next chapter that go into successful decision-counseling. These factors serve as guidelines and help to structure the legal counseling model laid out in the next chapter.

The present chapter also outlines some of the principles that govern ordinary decision-making. By keeping these principles in mind, lawyers can conduct their counseling sessions so as to avoid the pitfalls of inappropriate reliance on simple decision strategies. We also use these principles to structure the model found in the next chapter. However, effective counselors know that any theoretical principles will be of little value unless they are applied with sensitivity to the needs and capabilities of each client. The guidelines are prescriptive hypotheses that are expected to be beneficial sometimes for counseling some clients, not necessarily with all clients. They are not intended . . . to be used like many medical prescriptions automatically and without thought or imagination . . . [Any] one counseling strategy may not work well for all clients. . . . [E]ach client may respond in an idiosyncratic manner to any particular approach.[114]

---

[113] BAZERMAN, *supra* note 33, at 65.

[114] WILLIAM H. CORMIER & L. SHERILYN CORMIER, INTERVIEWING STRATEGIES FOR HELPERS: A GUIDE TO ASSESSMENT, TREATMENT AND EVALUATION 8 (1979).

CHAPTER 8

CLIENT COUNSELING

§ 8-1. THE LAWYER'S RESPONSIBILITIES IN COUNSELING CLIENTS

In legal counseling, a lawyer helps the client make a decision about matters within the scope of the attorney-client relationship. The lawyer's responsibility in this process is to ensure that the client considers and evaluates all of the available options.[1] As we noted in Chapter 1, the lawyer should empower the client, rather than making decisions for the client. This chapter describes a process where the lawyer makes sure that the client identifies all of the appropriate alternatives, thoroughly evaluates each one with the client, and helps the client to an option that best satisfies the client's goals.

During this process, the lawyer should generally be non-directive as to the client's ultimate choice, but directive as to the process followed in reaching that decision. This means that the lawyer directs the client through the process of making an effective decision, but the lawyer allows the client to make the ultimate decision.

Under some circumstances, however, the lawyer must be directive in dealing with the client's decision. The lawyer cannot facilitate the client's commission of a crime. Thus, the lawyer must be "directive" by telling the client that the goals or means are unlawful and the lawyer will not participate. Indeed, the lawyer may even be required to withdraw from the

---

[1] The following discussion assumes that the client is fully competent and without undue time pressure. If the client is not fully competent, the lawyer's responsibility changes. *See* MODEL RULES OF PROF'L CONDUCT R. 1.14 (a) (1994) ("When a client's ability to make adequately considered decisions in connection with the representation is impaired, whether because of minority, mental disability or for some other reason, the lawyer shall, as far as reasonably possible maintain a normal lawyer-client relationship.").

The comments to the Model Rules remind lawyers that even legally incompetent people may be able "to understand, deliberate upon, and reach conclusions about matters affecting" their own well-being. MODEL RULES OF PROF'L CONDUCT R. 1.14 (a) cmt. 1 (1994). Even incapacitated people should be treated with attention and respect. *Id.* As a practical matter, the lawyer will become more directive throughout the entire representation. This means not only identifying the client's options more openly, but providing more guidance in reaching a decision. *Cf.* David Luban, *Paternalism and the Legal Profession,* 1981 WIS. L. REV. 454, 493 (stating that the lawyer's assertion of control justified paternalism). For a thorough criticism of this view, see Paul Tremblay, *On Persuasion and Paternalism: Lawyer Decisionmaking and the Questionably Competent Client,* 1987 UTAH L. REV. 515 (1987).

On the other hand, competent clients may contract with their lawyers to make these decisions. Fully competent clients may decide not to be actively involved in the process of reaching a decision and contractually delegate that duty to the lawyer. *See* Alex Hurder, *Negotiating the Lawyer-Client Relationship,* 44 BUFF. L. REV. 71 (1996).

representation if the client persists in an illegal course of conduct.[2] In addition, lawyers may also have to be directive when clients choose a patently bad alternative. That is, lawyers may have an obligation to tell their client that they are making a bad decision.

A lawyer would commit malpractice if she allowed a client to choose a course that the lawyer knew was ineffective and flawed. At the very least, the lawyer must advise the client against that choice and explain why.

But it is not only the case in which the client is about to choose an obviously flawed course in which the lawyer should become involved in decision-making. As Anthony Kronman has said, "[The lawyer's] responsibilities to a client go beyond the preliminary clarification of his goals and include helping him to make a deliberatively wise choice among them."[3] The lawyer should assist the client in evaluating the alternatives. The client can fold the lawyer's concerns into the client's calculus of risks and benefits.

Experience tells us that many clients want advice about how to make their decision. Many clients see lawyers as expert problem solvers and they expect the benefit of the lawyer's multiple expertise. Not only do they want lawyers to identify the legal alternatives, but they also expect lawyers to analyze the situation and suggest the best course of action.

This chapter aims not only to equip lawyers with the skills necessary to help clients make good decisions, but also to equip lawyers to make good decisions for those clients who want their lawyers to do so. The process of considering alternatives, their risks and benefits, and deciding which alternative(s) to pursue, applies whether the client makes the decision in conjunction with the lawyer or the client directs the lawyer to make the decision alone. In both instances, the decision can be enhanced by following the decision-making guidelines set out in this chapter.

The role the lawyer plays should vary in different situations. The client may want more or less involvement from the lawyer. Some decisions require an elaborate decision-making process, while other decisions require a less complicated process. However, almost every legal counseling session requires certain common elements. They are:

- *Information:* Effective lawyers provide information about the law or the legal system.

- *Advice:* Effective lawyers advise their clients about the available ways to accomplish the clients' objectives.

- *Questioning:* Effective lawyers ask the client questions designed to clarify important facts and the client's objectives.

- *Discussion:* Effective lawyers discuss the various options with the client and help decide which ones best meet the client's goals.

---

[2] MODEL RULES OF PROF'L CONDUCT R. 1.16 (a)(1).

[3] *See* ANTHONY T. KRONMAN, THE LOST LAWYER 129 (1993).

§ 8-2. THE RHYTHM OF COUNSELING

Every counseling session takes on a distinct rhythm — description, discussion, and decision. This rhythm, which provides the overall structure of the conversation, incorporates the five stages of effective decision-making.[4] The following chart shows how each phase of the process described in this chapter corresponds to a stage or stages in effective decision-making and the basic elements that predominate during each stage.

RHYTHM OF COUNSELING	BASIC ELEMENTS	STAGES FOR STABLE DECISIONS
Description: 1. Assess the client's case. 2. Identify available alternatives.	Questioning Information Advice	1. Appraising the challenge 2. Surveying the alternatives
Discussion: 1. Agree on the alternatives under discussion. 2. Agree on the criteria to evaluate the options. 3. Apply the criteria in a rigorous and systematic fashion. 4. Fill out a Decision Sheet.	Advice Information Discussion Questioning	3. Weighing the alternatives
Decision: 1. Make an optimal choice. 2. Make comparative judgments. 3. Make and review the decision.	Discussion Questioning	4. Deliberating about commitment 5. Adhering in spite of negative feedback

§ 8-3. DESCRIPTION

Every legal counseling session should begin with an accurate, complete, and objective description of the subject under discussion and the decision

---

[4] IRVING JANIS, SHORT-TERM COUNSELING 137 (1982). *See also* IRVING JANIS & LEON MANN, DECISION MAKING 171-200 (1977).

to be made.[5] This includes the client's story, a general overview of the applicable law, the client's goals, and a preliminary list of available options. An effective description sets the stage for the hard work to come; i.e., the discussion and evaluation of each alternative. It narrows the focus so that the lawyer and the client can efficiently use their time to reach the best decision under the circumstances.

An effective description presents the client with the reality of the situation. It allows the client to view the matter and decide what to do. Effective decision-making begins when a person is confronted with a challenge to his or her current course of action. This challenge can be events or communications that convey threats or opportunities. The central question facing a decision-maker during this stage is whether the threat or opportunity is important enough to warrant the effort of making an active decision about it. Ignoring or rejecting the challenge leads to complacent pursuit of the original course of action without any change, simply continuing business as usual. Once the decision-maker gives a positive response to the first key question, he or she accepts the challenge and decides to decide.[6]

An effective description winnows the possible alternatives to an appropriate few. Although an almost limitless number of options are potentially available in every case, most of these will not be useful to the client either because of cost, the unlikelihood of success, or the client's personal distaste or preference. Furthermore, counseling sessions would be unbearably tedious if the lawyer dutifully listed every alternative in the universe and proceeded to discuss each one with the client. The lawyer serves the client well by eliminating those alternatives that are not feasible, rational, or appropriate. Of course, the lawyer must remain open to the possibility that the client will want to discuss some of the alternatives dismissed by the lawyer. But if the lawyer has learned enough about the client, the client's case, and the client's goals during the interview, an effective lawyer should be able to identify the alternatives that satisfy the client's goals.

Finally, an effective description sets the pace for the decision process. Ineffective decision-makers may have already made up their minds and be committed to one course of action, or they may delay reaching any decision at all.[7] An effective description backs the impulsive decision-maker up a few steps and focuses the attention of the reluctant decision-maker.

---

[5] *See* ROBIN M. HOGARTH, JUDGEMENT AND CHOICE 185-189 (2d ed. 1987). Hogarth suggests that effective decision-makers should begin by structuring the problem along several dimensions. This structuring involves accurate descriptions of the decision-makers, the alternatives, the evaluation criteria, the uncertainties, and the level of generality in which to address the problem. These elements correspond to the components of an effective description.

[6] *See* JANIS, *supra* note 4, at 136-137.

[7] *See id.* at 140-142 (discussing excessive delay and premature closure).

§ 8-3(a). ACCURACY, OBJECTIVITY, AND COMPLETENESS

A good description is accurate. It accurately describes the client's situation and the applicable law. Accuracy enhances the lawyer-client relationship by showing the client that the lawyer has heard and understood the client. An accurate description also avoids any misunderstanding between the lawyer and the client by preventing the lawyer from proceeding on the basis of a misunderstanding.

In a sense, a good description is objective. It describes the situation from the client's point of view but does not adopt that point of view. It puts some distance between the client's perceptions and the discussion. This should allow the client to realistically evaluate the consequences flowing from the available alternatives.[8] Objectivity, however, is not the same as neutrality. Neutrality implies that the person has not taken sides, but the lawyer who represents a client has taken sides. Objectivity simply requires the lawyer to look at the case honestly. It suggests a realistic appraisal of the strengths and the weaknesses of the client's case without skewing the matter in favor of the client.

A good description is also complete. It includes everything that matters to the client and to the case. It describes the case in sufficient — not exhaustive — detail. It provides a summary of the relevant issues and offers the client an opportunity to verify the lawyer's understanding of the matter.

Accurate, objective, and complete descriptions contain two elements. First, they include an assessment of the client's case. Second, they identify alternative solutions for the client to consider.

§ 8-3(a)(1). Assess the Client's Case

At the beginning of each counseling session, the lawyer should check with the client to see if anything has changed. The lawyer needs to find out if the client's goals have changed, if there is any additional information that the client can now provide, or if something has happened that will influence the outcome of the matter. The client may have decided not to pursue the original goals of the case. Or maybe the client has remembered important facts during the interim between the last meeting and the current session. Or something may have happened to the client that affects the representation. For example, in a litigation matter, court papers may have been served on the client in the interim. In any event, asking the client a few simple questions before proceeding with the counseling session will greatly enhance the quality of the counseling session.

---

[8] Ineffective decision-makers often overestimate the favorable consequences flowing from their desired option. *See* JANIS & MANN, *supra* note 4, at 84-85. They describe a conversation with a student of theirs who had just married. The student explained that before the marriage, his thoughts were dominated by the favorable consequences he believed marriage would bring. He only briefly considered the unfavorable consequences. He even avoided talking to people who might offer a negative view of marriage.

A simple way to begin the counseling session is for the lawyer to say, "Has anything happened that I should know about?" In many cases, the lawyer can anticipate some events and ask about them. For example, the lawyer and the client may have expected the other party to contact the client, so the lawyer can ask, "Has Mr. Smith called you?"

After determining if anything has changed, the lawyer can move into an assessment of the matter. This assessment should include the following:

- A description of the client's story, any additional facts, and the applicable law;

- Identification of the client's goals for the case; and

- A recognition of the importance of the decision to the client.

The description of the client's story, the facts, and the law should not be extensive. Lawyers may be tempted to lecture the client on all of the elements of the case and the nuances of the law. After all, lawyers have spent a lot of money on a law school education learning to think like lawyers. This is an opportunity to show off this ability. But most clients do not need elaborate descriptions of the law and it would waste time for lawyers to give it to them.

Instead, this description should set the stage for the discussion that follows by briefly putting the case into its legal context. In order to properly identify and evaluate the available alternatives, clients must appreciate how the law enables or constrains their choices. Avoid the temptation to launch into a long discussion of the latest cases. Simply summarize the client's story and then identify the applicable law at a fairly high level of generality. For example, the lawyer might relate the client's situation and then say, "My legal research shows that you might be able to recover your losses. You can also try to settle your case by not going to court." The lawyer should also restate the client's interests. This helps frame the identification and evaluation of the alternatives. Restating the client's interests focuses both the lawyer and the client on the purpose of the representation. These interests anchor the lawyer and the client in the attempt to achieve them rather than in some generic "case." It helps the lawyer avoid skewing the matter to the lawyer's ends and it helps the client retain control of the discussion.

§ 8-3(a)(2).   Identify the Alternatives

Identifying the alternatives sounds like a simple process: the lawyer or the client simply list the client's options. But there are a number of pitfalls that can undermine the client's ultimate choice. First, what counts as a viable option? There are many things that can be done in any given situation. Ineffective decision-makers do not generate a wide range of options for consideration. They may exclude options that seem too costly,[9] or they may ignore options that challenge the status quo.[10]

---

[9] IRVING JANIS, DECISION MAKING 174 (1977) (finding that smokers feared lung cancer but rejected chest x-rays as too costly).

[10] *Id.* at 372 (stating that decision-makers resist making changes either to the status quo or the way they make decisions).

Second, who chooses the options to be considered? The lawyer may unnecessarily limit the available options to those that the lawyer feels most comfortable discussing, and the client may exclude options either because the client is not aware of them or because they do not sound sufficiently "legal" to talk about with a lawyer. There is an additional danger that the lawyer will influence the client's choice by skillfully arranging the presentation of the options. It is best if both freely propose options.

Third, if both are to present options, who goes first, the lawyer or the client? The lawyer may unduly influence the client's decision by speaking first and overwhelming the client. In some instances the client should go first while in other instances the lawyer should go first. It is best if both the lawyer and the client generate their own list of options and then compare them.

No matter who goes first, however, the quality of the relationship between the lawyer and the client will determine whether or not the lawyer will dominate the client. Lawyers who have built strong relationships with their clients can be more flexible with their counseling sessions than lawyers who have not built strong client relationships.

The following proposals help mitigate undue lawyer influence, and, at the same time, they permit the lawyer to help the client generate options. They also help the lawyer steer the decision process towards a wise and prudent decision.

The lawyer and the client should choose options that:

- Satisfy minimal acceptance criteria

- Cover a wide range of possible solutions

- State the options at a medium level of generality

§ 8-3(a)(2)(i).   Minimal Acceptance Criteria

The lawyer should choose options that meet minimal acceptance criteria. Those criteria are: 1) the option satisfies a minimum of client goals; 2) the option is acceptable to the client personally; and 3) the option is legitimate, i.e., it is not forbidden by law, ethics, rules of procedure, etc. Using these minimal criteria ensures that the lawyer and client will consider a wide range of options. Because the client may eventually choose an option from this list, it is important not to unduly limit the client's choices.

Any acceptable option must minimally satisfy one or more client goals. That is, the option must either advance the client's goal slightly or, in cases where the client has multiple goals, advance at least one of those goals. The lawyer should not exclude from discussion options that do not seem perfect. No option may successfully advance all of the client's goals or achieve complete success. In most situations, the client must choose an option that advances some goals but not others, or one that achieves only limited success. In those cases, the client's ultimate choice comes from imperfect options.

The option must be acceptable to the client. The client may have already declared some options out of bounds based on personal, religious, or social objections. The lawyer should try to find out these limitations during the interview phase. These objections can then serve as a way to filter out some of the limitless options that may be available.

The option must be legitimate. In theory, every litigant might eliminate the opposing parties by contracting for their death. But that would be illegal! In reality, the law serves as another filter on available options. Aside from silly possibilities, the law may prevent the lawyer from raising certain options. Raising these options may violate the Rules of Professional Conduct or the substantive law. The law may also preclude using certain devices because they may be procedurally or substantively barred.

Thus, the lawyer should include a wide range of options that minimally serve the client's goals and then filter those options through the client's and the law's limitations.

§ 8-3(a)(2)(ii).   Cover a Wide Range of Options

The initial options should present a variety of possible solutions to the client's problem. A wide range of solutions guards against the biases of the lawyer and the client. It helps move the client beyond a commitment to the status quo or the lawyer's commitment to the familiar solutions.[11]

Generating a wide range of options allows the lawyer and client to compare each one against the others. In this way, the client can be confident that he has selected the option that accomplishes more than other options. In addition, generating a wide range of options allows the lawyer and client to put options together in new combinations. Good decisions often result from this creative sifting and recombining, whereas decisions that consider fewer options raise the possibility that the best option may never be generated.

The lawyer and the client should each independently generate a list of options. The client legitimately expects the lawyer to identify the options that, in the lawyer's expertise and experience, will accomplish the client's problem. Clients come to lawyers because they believe that the lawyer has something to offer, and clients expect lawyers to know the law and how to solve their legal problems. Thus, lawyers should help to preliminarily identify some alternatives for the client to consider.

At the same time, lawyers should have clients create a list of options. The empirical studies cited in earlier chapters show that many lawyers do not simply offer advice. They tend to dominate their clients.[12] Clients are alienated by this approach and, at least in some instances, begin to resist the lawyer's efforts.

---

[11] *See, e.g.,* JANIS & MANN, *supra* note 4, at 75, 95-96. They describe a pattern of defensive avoidance where decision-makers not only avoid being exposed to information that challenges the status quo, but also selectively distort unavoidable, challenging information by discounting its significance or bolstering the decision maker's commitment to the status quo.

[12] See discussion in Chapter 2.

This creates a delicate situation for the lawyer. Clients expect lawyers to show some expertise but not to dominate the case. In the end, some lawyers handle the cases so as to maximize the lawyer's interests, and clients withdraw from involvement with the lawyer and the case.

Effective lawyers form a partnership with their clients, with each contributing to the representation. Prior to the counseling session, the lawyer should prepare a list of alternatives that best accomplish the client's goals. The lawyer can identify options that the client may not be aware of and exclude options that are not possible to pursue.

The lawyer should begin this section with a framing statement. For example, the lawyer could state along these lines:

> At this point, we need to identify some options that you can consider. I've made a list of options that I think can help you accomplish your goals. We can talk about them in a minute. I am also interested in any options that I may have missed or left off this list. Each of us may come up with ideas that the other has not thought of. Two heads are better than one. We can put our ideas together and decide what to do. here is the list. What do you think?

Another possibility is for both the lawyer and the client to generate a list of options prior to the counseling session. That way, the client can generate options while he has the time to reflect and ask advice of friends and family. The lawyer should have the client also prepare a list. If the client prepares his list before he sees the lawyer's list, the client may come up with creative options. If the client sees the lawyer's list first, the client may merely rely on the lawyer.

The lawyer should remain sincerely open to hearing what the client has to say. The legal system gives lawyers a powerful lens through which to view the world. Like any lens, it helps focus our vision acutely for a particular task. But it also distorts our vision when used in situations that are not suited to its properties. An astronomer would not look at the stars with a microscope and a biologist would not use a telescope to look at microbes. Similarly, a legal perspective may not be useful for every task. It may distort some things and leave others out.

Some people have trouble generating lists of alternatives. They have trouble "thinking outside the box." They may limit themselves to the most obvious, the most familiar, or the most "legal-sounding" ones. Effective decision-makers are aware of this problem and structure the decision process to avoid it. One of the simplest ways to ensure that the lawyer and the client consider a variety of options is brainstorming.

Brainstorming is a technique frequently used by decision-makers to quickly generate a lot of material. The rules for brainstorming are simple.[13] They are:

---

[13] *See* JANIS, *supra* note 4, at 168-170.

- *Produce as many alternatives as possible:* List whatever comes into mind in connection with the client's case. Go from one idea to another. Produce as much material as possible.

- *Don't judge anything at the beginning:* People have a tendency to temper their ideas by hyper-critical notions. There will be time to evaluate these ideas later. Any idea, no matter how impractical or impossible it sounds, should be listed.

- *Be creative:* Deliberately think about novel or unconventional ways to address the client's situation. Often, these so-called impractical choices may be the best solution for the client.

- *Think broadly:* Use anything for further ideas. Build on previously listed ideas to come up with more ideas.

- *Consult freely:* Use other resources. This includes people as well as written material. Effective decision makers use whatever expertise is available.

- *Avoid binary roadblocks:* Stay away from "either/or" thinking. Most decisions are not simply choices between two mutually exclusive options. Rather, there are often intermediate stages for each choice. Even if there are only two choices, they can be conditioned upon the performance of certain factors. In short, people can always come up with creative and effective ways to address even difficult situations.

A brainstorming session with the client can be a very efficient way to make decisions. When the lawyer and the client have plenty of time to reach a decision, the client can generate a list without the lawyer. The lawyer can tell the client the brainstorming rules and ask the client to meet with a trusted advisor to create a list of options. This list can then be considered at the next session along with the lawyer's own list. The benefit of this latter approach is that it allows the client to come up with options outside of the lawyer's influence. The client can then come to the counseling session with some momentum and confidence.

Once a list of options has been generated by brainstorming, the lawyer and the client should review the list with an eye toward eliminating some options and combining others. The lawyer and the client should review the list and leave any option that minimally advances the client's goals on the list. They should eliminate any that are illegal or impossible to pursue. Finally, they should combine any fragmentary options together. This can be done by grouping together options that have a similar theme, that seem to be parts of a larger, more general option, or that gain strength when combined.

§ 8-3(a)(2)(iii).   Generality of Options

The lawyer should identify options at a fairly high level of generality. She should not identify each detail or step in the process. This is the time to orient the client's thinking toward overall solutions rather than minutiae. The details can be explored later.

Identifying numerous detailed options runs the risk of fatiguing the lawyer and the client. Both the lawyer and the client may well run out of time and energy as they plod through every aspect of every alternative. Instead of reaching a good decision by covering a wide range of options, the client may reach a bad decision out of mental fatigue.

A high level of generality presents the options more fairly. For example, a client may have the option of litigation or mediation. If a client has several affirmative defenses as well as several counterclaims, the sheer number of them may make it seem as though litigation is a better option. The amount of time spent on the litigation options will overwhelm, practically and psychologically, the lawyer and client. Instead, a presentation that tells the client that there are two ways to resolve the matter (e.g., going to court or going to mediation) puts the options on more even terms. The client can then evaluate them more objectively. When the lawyer and the client have produced the final list of options to consider, they can move to the discussion phase of counseling.

§ 8-4.   DISCUSSION

After the lawyer and the client have assessed the client's case and identified available options, it is time to discuss and evaluate those options. Stated simply, the lawyer and the client talk about and judge the list of alternatives. But the lawyer's responsibility in this process is more important and more complex than it might initially appear. Effective counselors help clients to avoid the typical mistakes of ineffective decision-makers. The suggestions in this section are designed to allow lawyers to enable clients to avoid these mistakes.

Often, people who must make decisions under high stress use various tactics to avoid making the decision. They procrastinate, they shift responsibility, or they bolster their commitment to the status quo or to an inadequate alternative.[14] The client who procrastinates or shifts responsibility may never make it to a counseling session. There may be little a lawyer can do if the client will not return phone calls or if the client denies responsibility for making a decision.

Assuming that a client makes it to the office, the lawyer should be aware of the possible flaws in the client's evaluation of the available alternatives. According to social scientists, decision makers use a variety of tactics to bolster their commitment to either the status quo or to an ineffective alternative.[15] These tactics include doing the following as to their hastily chosen position:

- *Exaggerating favorable consequences:* This is the most obvious tactic people use. By exaggerating the favorable consequences, people create an unrealistic picture of how a choice will affect them.

---

[14] *See* JANIS & MANN, *supra* note 4, at 87.

[15] *Id.* at 91-98.

- *Minimizing unfavorable consequences:* Even if people don't exaggerate the positive consequences, they may avoid acknowledging the likelihood and the extent of any negative consequences.

- *Denying the impact of negative consequences:* People may acknowledge the negative consequences but minimize the effect it will have on them. They may convince themselves that "things won't be so bad" or that "I can handle anything that happens."

- *Exaggerating the remoteness of the triggering event:* People may postpone a decision because they believe that the events that may force their choice will not happen in the near future. The difference between effective and ineffective decision makers often turns on the accuracy of this determination.

- *Minimizing the degree to which the matter affects other people:* People may believe that the consequences of any decision will only affect themselves. They forget that third parties — business associates, spouses, children, other constituencies, or the public — may be affected by whatever choice they make.

- *Minimizing personal responsibility for the choice:* People under pressure may assure themselves that the questionable decisions they make have been forced on them by outside pressures. The person does not shift the responsibility for the decision to anyone else. Rather, the decision-maker understands that she must make the decision but claims that circumstances gave her no alternative.

People use various tactics. Some personality types may be inclined towards one strategy, but external pressures may push them toward others. In any event, these tactics undermine effective decision-making by preventing a full and realistic consideration of the available options. The ineffective decision-maker may simply avoid discussing some options, exaggerate the consequences of other options, or refuse to commit to any choice at all.

§ 8-4(a).   CLIENT/LAWYER COLLABORATIVE DELIBERATION

During counseling, the lawyer should not merely sit back and allow the client to engage in ineffective decision-making. The lawyer can help the client by joining the client in collaborative deliberation and by structuring the process so that the client is likely to consider the relevant factors.

In the following excerpt, Kronman describes the important role that the lawyer should play in the deliberative process.

Anthony Kronman, The Lost Lawyer 130-131 (1993)[16]

* * *

[A] lawyer needs to place himself in the client's position by provisionally accepting [the client's] ends and then imaginatively considering the consequences of pursuing them, with the same combination of sympathy and detachment the lawyer would employ if he were deliberating on his own account. The kind of deliberation that is required in such cases might be termed "third personal," for it takes as its starting point not the ends of the person deliberating, but someone else's, and hence requires an additional, preliminary act of imagination that first-personal deliberation does not- the imaginative assumption of this foreign starting point itself. In every other respect, however, third-personal deliberation resembles its first-personal counterpart.

The lawyer's third-personal deliberations yield an independent judgement concerning the soundness of the client's decision, a judgement that is in principle distinguishable both from the client's declared views and the conclusion the lawyer would reach starting from his own personal values instead (though obviously in any given case these judgements may coincide). Of course, the lawyer's third-personal judgement is open to revision as the client presents new facts and elaborates his objectives. But by the same token, the client may change his own mind when he hears what his lawyer has to say. The process might thus best be described as one of cooperative deliberation, with the lawyer attempting to see things from the client's point of view, only more clearly, and each party being prepared to revise his or her initial judgement in light of arguments and insights the other presents . . . [17]

* * *

§ 8-4(b). STRUCTURING THE DISCUSSION

The lawyer should structure the process so that the client considers the relevant factors in making a decision. The process outlined in this section is designed to enable the client to avoid the problems of ineffective decision-making. Although many different styles can be effective, the most effective discussions include the following elements:

- The lawyer and the client agree on the options under discussion.

---

[16] Copyright 1993 by the President and Fellows of Harvard College.

[17] Kronman, *supra* note 3 at 130-31. Kronman suggests that the lawyer use the "third personal deliberation" method when a client's goals are ambiguous, conflicting, or confused or the client is in danger of making an impetuous decision. However, we believe that the method that Kronman describes will be of value to the client throughout the decision-making process. Throughout the process, the lawyer and client can use the lawyer's "third personal" assessment to evaluate the client's judgment.

- The lawyer and client agree on the criteria to be used to evaluate them.

- The lawyer and client apply the criteria in a systematic and rigorous fashion.

§ 8-4(b)(1).   Agree on the Options under Discussion

The lawyer and the client have already ventured down this road by generating a broad list of options to consider. Some of the options may have been eliminated already. If the list has been winnowed to a manageable number, the lawyer and the client can then move on and evaluate them. But if the list is still too long, the lawyer and the client should spend more time combing through the options.

The lawyer can introduce the consideration of options with the following framing statement:

> We're now ready to look at the options and choose one. We need to work together on this so don't be afraid to raise any issues with me as we discuss these. Before we do that, let's look at the list one more time. Are there any options that we should not talk about now for any reason? . . . Are there any that seem to be pieces of other options? . . . Are there any that you want to eliminate on second thought? . . . Are there important options that we have missed?

Once the list is set, the lawyer should ask the client to choose the order in which the options will be discussed. This concedes control over the sequence of topics to the clients. It signals that the lawyer will not dominate the conversation.

§ 8-4(b)(2).   Agree on the Criteria used to Evaluate the Options

Many decisions will simply require the client to identify the good and bad things that will come from choosing an option. Often what is good and bad will be self-evident. Staying out of jail is usually a good thing, while going to jail is ordinarily a bad thing. But many times the criteria will not be so clear. A delay may be good in some circumstances and bad in others. Expensive litigation may be a serious negative factor for some clients but not for others. Whether or not something should be considered a positive or a negative factor ultimately depends on whether or not it advances the client's legal and personal goals.

Effective decision-makers avoid choosing the first option that minimally satisfies their interests.[18] They use criteria that evaluate their goals and differentially weigh those criteria.

---

[18] HERBERT SIMON, MODELS OF MAN 204-205 (1957) (satisficing — choosing a "just good enough" solution — is an inescapable part of a human's bounded rationality).

Under the authoritarian model, lawyers decided what criteria to use. These lawyers ignored any considerations that were not "legal" or "logical."[19] Under a pure client-centered model, lawyers deferred to the clients to apply whatever criteria they wished. However, both models failed to take into account the ordinary biases people bring to decision making. Both the lawyer and the client are subject to weaknesses when evaluating pros and cons.[20]

An effective counselor takes an active role by identifying criteria that seem useful in light of the client's goals.[21] The effective legal counselor also asks the client what criteria to use. In addition, the effective legal counselor shares his perceptions as to the criteria's usefulness. Making this a joint project makes it more likely that the client will make the final decision after consideration of many different perspectives.

The legal counselor should first ask the client what criteria they should use to evaluate the various options. The lawyer might then identify additional criteria and ask the client's if they should use them. The lawyer should not raise criteria that would not advance the client's goals. If the client proposes criteria that do not appear to the lawyer to advance the client's goals, this may be a signal to the lawyer that the client has goals that have not yet been identified. The lawyer and client may need to back up and re-evaluate the client's goals.

Good decision-makers also know that not every factor has equal weight.[22] Some consequences will be more important than others. The lawyer should ensure that the client weighs the pros and the cons appropriately and does not fall into the trap of treating each one alike.

This can be outlined in framing statements like these:

> To make a good decision we have to use good guidelines. During our first interview, you mentioned that you needed to get this over with before school let out in the spring. You also mentioned that you wanted to avoid angering your ex-spouse. These two things seemed to be the most important factors to you. Are there other factors that we should consider in making this decision? You said that you weren't worried about your costs. If you still feel that way, then we should weigh time and the possibility of upsetting your spouse more heavily than cost as we look at these options.

---

[19] See, e.g., ROBERT M. BASTRESS & JOSEPH D. HARBAUGH, INTERVIEWING, COUNSELING, AND NEGOTIATING: SKILLS FOR EFFECTIVE REPRESENTATIONt 61 (1990) (quoting a lawyer who described his technique of asking questions so that he was not "fed information which I have no need to know.").

[20] For example, both the lawyer and the client may use the availability or the representativeness heuristic to evaluate the options. See, e.g., RICHARD NISBETT & LEE ROSS, HUMAN INFERENCE: STRATEGIES AND SHORTCOMINGS OF SOCIAL JUDGEMENT 17-42 (1980). These perceptual flaws may lead to an inaccurate weighing of the options and, therefore, to a less than optimal decision.

[21] See, e.g., MAX H. BAZERMAN, JUDGEMENT IN MANAGERIAL DECISION MAKING 4 (1994) (rational decision-makers identify all relevant criteria).

[22] Id. (rational decision-makers know the relative value of each of their decision criteria).

§ 8-4(b)(3).   Apply the Criteria in a Rigorous and Systematic Fashion

Once lawyer and client have established the criteria and their weight, good decision-makers use a system to thoroughly identify and evaluate all of the consequences that attach to each available option. Benjamin Franklin outlined the procedure that has become commonplace: draw a line down the middle of a sheet of paper. For each option, list the pros on one side of the page and the cons on the other. Tally up the pros versus the cons and choose accordingly.[23] While many decisions can be made following this simple procedure, some decisions require a bit more care.

First of all, it is not always clear whether something is a pro or a con. For example, spending money can either be an investment or a completely wasteful expense. The lawyer and the client may know that consequences will flow from the decisions they are making but they cannot always tell whether they will be positive or negative. Deciding to put them on the pro side of the page or the con side requires the client to evaluate the consequences and decide where they go.

Second, both tangible and intangible consequences will flow from clients' decisions. These include the client's self image, relationships, and moral matters that cannot be measured but nevertheless are likely to be important to the client. There is a risk that some consequences will be overlooked unless the client approaches the decision in a systematic fashion.

Finally, all decisions will have consequences for people other than the client. These consequences may be also be overlooked unless the lawyer and the client systematically consider them.

Effective decision-makers also evaluate the likelihood that any consequence will occur; and, if it does, how important that consequence is. For these reasons, we suggest that lawyers and clients follow a process in which they

- identify all of the consequences that may flow from a decision
- decide whether each consequence is a "pro" or a "con"
- evaluate the importance of each consequence, and
- assess the likelihood that each consequence will occur.

This procedure allows lawyers and clients to systematically evaluate each option. It guards against either the lawyer or the client short-circuiting the decision-making process.

§ 8-4(c).   THE DECISION SHEET

To insure that the lawyer and client thoroughly evaluate each option, they should fill out the Decision Sheet, which is located at the end of this

---

[23] *See* JANIS, *supra* note 9, at 149 (*quoting* Franklin's letter to the famous scientist, Joseph Priestly). Franklin suggested taking several days to fill out his sheet. This "moral and prudential algebra" consisted of striking out all the items on the list that nullified each other and basing his decision on the factors that remained.

chapter.[24] Some decisions may be relatively simple, and may not require the thorough evaluation required by our decision sheet. We have included a thorough decision sheet that will enable a client to consider many factors when making an important decision. For simpler decisions, a simpler decision-making sheet may be appropriate. Feel free to alter our proposed sheet to fit your client's needs.

Filling out a sheet helps the lawyer and the client keep all of the options and their consequences in mind. Without some way to organize this information, clients may overload their decision-making circuits and choose an option that is "just good enough."[25] Writing down the options and their consequences also gives clients a document to review after the meeting. This sheet can help clients who can not reach a decision during the conference. It also can help clients who have made a decision to review their thinking and to either confirm their choice or change their mind.[26] Finally, the Decision Sheet serves as a record of the counseling session. The lawyer should keep copies of the filled out sheets in the file to document what was discussed with the client.[27]

Here is how lawyers should approach the Decision Sheet procedure. Separate the possible consequences flowing from each decision into the following categories:

- The consequences to the client.

- The consequences to others.

- The consequences for the client's self-image.

- The consequences for the client's reputation.

Decide whether each consequence is a plus or minus. Then decide how likely it is that the consequence will occur. Use a 1-5 scale with 1 meaning "virtually certain to happen," 3 meaning "more likely than not to happen," and 5 meaning "not likely to happen at all." Next decide how important the particular consequence is. Use a 1-5 scale with 1 meaning "Very important," 3 meaning "somewhat important," and 5 "meaning not important at all."

§ 8-4(c)(1).   The Consequences to the Client

These are generally the most obvious elements in this process because they coincide with what most people consider the pros and cons of an

---

[24] The elements of this process and the Decision Sheet procedure have been adapted from Irving Janis' work. See IRVING JANIS, COUNSELING ON PERSONAL DECISION 65-70 (1984); JANIS, *supra* note 4, at 168-177; JANIS & MANN, *supra* note 4, at 135-169.

[25] *See* SIMON, *supra* note 18, at 205.

[26] *See, e.g.,* JANIS & MANN, *supra* note 4, at 377-379 (suggesting that reviewing a written sheet helps diagnose flaws in decision process).

[27] Filling out a decision sheet does not guarantee that a client will make the most optimal decision. The client may psychologically resist a decision for a number of reasons that the lawyer cannot control. At best, the decision sheet is a tool the client can use and, when properly filled out, gives clients the best opportunity to consider thoroughly all of their options. *See* JANIS & MANN, *supra* note 4, at 379 (suggesting balance sheet may fail to overcome psychological resistance and calling for more powerful psychological techniques). Going any further may be beyond the scope of the lawyer-client relationship, however.

option. These are any identifiable consequences that are likely to flow from an alternative. They include both tangible consequences and intangible consequences. Tangible consequences are measurable effects of the decision. They can include the expense of representation, the increased sales of a business, or the additional overhead for a business contemplating moving to a new location.

Intangible consequences are the unmeasurable but recognizable effects of a decision. These include additional publicity for a business about to enter a new contract, a new work environment for the client leaving a job, or the added stress on the client from a lawsuit. Any cost or benefit that accrues to the client should be included in this category.

§ 8-4(c)(2).   The Consequences to Others

The second category includes the costs and benefits to others. These include both the tangible and the intangible consequences that will flow to anyone else who may be affected by the decision. This requires the client to consider how an option will affect the other side, the client's family, and other third parties.

Tangible consequences may include the extra litigation costs imposed on the other party, the monetary savings to the other party to a business deal, or the effects of closing a factory will have on a town. Intangible consequences may include the effects of moving children to a new school, the enhanced curriculum at that school, or the good will generated by opening a new factory.

Clients and their lawyers should deliberately think about these effects because they may be important factors to the client in the long run. In our view, the client should have the opportunity to consider the effect any option will have on third parties, even if they are not parties to the lawsuit or involved in the matter. In the end, the client should have the option to determine what weight to give to the interests of others, but they should be identified as factors that he can consider in making his decision.[28] Chapter 9 discusses how the lawyer might raise moral considerations with the client without imposing the lawyers values on the client.

§ 8-4(c)(3).   Consequences for the Client's Self-Image

Effective decisions are consistent with a client's self-image. They are consistent with her self-perceived values and attitudes. The client may not be fully supportive of decisions unless they are consistent with the client's self-image. This lack of support undermines people's resolve and may cause them to change their minds or not follow through on what must be done to carry out their decision.

---

[28] THOMAS L. SHAFFER & ROBERT S. COCHRAN, LAWYERS, CLIENTS, AND MORAL RESPONSIBILIY 39 (1994) (stating that lawyers should help their clients exercise moral responsibility).

The client should consider whether this is the kind of decision a person like him would make. The lawyer can ask: "How will you feel about this choice?" This question implicitly asks the client to decide if, after choosing this option, he will feel as though he is living up to his ideals? The client then considers whether or not this consequence is a pro or a con, how likely it is to occur, and how important it is to the client.

§ 8-4(c)(4).   Consequences for the Client's Reputation

Here the client considers how other people will perceive him as a result of choosing a particular option. People have a certain image of themselves that they wish to convey to others. A business executive wants to appear decisive; a parent wants his children to perceive him as loving; a fired worker does not want to be seen as a doormat. If your client is a corporation or other organization, the organization's representative will want to consider the reputation of the organization as a part of the decision-making process.

People are part of a social network. They do not exist apart from the groups to which they belong. An individual may be a lawyer's client but he may also be a father, a partner in a medical practice group, a member of a faith community, and a citizen. It is likely to be important that a client's actions allow him to continue to play all of these roles and to remain a respected member of these groups.

A client may not persist in the face of opposition if he chooses an option that undermines the perceptions of people and groups who matter to him. As Janis and Mann point out,

> [a]nticipated social feedback, which includes being criticized and ridiculed by a group as well as receiving praise and respect, can play a crucial role in determining the decision maker's judgement of the best alternative, his willingness or unwillingness to commit himself, and his willingness to stick to a decision or reverse it after he encounters distressing setbacks.[29]

As before, once the client identifies the consequences to his reputation, he then decides whether they are pros and cons, how important they are to him, and whether they are likely to happen.

§ 8-4(c)(5).   Reviewing the Decision Sheet

This system makes explicit what most people do implicitly when they are called on to make a decision. It enables a lawyer and a client to make decisions with the confidence that they have considered most of the relevant factors. Effective decision makers consider all four categories.[30] The final decision depends on the relative strengths of the various consequences from each category.

---

[29] *See* JANIS & MANN, *supra* note 4, at 139.

[30] *Id.*

Once the client has completed the sheet, the lawyer should review it. The lawyer should focus on categories that have relatively few entries to ensure that nothing has been missed. The lawyer should give some examples of consequences that may have been excluded and ask the client to consider them. By the same token, the lawyer should review the categories that have a lot of entries and ask the client whether or not all of them are significant and whether any of them have been missed.

This system not only enables the client to make wise decisions, it also allows the lawyer and the client to anticipate the most likely challenges to the decision. It prepares the client for any negative feedback she may receive.[31] This system introduces the client to potential sources of conflict. The client then can practice dealing with the criticism in the safe environment of the lawyer's office. The client may decide that he is not willing to endure such criticism and reject the option that leads to being criticized. On the other hand, the client may choose the option anyway. When the expected criticism materializes, the client will have the benefit of having considered how to deal with it in advance.[32]

The lawyer and the client should fill out the decision sheet completely and accurately. The decision will be undermined if some categories are given cursory consideration or some consequences are not honestly evaluated. One of the most common mistakes is to fail to consider doing nothing. This may not be a very good option, but explicitly considering doing nothing allows the client to confidently move past the status quo. The lawyer should ask the client to consider not only the costs from acting but the costs and benefits from not acting.

The lawyer must also guard against the biases that often skew perception.[33] These biases may distort the evaluation of the pros and the cons. The tendency toward optimism may lead a lawyer or a client to overestimate the amount of a jury verdict or its likelihood.[34] Recent events may skew a client's perception about certain matters.[35] For example, a client who has just been fired may be very eager to take revenge on his employer. He may have also read a recent story about wrongful discharge lawsuits. These events may color the client's perceptions of the value of his case and the amount of risk he should tolerate.

---

[31] *Id.* at 148.

[32] *See* JANIS, *supra* note 4, at 182-192 (preparing decision-makers for actual events by providing realistic information about the consequences of decisions).

[33] *See* BAZERMAN, *supra* note 21, at 12-47 (outlining common cognitive biases that interfere with rational judgement). See also the discussion in Chapter 7.

[34] *See* NISBETT & ROSS, *supra* note 20, at 25 (describing "gambler's fallacy" where gambler believes his color or number is due because of its absence in previous runs).

[35] *See id.* at 45 (vivid information is more likely to be remembered and recalled than non-vivid information). *See also* AMOS TVERSKY & DANIEL KAHNEMAN, *Judgement under Uncertainty: Heuristics and Biases,* SCIENCE 1124, 1127 (1974) (recent and vivid events likely to be recalled therefore biasing predictions about similar events).

The lawyer must be particularly careful in framing the options. As we discussed in Chapter 7, whether a choice is framed as a "gain" or a "loss" will influence its attractiveness.

The lawyer should make sure that the client considers all the options. The goal is to allow the client to make the best decision under the circumstances. The lawyer should create an environment in which that can happen. The lawyer must be willing to point out factors that the client may have missed and to question assessments that may be inaccurate. The lawyer may have to be assertive in making the client consider consequences. Indeed, the lawyer may have to challenge some of the client's statements. In the end, however, decisions reached this way will be better and less susceptible to second-guessing than decisions reached any other way.

§ 8-5.   DECISION

§ 8-5(a).   CHOOSING THE OPTION THAT BEST MEETS THE CLIENT'S VALUES AND GOALS

Deciding which option to choose is the third phase of counseling. After the available options have been identified and evaluated, the client must choose which course to follow. Although there is no script to follow, there are some guidelines that will lead to better decisions in the long run.

The client should make the decision because it is primarily the client who will suffer the consequences of the decision. It is the client's case and the client's life. The lawyer is responsible for guiding the client through the process. The lawyer should give her opinion if the client asks; but the lawyer should not take the decision from the client.

§ 8-5(a)(1).   Making an Optimal Choice

The Decision Sheet that the client filled out provides a basis for the client to measure one option against the others. The Decision Sheet provides a way for the client to see what can be accomplished from each option and at what cost. If these sheets are filled out thoroughly, the lawyer and the client can quickly focus on the most optimal options.

The chosen option should represent the most significant improvement over the status quo. The client should not choose any option if none of them improves the client's current situation. People sometimes get caught up in the momentum of decision-making and forget that doing nothing is often an option. Of course, many clients will not have the luxury of choosing the status quo. They may be defendants in lawsuits. But even these clients may benefit from a decision sheet that lists the consequences of doing nothing. Even a defendant can take a default judgement.

The lawyer should be aware of the hidden problems that can undermine decision-making. The cognitive biases, heuristics, and schemas discussed in the previous chapter all influence how the lawyer and the client view the alternatives, evaluate them, and choose one over the other. It is impossible to do away with these things completely. Nevertheless, the lawyer can improve the client's decision-making process if the lawyer remains aware of them and of how they can influence decisions. If the lawyer notices a hole in the client's consideration, it may be the result of one these biases, heuristics, or schemas. The lawyer can discuss this with the client and simply point out the problem.

For example, suppose a client is inclined toward choosing litigation. The client stubbornly underestimates the negative consequences of litigation and overestimates the positive consequences. The client accepts the most optimistic litigation scenarios and rejects the most pessimistic ones. The lawyer must ensure that the client realistically considers the options and chooses the one that has the most realistic chance of accomplishing the client's goals. At the very least, the lawyer must ensure that the client understands the risks involved in any course of action.

Finally, the decision should reflect the client's values, including the client's moral values. The client may have already identified his values during the course of the representation and the lawyer can assist the client in evaluating how these values might influence the decision. Anthony Kronman's third personal method of collaborative decision-making, discussed earlier in this chapter, is important here. Generally, the lawyer should provisionally assume the client's values and discuss the client's decision from that perspective. One way of raising the question of the client's values, without imposing the lawyer's values on the client is to ask the question, "What do you think would be fair?" The following chapter provides a more developed discussion of how and why the lawyer should raise such issues in the law office.

Representation of corporations and other organizations can raise special questions for the lawyer at the decision-making stage of counseling. It is likely that the lawyer will deal with a corporate officer or agent who will have authority to make decisions for the organization. What values are the lawyer and corporate representative to apply when making decisions? Obviously, corporate profits will be a relevant consideration, but it should not be the only consideration. Increasingly, corporations are held to a standard of social responsibility by the public and the state. As a matter of the corporation's self-interest, the corporate representative and the lawyer should consider the public image of the corporation when making decisions. There may also be corporate resolutions that might guide the corporate representative and lawyer. Finally, in difficult cases, the corporate representative might look to her own values for assistance in resolving issues; it is likely that she was chosen for decision-making responsibilities because of her wisdom.[36]

---

[36] *See* E. Mitchell, *Cooperation and Constraint in the Modern Corporation: An Inquiry Into the Causes of Corporate Immorality,* 73 TEX. L. REV. 477, 478 (1995). Under Model Rule 1.13, if the corporate representative seeks to act in a way "that is a violation of a legal obligation to the organization, or a violation of law which reasonably might be imputed to the organization, the lawyer shall proceed as is reasonably necessary in the best interest of the organization." These actions might include asking for reconsideration, advising a separate legal opinion, or "referring the matter to higher authority in the organization."

§ 8-5(a)(2). Making Comparative Judgments

The client should compare each alternative to all of the other alternatives before settling on a final choice. Lawyers should guard against the tendency to satisfice, i.e., choose the first alternative that minimally satisfies the client's goals. Once people choose a course of action, they often freeze their consideration of other competing options. They will tend to see everything else in light of the chosen option rather than in light of whether or not it accomplishes their goals. Indeed, people will tend to reinterpret the other options to make the chosen option seem more favorable than it is.[37] This may prevent the client from choosing a later option that is better overall.

Lawyers should also help clients avoid the tendency toward "elimination by aspects."[38] This occurs when people evaluate options by sequentially comparing them to one criterion after another. The decision-maker eliminates options that do not fit a single criterion. They may eliminate every option, thereby choosing the status quo by default. Elimination by aspects may also result in choosing an option that accomplishes the client's goals, but only in a mediocre way.[39] Elimination by aspects fails to consider the relative weights of various consequences. It treats all consequences as having the same weight. Thus, any failure is fatal. But in most situations not all consequences have the same importance. Some consequences matter more than others to a client.

A properly filled out Decision Sheet is an important tool. It helps the lawyer and the client evaluate the consequences based on their relative weight. This enables clients to more realistically compare all of the options against each other.

The lawyer should warn the client about the tendency to eliminate by aspects, and the lawyer should help the client avoid this by asking the client to clarify how important each of the consequences really are. The Decision Sheet helps do this by asking clients to rate both the likelihood and the importance of each consequence.

§ 8-5(a)(3). Making the Decision

Making decisions is not a mechanical process. Making good decisions is hard work. The lawyer should provide a comfortable physical and emotional environment in which the client can make decisions. The client should be able to sit in a comfortable location and have easy access to any materials that need to be reviewed. A conference table serves this purpose well. The lawyer and the client can sit side-by-side. Any papers or other material can be spread out on the table for easy reference by the lawyer and the client. Interruptions should be eliminated or kept to a minimum.

---

[37] *See* Janis & Mann, *supra* note 4, at 91.

[38] *See id.* at 31-33.

[39] *Id.* at 32.

The lawyer should also create a comfortable emotional environment for the client. The lawyer should reserve adequate appointment time for the client to make the choice. Clients should not feel pressured to make decision. The lawyer should use active listening skills to reflect the client's feelings and concerns about making the decision. Projecting empathy, acceptance, and genuineness helps put the client at ease. Just as these factors enhanced the relationship earlier between the lawyer and the client, they now further solidify the trust the client must have when making significant decisions.

The client may need more time to consider his options. He may need additional information or may need to consult trusted advisors. The lawyer should explain any deadlines that must be met and allow the client to take additional time to make the decision if possible. Of course, the lawyer should give herself sufficient time to complete any legal work for the client. The law may impose absolute deadlines that the client cannot ignore. Within these constraints, however, the lawyer should give the client as much time as the client needs to reach a decision.

§ 8-5(a)(4).   Reviewing the Decision

The lawyer and the client should review the decision once the client has made his choice. This review allows the client to look at the chosen option in isolation from all of the others. It helps the client see the consequences of the chosen option more clearly and without comparison to other options. A final review solidifies the choice, insures that the client understands the decision, makes the client more confident that the decision is well thought out, and makes it more likely that the client will complete any necessary follow-up actions.

The final review gives the lawyer and the client a chance to correct any flaws in the decision process. The lawyer should make sure that the client has considered all of the available information from a wide variety of sources. This information should include realistic appraisals of the benefits and the costs attached to any decision. The consequences identified on the decision sheet should be reviewed. They do not have to be covered in great detail, but simply restating them gives the client one more chance to think about them.

The final review allows the client to consider his ability to cope with the consequences of his choice. Clients will often have to perform some follow-up actions to implement decisions. Even simple matters like returning to the lawyer's office to sign documents require a commitment from the client. More significant decisions may require wholesale changes in the client's life or subject the client to serious scrutiny and criticism. If a client cannot cope with the stress these follow-up actions entail, the client is less likely to cooperate with the lawyer as the case proceeds or comply with the agreed-upon settlement. The lawyer should identify the various obstacles that may arise and encourage the client to realistically appraise his ability to cope with them. The lawyer should encourage the client to think about ways to handle these matters in advance. For example, if the client is likely to be criticized, the lawyer should help the client decide whether or not to respond to the criticism directly or to ignore it.

Allow the client to change his mind. The lawyer should advise the client that many people have second thoughts about their decisions. Within the constraints of the law (deadlines, agreements, etc.), the client is free to reverse course.

The lawyer should remain available for future consultation with the client. The client should feel comfortable contacting the lawyer for any additional consultation about the matter. The client may have second thoughts about the chosen option or may want to discuss some considerations that the lawyer and client did not think of during the counseling session. The lawyer should make it clear that she remains available to the client for these discussions.

§ 8-5(b). HOW TO STRUCTURE THE DECISION PHASE

As we have warned throughout this book, there is no script to follow when interviewing and counseling a client. The effective lawyer guides the client through the decision process without taking the decision from the client. The effective lawyer understands the dynamics of decision making but does not impose a rigid, unnatural structure on the process. Rather, the effective lawyer uses her understanding of the process to establish guidelines. The lawyer remains flexible and adapts these guidelines to the client, the situation, and the lawyer's own style.

Here are a set of questions that lawyers can use as guidelines when helping a client make a decision.[40] These questions will help the lawyer structure this decision. Remember, an effective lawyer will not have to ask these questions verbatim nor cover each one explicitly in every case. Rather, the effective lawyer will monitor the decision process to make sure that these matters are covered in one way or another.

1. "Which alternative looks best?"

Here is where the lawyer asks the client to consider which option best accomplishes the client's goals. The lawyer should urge the client to weigh the consequences, compare all of the options against each other, and choose the one that best serves the client's needs.

2. "Is this option just good enough?"

Here, the lawyer lets the client consider whether or not the client satificed. That is, whether or not the client opted for this particular option because it was the first one that seemed to minimally satisfy the client's needs. It is important for the lawyer to ask this question directly. By doing so, the client is given the opportunity to step back from the decision itself and take a look at his decision process.

3. "Does this choice satisfy all or most of your goals?"

This question is related to the previous question. It asks the client to examine the process he used to reach his decision. It guards against satisficing by expressly negating the minimal satisficing criteria.

---

[40] *See* JANIS, *supra* note 4, at 177-178.

4. "Does this choice feel right to you?"

This question helps the client decide if the choice is really the best one. People may choose an option because it seems to be the most reasonable one when they really prefer another option. The client may be reluctant to voice this concern for fear of being too emotional or irrational. This question gives the client permission to use feelings as a way to test a decision.

5. "If the choice does not feel right, what is missing, information or something else?"

The client may not feel comfortable with a decision because he needs more information. The client may also want to consider other matters before proceeding. For example, the client may want to know more about the personal effect the decision will have on third-parties or may want to ask other people for advice before making a final commitment.

6. "What information do you need to make this decision?"

The lawyer can ask this question if the client says that he needs more information. It is the lawyer's job to make sure that the client does not make a decision without considering all of the information that the client needs. The lawyer may be able to provide this information. For example, the client wants to know how long a case takes to get to trial. The competent lawyer can answer this question. If the lawyer cannot provide the information, the lawyer should find the answer or arrange for the client to get the information.

7. "Which would be the fairest option?"

This question brings the morality of the decision to the table, but in a way that allows the client to look to his own moral values for guidance. To fail to ask a question such as this, when the lawyer is asking questions from every other angle, suggests that moral values have no place in the law office. The following chapter discusses this issue in greater detail.

8. "Is there anyone else that you would like to talk to about this choice?"

The lawyer should ask this question even if the client expresses confidence in his choice. Lawyers should encourage their clients to talk to other people before making important decisions. Effective decision-makers use all of the resources available to them. Other people are important resources. Consulting others can provide technical expertise, additional information, or an alternative perspective on the matter. They may be experts on a matter crucial to the final decision. Suppose a client must make a decision involving the custody of children. If the client is concerned about the effect the decision may have on the children, a child psychologist can provide expert advice.

Other people may also have particular knowledge about a matter that will help frame the decision and its consequences for the client. For example, a client who needs to know the city's plans for development before purchasing a business franchise can consult the city's planning office.

Finally, talking to another person brings a different perspective to the decision. The lawyer and the client may become so involved in the process that they are unable to view matters objectively. The lawyer may not be able to check his self-interest in the outcome of the case. A third party who is not involved in the decision and who will not be affected by it may be able to provide an objective perspective. Clients should also be encouraged to consult trusted non-legal advisors. These people can help the client explore the personal, non-legal dimensions of their decisions. They bring a different perspective to the client's decision.

9. "Are you prepared to do what must be done to implement this choice?"

Ineffective decision-makers often overestimate their resolve to follow through on their choices. They get caught up in the euphoria of making the decision. They falter when the time comes to actually make the changes necessary to implement their choice. Unless the client has chosen the status quo, any decision is likely to necessitate a change in the client's life. Change in the abstract is easier than change in reality. The client must confront the transition from the abstract to the concrete. This question prepares the client for this transition. The lawyer should explore the specific things the client will have to do.

For example, clients who choose litigation should be asked if they are willing to be deposed, to face the criticism of their peers, to spend the time away from their work and family, and to be available for extensive consultation with the attorney. The lawyer should explore these matters even if the client has considered them on the decision sheet. Reviewing these matters at this stage gives the client an opportunity to verify his commitment to the chosen option.

10. "What contingency plans do we have to make?"

Decisions are not made nor implemented in a vacuum. The effective lawyer will make the client aware that most decisions are contingent. Circumstances may change and make the chosen option no longer viable. Other factors may arise that make the choice less attractive. Clients should be warned about any possible barriers to implementing their choice. They should be asked to make a contingency plan. The client may agree to meet again with the lawyer in the event that the original choice fails. The client may want to rank the remaining options in the order of preference and give the lawyer authority to proceed down the list as options are eliminated. No matter which method the client chooses, the effective lawyer will make sure that the client makes some contingency plan.

§ 8-6. MODIFYING THE MODEL TO GIVE CLIENTS BAD NEWS

Not every representation has a happy ending. Clients may be in situations in which no available choice is a pleasant one. In the following excerpt, Professor Linda Smith outlines a process for giving clients the "bad news" that there they cannot avoid pain or loss.

Linda F. Smith, *Medical Paradigms For Counseling: Giving Clients Bad News,* 4 Clinical L. Rev. 391-393, 417-427, 430-431(1998)[41]

* * *

[S]ometimes there are no choices that will achieve the client's goals. The abandoned spouse cannot prevent the divorce or avoid an order for visitation, the thief cannot stay out of jail, the business cannot escape paying damages, and the tenant will be evicted. Of course, the amount of visitation, jail time or damages can be greater or smaller and the eviction may be delayed a bit; but the outcome the client wants to avoid is inevitable. These are particularly hard cases for the lawyer-counselor where the formula of identifying alternatives and predicting consequences can seem like a cruel joke. In these cases the lawyer must also be able to tell the client "bad news." At these junctures, the skill of informing and explaining empathically takes priority over the paradigm of offering the client choice. . . .

"Bad news" counseling in the legal arena should . . . involve an understanding and positive discussion with "flexibility, reassurance and empathy." [The following] basic principles . . . should guide a "bad news" legal counseling session.

1) Be Prepared. Because clients will usually desire (and may need) a good deal of information, the lawyer should avoid communicating "bad news" until she is prepared to fully explain the situation. In most instances, this may mean delaying the "bad news" counseling until after the interview and providing it during a follow-up counseling session. Even when the lawyer may know early in an interview that a client's goal cannot be achieved, it will be wise to delay that discussion. Time will allow the lawyer not only to prepare a comprehensive explanation, but to engage in creative problem-solving. The lawyer will be able to consider whether there may be alternatives to achieving the most important aspects of the client's goals.

If, during the interview, the lawyer hears a client insist upon an outcome that seems highly unlikely, the lawyer should decline to tell the client how hopeless the case is. Instead, the lawyer should empathize with the underlying feeling and encourage the client to explore what the most important aspects of a solution might be. . . .

2) Be Self-Aware. Ironically, being overly prompt with bad news may come from the laudable goals of providing the client with information (e.g., no consent is required for a no-fault divorce) and performing effective service (e.g., obtaining alimony).Yet the client who is still in denial about the separation and divorce is not emotionally ready to consider this information or to make such a decision. The attorney must help her process the

---

"bad news" that her marriage is over before they can consider various realistic options. . . .

3) Conduct the counseling session in person, in private, and with sufficient time. Once it is clear that "bad news" must be conveyed and the lawyer is prepared to do so, the lawyer should arrange a personal counseling session with ample time for the difficult conversation.

4) Be clear, direct and candid in giving information. The lawyer should open with a "warning shot," to control the conversation and get to the point promptly.

While in other settings it may be best to reflect the client's prior statement of goals in a counseling session involving serious and significant bad news, it may be dysfunctional to do so. As an illustration, although the criminal defendant facing a likely conviction may have enunciated his goal of "getting this #$%! case dismissed and suing the cops for harassment," reasserting this goal at the beginning of a counseling session would mislead rather than reassure the client. Instead, the lawyer should reframe the client's goals in a way which will be consistent with both the prior session and the counseling that is to come. ("I know you want to make informed decisions about this case and your situation.")

Similarly, the client should not be invited to select which option to discuss first if this will make it either intellectually or emotionally more difficult to hear the bad news. Focusing on alternatives which have a slim chance of success can dysfunctionally allow the client to avoid facing a difficult reality. Similarly, the client may need to understand the most probable but worst case scenario before considering compromise. Until the client comprehends the likelihood of conviction and punishment, he may be unwilling and unable to have a useful discussion of a plea negotiation. Instead, it would be preferable for the lawyer to announce the topic on which information must be conveyed. ("We need to discuss the charges you are facing so you'll understand both what is likely and what is possible in this case.")

[T]he lawyer will educate the client by explaining the legal standards and how they apply to the facts of the case and by describing what will likely happen next. Lawyers . . . should avoid jargon, be candid and direct, and check to see if the client is following the explanation.

It seems that many well-meaning attorneys may hurry through this discussion, giving the client a negative prediction but not showing the client why the facts and the law would bring about that outcome. The lawyer may feel more powerful and affirmed if the client simply accepts his prediction. It may even feel cruel to the lawyer to draw out all the "bad facts" that have led the lawyer to conclude that "any jury would convict." Clients may argue or may change the subject, seeking to avoid difficult news. But the lawyer must not allow the client to remain in a state of denial. Only after the lawyer has communicated all his reasons for his predictions will the client be as capable as the attorney to make informed decisions. . . .

5) Convey empathy and caring. Of course, while divulging this information, the lawyer should show empathy for the client and take note of the client's concerns and agendas. In fact, such empathy may be necessary to help the client take in the "bad news." . . .

It is most important for the client to understand the legal standard and how it applies to his case. Linking the law with the facts allows the client to understand, and requires the client to rely less upon the lawyer's forcefulness or estimated risk (99%) of loss. . . .

6) Attend and respond to the client's level of knowledge.

7) Attend and respond to the client's emotional reactions. Once they hear "bad news," clients . . . will respond in a variety of ways. . . . Patients frequently respond with disbelief or denial; and clients who feel wronged may also respond by expressing disbelief. The lawyer should understand this as the client's emotional difficulty in accepting the situation, rather than an argument over the lawyer's analysis. Accordingly, the lawyer should empathize with the client who feels unfairly treated. The lawyer should explore the client's feelings if they are unclear. If the client needs further information to understand the law and how it applies in his case, of course the lawyer should explain. But it is most important that the lawyer avoid having an argument over his analysis. If the client expresses anger at the lawyer's inadequacy or threatens to get a "real lawyer," there, too, the lawyer should empathize with the feelings and recognize the client's right to seek other representation. Where the client is disbelieving, in denial, angry or blaming, the lawyer may well have emotional reactions to the client's statements and accusations. The lawyer, though a professional, is emotionally involved in his work. He should step back and consider his own feelings. The lawyer should describe his feelings rather than act them out. Rather than lashing out that the client won't find better representation, the lawyer should acknowledge his emotion and then focus upon the client's case. . . .

As doctors have to avoid over-reassurance, lawyers too must be careful to stick with their candid opinions rather than alter them to appease protesting clients. Even though the client protests "I can't believe they would convict me!" the lawyer should not alter his prediction of "almost certain conviction" to "you never can tell what a jury will do — it's a roll of the dice." Whatever the lawyer's candid considered opinion, it should not waiver because the client complains. . . .

8) Conclude with a proposed plan which takes into account the client's personal perspective. As doctors turn to the treatment plan following the information, once the lawyer has conveyed the essence of the "bad news" he should discuss how the case can be handled. Here alternatives will be discussed — but in light of the crucial information about the weakness of the client's case. In light of the likelihood of conviction, the client should consider negotiating a plea agreement and needs to know what sort of fine or incarceration will form part of that arrangement. If eviction is certain, the client must decide whether to seek more time to move or to leave as soon as possible to minimize damages. The businessman who has wrongfully

terminated an employee needs to consider whether to reinstate him or to pay damages. Depending upon the case and the client, the choices may be equally desirable (or undesirable); or one approach may be obviously the least risky way to approach a bad situation. If one approach clearly holds greater possibility for minimizing the harm the client fears, the lawyer should be clear about that. Clients may well be overwhelmed by the "bad news" and the lawyer can assist by being clear about which option most closely approaches the client's goals.

Patients consistently report that they would like an opportunity to talk and ask questions. Although the "bad news" may be overwhelming for some clients, lawyers would do well to invite their clients' questions and concerns. A client coming to terms with a difficult legal situation and facing undesirable consequences may well need some time to explore the "what ifs" and "why's" of the situation.

Doctors are encouraged to refer their patients to others who have faced similar situations and to help the patient rally his own resources. While it would be odd for a lawyer to arrange for a client to meet a homeless person before being evicted or an incarcerated person before pleading guilty, there is much to be gained from helping the client re-orient to the unpleasant reality. It is appropriate and necessary to explore the "non-legal" consequences of any course of action. The abandoned spouse may benefit from referrals to therapy and social groups that serve divorced single parents. The lawyer may want to help the tenant consider whether she could stay with relatives or friends, if she would need to put her belongings in storage, how she would seek permanent housing and what shelter facilities might exist as she faces an inevitable eviction. The criminal defendant should be invited to discuss what he knows of prison and if he wants to learn more before deciding upon a plea which will involve incarceration. In these ways lawyers must be willing to enter the client's world, as Sarat's and Felstiner's attorneys typically resisted doing.

With this approach the lawyer-counselor should be able to engage in counseling sessions which, of necessity, involve telling clients that their goal is probably impossible and the outcome they most fear is likely to be ordained under the law. . . .

It many instances it may be best to retain the structure of the "client-choice" counseling session. The lawyer will simply give the "bad news" in the course of describing an alternative. The negative legal prediction will be part of a much larger legal picture and explain why there is a some risk of loss or why a particular element of damages will not be available. . . .

In other circumstances, it may be clearer for the client to understand if the "bad news" aspect of the case is separated from an alternative and explained at the outset. Imagine the client who has various goals which can be accomplished (or are likely to be accomplished) in more than one way; however one goal is simply unachievable. The lawyer may choose to discuss that unachievable goal prior to describing any alternative. Otherwise, the lawyer will end up predicting failure to achieve that goal each time for each alternative. Such a conversation may seem as if the lawyer is trying to hide that particular bit of bad news. It may be more emotionally supportive to directly give the one bit of bad news at the outset, and then follow with the alternatives which will be primarily positive. . . .

Whether the "bad news" aspects of a case with substantial choice should be communicated at the outset or during the discussion of an alternative will likely vary from case to case and from client to client. The more focused the client has been on a goal which is impossible, the more important it will be to raise it early and deal with it directly. . . .

The medical studies indicate that in addition to information, empathy and hope, patients want their doctors to share their feelings. It is certainly plausible that some clients want this as well. Of course, medical problems are usually not the result of bad or illegal actions by the patient. Hence, in most cases medical professionals should be able to feel pain or concern or empathy for the patient who is ill or the parent whose child is disabled. And genuinely sharing this feeling of sadness (rather than maintaining a cold professional distance) should be possible. . . . Lawyers may be disinclined to share their genuine feelings with clients, imagining that they will dislike the client or disapprove of the client's goals. In those cases it could be unwise to share such genuine negative feelings about the client's case. However, it may not always be unwise. If the attorney-client relationship is strong enough, it may be possible and helpful for the lawyer to admit his emotions. If he is frustrated with what seems like nit-picking by the client, it would be more functional for the lawyer to admit his frustration than to act in a curt and cursory way. In other cases the client may be confused and genuinely want to know the lawyer's feelings. . . .

Of course, in many instances lawyers will agree with and approve of their clients. And in some cases the clients may want and be able to deal with the lawyer's feelings. While the lawyer may not feel sympathy for all aspects of a client's case, usually the lawyer can relate to some part of it. . . . The medical studies suggest that where lawyers sympathize with and approve of their clients, the clients will benefit from hearing this.

Even if lawyers try to avoid sharing emotions with clients, they will fail. Lawyers, like doctors, have emotions about their work. They want to succeed. They want the approval of their clients and of others. Accordingly, when things go wrong, the lawyer's emotions of frustration may well slip out in any event. . . . If a lawyer's emotions about a case intrude in a manner that could harm the attorney-client relationship, this is an additional reason for the lawyer to consider forging a genuine relationship and sharing his true feelings as well as his legal analysis with his clients. . . .

When lawyers must give clients "bad news," they should draw upon the lessons that emerge from the world of medical counseling. Lawyers must be direct and candid about the state of affairs. They must fully describe how grim the situation appears and explain why this is their opinion. They must enter into a dialogue in which the client's questions are answered and the client's feelings are respected and responded to. Lawyers must be self-aware in order to avoid responding dysfunctionally to the client's reactions. They should show empathy and communicate hope to the "whole person" who is the client. Only after delivering and processing "bad news" in this way can the lawyer counsel the client about choices and plans for the future.

———————

Professor Smith's excerpt fits within the model we have outlined in this chapter. She essentially suggests that lawyers

- thoroughly describe the factual and legal circumstances that give rise to the bad news,

- discuss the client's situation and options with care and compassion, and

- enable the client to make the best decision possible under the circumstances.

§ 8-7. CONCLUSION

This chapter has set out a model for lawyers to use when they help clients make decisions. It sets out a structure based on the rhythm of description, discussion, and decision. It suggests that lawyers structure the decision process to help clients avoid the problems associated with ineffective decision-makers. It also suggests a model form that lawyers can adapt to each client's decision. Finally, the chapter explains how to adapt and use this model when lawyers must help clients make unpleasant and difficult choices.

Option:						
Tangible and Intangible consequences to client:						
Tangible	Intangible	pro	con	NE	Occur 1-5	Important 1-5

Tangible and Intangible Consequences to Others:

Tangible	Intangible	pro	con	NE	Occur 1-5	Important 1-5

Consequences to Self-Image:

	pro	con	NE	Occur 1-5	Important 1-5

Consequences for reputation:

	pro	con	NE	Occur 1-5	Important 1-5

CHAPTER 9

MORAL CHOICES IN THE LAW OFFICE: WHO GETS HURT? AND WHO DECIDES?

§ 9-1. INTRODUCTION

Almost all decisions made in the law office have moral implications. Those decisions generally benefit some people at the expense of other people. In a divorce, will the client take actions that will harm his child or spouse? In structuring a business deal, or writing a will, who will benefit? Who will lose? Will the officers of a corporation consider the effects of its actions on workers, on consumers, on competitors, on the environment, on the community? Lawyers and clients must resolve questions like this all the time.

At the beginning of this book, we identified three lawyering models. Authoritarian lawyers control decisions in the law office; client-centered counselors structure the decision-making process so that clients resolve decisions in accordance with client interest; and collaborative lawyers and clients resolve issues together. Each model approaches moral issues that arise in the law office in a different manner.[1] In the following sections, we consider how lawyers under each model might address moral issues.

As you read the following sections, ask: Does one style of lawyering fit your personality better than the others? Should a lawyer choose one style of lawyering for all of her cases? Would different styles of lawyering fit better with different types of cases? With different types of clients? What style of lawyering are clients likely to want? Might different parts of the same case call for different styles of lawyering? Should your style of lawyering vary, depending on the style of lawyering on the other side?

§ 9-2. AUTHORITARIAN LAWYERS: THE GURU AND THE GODFATHER

In their book, *Lawyers, Clients, and Moral Responsibility*,[2] Thomas Shaffer and Robert Cochran identify two questions that define the moral

---

[1] For a discussion of each of these models, including essays by proponents of each, see Symposium, *Client Counseling and Moral Responsibility*, 30 PEPP. L. REV. 591-639 (2003). The contributing participants/authors to that symposium were Robert F. Cochran, Jr., Deborah L. Rhode, Paul R. Tremblay, and Thomas L. Shaffer.

[2] THOMAS L. SHAFFER & ROBERT F. COCHRAN, JR., LAWYERS, CLIENTS, AND MORAL RESPONSIBILITY (1994).

relationship between lawyer and client.[3] Those questions are: 1) Who controls the important decisions in the relationship? and 2) Are the interests of others taken into consideration in making those decisions? As to authoritarian lawyers, the answer to the first question is easy. Authoritarian lawyers, by definition, control decisions in the law office. But note that authoritarian lawyers can give two very different answers to the second question. Shaffer and Cochran have metaphors for each. The lawyer as guru[4] takes control of the relationship and considers the interests of others; the lawyer as godfather also takes control of the relationship, but ignores the interests of others. We consider each.

§ 9-2(a). THE LAWYER AS GURU[5]

The following story illustrates the lawyer as guru. Where does the lawyer go wrong (if he does)?

Harrop Freeman, *The Rabbi and the Horse-whip Lawyer*,[6] adapted from HARROP A. FREEMAN & HENRY WEIHOFEN, CLINICAL LAW TRAINING: INTERVIEWING AND COUNSELING 183-85 (1972)[7]

Mrs. G, when she came to my office was a young married woman in her late twenties and the mother of three children ages $1^1/_2$ to 5. My first interview revealed that she married at age 20 or 21, promptly after finishing college, to a respectable businessman in the city. They occupied a modern home which was owned by the entireties of the value of $350,000.00. She had a car of her own. She had domestic help. She had a reasonable amount of money to spend on her person and for her happiness and convenience.

Her husband was in the early thirties, very devoted, engaged in a family business which took considerable amount of his time including some

---

[3] Other articles and books have explored the place of lawyer/client moral discourse. *See* MONROE H. FREEDMAN & ABBE SMITH, UNDERSTANDING LAWYERS' ETHICS 6-11, 45-69 (3d ed. 2004); DAVID A. BINDER ET AL., LAWYERS AS COUNSELORS: A CLIENT-CENTERED APPROACH 391-93 (2d ed. 2004); DAVID A. BINDER ET AL., LAWYERS AS COUNSELORS: A CLIENT-CENTERED APPROACH 282-84 (1991); ROBERT M. BASTRESS & JOSEPH D. HARBAUGH, INTERVIEWING, COUNSELING, AND NEGOTIATING: SKILLS FOR EFFECTIVE REPRESENTATION 334-35 (1990); Jack L. Sammons, *Rank Strangers to Me: Shaffer and Cochran's Friendship Model of Moral Counseling in the Law Office*, 18 U. ARK. LITTLE ROCK L.J. 1 (1995); Thomas L. Shaffer & Robert F. Cochran, Jr., *Lawyers as Strangers and Friends: A Reply to Professor Sammons*, 18 U. ARK. LITTLE ROCK L. REV. 69 (1995).

[4] Within the Hindu faith, the guru is far more directive than leaders within most Western religious traditions. This direction extends to the details of religious, moral, business and family matters. *See* Raymond B. Williams, *The Guru as Pastoral Counselor*, 40 J. OF PASTORAL CARE 331 (1986). "[The Guru's] Disciple must keep his defenses lowered and confidently yield to the Master." Dima S. Oueini, *The Guru and His Disciple*, 45 THE UNESCO COURIER 16 (Sept. 1992).

[5] For a fuller discussion of the lawyer as guru, see SHAFFER & COCHRAN, *supra* note 2 at 30-39.

[6] We have updated this story to reflect modern divorce law and house prices.

[7] Copyright © 1972 by The West Group. Reprinted with permission.

evenings, and which required him to go to the city on buying trips occasionally. He was a mild, gentlemanly type, a sober, responsible sort of citizen, without apparent faults.

Mrs. G is a very attractive Jewish woman. She got herself involved with a married man (Mr. X), the father of two children — a very handsome Italian-Catholic who professed love for her and promised to get a divorce and marry her. An affair developed between them, quite discreet at the beginning but ultimately fairly obvious. Mrs. G insisted that the affair was beautiful and that no misconduct had been indulged in. Peculiarly, in the first instance she insisted that she went "out to dinner" with him (I was not so naive that I did not know that dinner involved dessert). She ultimately did acknowledge that she spent some time in a hotel in New York and in an apartment that he maintained locally. When she came to me, she wanted a divorce and she wanted custody of her three children. All of this with the anticipation of marrying Mr. X.

Mrs. G acknowledged to me that Mr. G was a good, devoted husband and that she had no charge of any kind to make against him. . . .

My reaction to all of the above was that Mrs. G was a silly, stupid person in spite of her education. My reaction was that she could use an old fashioned horse whipping and I told her so frankly. I told her that she had sex confused with love. I told her that I did not think there was any future in the proposed divorce. I told her that I felt that if the third person was such an individual that he would abandon his own wife and two sons, I could not see any hope in the future of a home with him and her three children. In short, I attempted to dissuade her from the idea of a divorce. However, she insisted that her happiness was with Mr. X and that she still wanted my services in trying to secure a divorce and custody of the children.

I had several conferences with Mr. G and his attorney. The husband's position was that he was quite willing to forget the past and continue to make a home for her and the children. In the alternative, he would give her a divorce providing he retained custody of the children and in that case he would extend liberal visitation rights.

I finally got Mrs. G and her lover to secure counsel and guidance from Mrs. G's Rabbi. They promised him after much discussion that each would go his separate way and try to fill his legal and religious obligations without seeing each other for a year. However, after about two weeks of this, Mrs. G called the Rabbi and told him that she would have to break her promise because her love for the third person was so great.

Subsequent conferences with the wife resulted in my counseling her as follows: She could procure a divorce and rush into the arms of her lover and leave her husband under a written agreement covering custody and visitation [with child custody in her husband]. [Or, she could remain with her husband. It was my opinion that a judge would be unlikely to give her custody.] Her reaction was that she would agree to a divorce with custody of her children with the father. Papers were drawn. But when it came to putting her signature to them she shifted her position and refused to execute the agreement. She insisted that she wanted the children and her lover. I told her that she [would probably] not get this under the law and that if she were to try she would [be] declared not entitled to custody.

I might say that I am a poor counselor in this sort of situation because I felt that Mrs. G was being used. I told Mrs. G that I felt that the lover never had any intention of marrying her, that he was putting a veneer on a sordid arrangement, that she was heading straight to destruction — even worse. I pointed out that marriage was economic, family, societal, etc., and not merely lovers coming together. I outlined how much she had: a good husband, good home, children, economic security, social position, acceptance by friends and society. My reaction was one of such complete disgust that I had all I could do to keep from tossing Mrs. G out of my office on her ear. I felt that I should continue to try to reason with the lady and did so, but evidently the die was cast. Finally, I gave it to her quite frankly as I had stated before — she could have her children and the separation; she could have a divorce and her husband would retain custody of the children. She [was unlikely to get] both. She was not entitled to both. She herself was seeking her own vanity and selfishness. The children's future was not with the lover even if she should marry him. If she was not agreeable to my counsel and advice, she might try another lawyer.

The result of the above was that she left my office in tears, went home to the children, took them to her sister's home, whereupon her husband promptly brought the children back to the home.

Mrs. G did go to another lawyer. What happened there I cannot say. I know that Mr. G ran out of patience with his wife and gave up hope of trying to arrive at anything amicably with her. He himself instituted a divorce . . . and the parties are divorced. Mrs. G got very little alimony. The children are in the custody of the father. Surprisingly, or perhaps I should say not surprisingly, Mrs. G is not married to her lover. He is not divorced. He is not even now seeking a divorce. Mrs. G lives with her sister and daily attends the children at her former husband's home as if she were the maid.

I am sure that Mrs. G is completely dissatisfied with my service and I have seen her on the street, but she has turned her head the other way as if she did not see me or didn't know me.

To me, the above situation was most exasperating. I felt that Mrs. G was an amoral, spoiled brat. I do not even believe that she loved the third party in the true sense of the word love. I think she simply wanted to assuage her own conscience by convincing herself that the dirty affair was love.

* * *

It seems that the Horsewhip lawyer correctly described the law, he correctly predicted the consequences of the client's choices, and he probably (given the little bit that we know) was right on the morals of the case — he was concerned about what appeared to be the innocent parties in the case, the client's husband and children. If so, where did he go wrong, if he did?

In our view, this lawyer was ineffective as a counselor-at-law. He was too domineering, too quick to reach conclusions, too unwilling to let his client wrestle with the implications of (what should have been) her choices. We get the sense that the lawyer learned very little about the client. There may have been deeper reasons for her desire to leave her husband. If there were, the lawyer would never have learned them. If we assume that the lawyer was right on the morals of the case, his moral counsel was ineffective. He may have even hardened his client's resolve to get her way. If he had taken a bit of time to get to know his client, he might have had an opportunity to influence her.

The directive lawyer is part of a venerable tradition among American lawyers. David Hoffman, who in the 1830s drafted the first guidelines for American lawyers, said, "[The client] shall never make me a partner in his knavery."[8] Judge George Sharswood said, "It is the duty of counsel to be the keeper of the conscience of the client; not to suffer him through the influence of his feelings or interest to do or saying anything wrong. . . ."[9] Judge Clement Haynsworth put it, "[T]he lawyer must never forget that he is the master. He is not there to do the client's bidding. It is for the lawyer to decide what is morally and legally right. . . ."[10]

In recent years Professors Deborah Rhode, David Luban, and William Simon have also argued that lawyers should take control of moral issues that arise in representation. In her book, *In the Interests of Justice*, Rhode argues that "[l]awyers can, and should, act on the basis of their own principled convictions, even when they recognize that others could in good faith hold different views."[11] David Luban argues in his book, *The Good Lawyer*, that "when professional and moral obligation conflict, moral obligations rule the day."[12] William Simon argues in his book, *The Practice of Justice*, that "[l]awyers should take those actions that, considering the relevant circumstances of the particular case, seem likely to promote justice."[13] They provide little, if any, discussion of the role that the client might play in determining what moral standards should control the representation.

---

[8] *Resolutions on Professional Deportment,* No. XIV, *in* I Hoffman, A Course of Legal Study 752-75 (2d ed. 1836), *quoted in* Thomas L. Shaffer, American Legal Ethics (1985).

[9] George Sharswood, *Essay on Professional Ethics* (1854), 32 Reports of the American Bar Ass'n (1907), *quoted in* Shaffer & Cochran, *supra* note 2, at 225.

[10] Clement F. Haynsworth, *Professionalism in Lawyering*, 27 S.C. L. Rev. 627, 628 (1976). For a more developed critique of the directive approach, see Shaffer & Cochran, *supra* note 2, at 30-39.

[11] Deborah L. Rhode, In the Interests of Justice: Reforming the Legal Profession 58 (2000).

[12] David Luban, *The Adversary System Excuse, in* The Good Lawyer: Lawyers' Roles and Lawyers' Ethics 118 (1984, ed. David Luban).

[13] William H. Simon, The Practice of Justice: A Theory of Lawyers' Ethics 138 (1998). It may be that there will not be a great deal of difference between Deborah Rhode's "[lawyers'] own principled convictions" standard and Simon's legal ideals standard. The

Though we admire the guru lawyer for his commitment to moral values, there are risks, moral risks, in the life of a guru. First, there is the danger that the guru lawyer will be wrong. Humility is justified when approaching the moral issues that arise in the law office. These issues are likely to be difficult. We do not suggest that there are not objective moral standards, but none of us has perfect ability to discern those standards or to determine how they should apply in particular cases. There is a danger that lawyers will be confident of their moral judgment when confidence is not justified. Two consciences, in conversation, are more likely to get to the moral truth than one.

Our second concern with the guru lawyer is that he robs the client of the opportunity to grow morally. People grow morally through exercising moral judgment. They develop virtues (courage, truthfulness, faithfulness, and mercy) through practice, as an athlete develops physical skills through practice. Lawyers who prevent clients from moral exercise — from deliberating, making moral judgments, and acting on them — deny clients the chance to become better people. The guru's authoritarian lawyering can provide only limited moral growth for the client. The greatest moral growth will come to the client if the client chooses to be good, rather than being told to do the good.[14]

§ 9-2(b).   THE LAWYER AS GODFATHER[15]

The second authoritarian lawyer, the godfather, also controls the representation, but he ignores the interests of others. The godfather lawyer, like the godfather of the Mario Puzo novels, tells his clients, "You just leave it to me." He takes care of his people, often at the expense of other people.

Arnie Becker of the "LA Law" television show was a godfather lawyer. In the pilot movie,[16] one of Arnie's divorce clients, Lydia Graham, wants to settle her divorce under terms proposed by her husband. At the initial interview, the following exchange takes place between Lydia and Arnie.

Lydia: I just don't want to get into an ugly pitched battle with name calling and recriminations.

Arnie: I respect that feeling entirely.

Lydia: Barry and I may not have wanted to be married to each other but we're still parents to our children. We're still civilized adults who won't get down in the dirt and grovel over who gets the dishes.

"legal ideals" that a lawyer discerns are likely to look a lot like the lawyer's ideals. There is a danger that Simon's model would cloak the lawyer's moral judgment in legal garb, giving it the authority of law.

[14] See ROBERT P. GEORGE, MAKING MEN MORAL (1994).

[15] For a fuller discussion of the lawyer as godfather, see SHAFFER & COCHRAN, supra note 2, at 5-14.

[16] L.A. Law (1986) (Written by Steven Bochco & Terry Louise Fisher).

[When Lydia discloses that her husband moved out on December 21, Arnie suggests that her husband is having an affair.]

Arnie: Men are creatures of habit, Lydia. In nine years I've never once seen a man initiate a divorce, and certainly not four days before Christmas, unless he had another woman to replace the one he was leaving.

* * *

Lydia: You're deliberately trying to turn this into something ugly.

Arnie: No, what I am deliberately trying to do is to protect your rights under the law. Let me be blunt, for your husband, divorce is a fiscal inconvenience, but for you, this could be the most important financial decision that you'll ever make in your life. And I personally, as well as professionally, don't think that such a decision should be made casually. Do you?

Arnie, on his own initiative, hires a private detective, has Lydia's husband followed, and discovers that the husband is having an affair with a younger woman. Arnie presents revealing, inflammatory pictures of the husband and paramour to Lydia. She is outraged at her husband and allows Arnie to "coerce"[17] a very favorable settlement from the husband.

Lydia is outraged at her husband, but she is also outraged at Arnie. The following is their final exchange in the movie:

Arnie: Well, I guess we socked it to him pretty good, huh?

Lydia: I think what you did was despicable. I'll never be able to look at him again with any kind of respect or affection.

Arnie: Lydia, you came in here looking for somebody to do your dirty laundry, what did you expect?

Lydia: Well, it stinks.

Arnie: Well, dirty laundry usually does. It's messy and it's nasty and it turns up a whole lot goo, but it's a lot more civilized and a hell of a lot more lucrative, than putting a bullet between his ears.

Lydia: It's all so easy for you. Just sock it to him and get the money. Well, I lost my life, my children lost a family, and there's no amount of money that would compensate for that.

Arnie: Gonna give it back?

Lydia: (Sob) No.

---

[17] Arnie implicitly threatens to turn the husband over to the IRS for tax fraud.

Arnie: Lydia, maybe you hate me today. That's understandable . . .
                but two weeks from now you're going to be recommending
                me to a friend, two months from now you'll be inviting me
                over for dinner.

Who gets the better of the argument? Did Arnie do a good thing?

In his defense, Arnie would argue that he only provided more information to the client. He increased her knowledge. He empowered her. Her
husband *was* cheating on her. But note that Arnie gave his client only a
selected type of information, information that was likely to inflame her
passions against her husband. He did not, for example, give her a booklet
on the negative effects of parental conflict on children. Arnie manipulated
her by the choice of the information that he gave her. At times godfather
lawyers, like Arnie, manipulate their clients. Godfather lawyers with more
compliant clients just tell them what to do.

Arnie might also argue that the client was in the midst of emotional tur-
moil and was not thinking clearly. She, as clients often do, was merely
thinking in the short run; he was thinking in the long run. The decisions
made during legal representation concerning assets, alimony, and child
support will probably have consequences for her and her children for the
rest of her life. Arnie may be right. In two weeks, the client may be rec-
ommending Arnie to her friends; she may come to thank him.

Arnie's argument is that this was an occasion for lawyer paternalism.
Godfather lawyers are paternalistic. Paternalism is limiting someone's
freedom for the sake of her own good.[18] Godfather knows best. As we have
previously argued, the law office is not the place for paternalism. A client,
at least one that is an adult, should have the opportunity to make his own
decisions.[19] For the lawyer to control decisions is inconsistent with client
dignity. In addition, it is likely that the lawyer does not know best. Clients
are likely to be better judges of their own interests. Arnie may not be right.
The acrimony between Lydia and her husband may be very damaging to
the children. That may be a greater loss to the client and the children than
any financial gain. Like many lawyers, Arnie saw only the client's financial interest.[20] Money may not have been Lydia's most important value. It
is right for the lawyer to be concerned that clients may make hasty decisions. One of the lawyer's jobs is to make the client slow down and consider
the long-term implications of her decisions, but it is not the business of the
lawyer to manipulate the client toward his view of things.

---

[18] *See* Dennis Thompson, *Paternalism in Medicine, Law, and Public Policy, in* ETHICS
TEACHING IN HIGHER EDUCATION 246 (D. Callahan & S. Bok eds., 1980), *quoted in* David
Luban, *Paternalism and the Legal Profession*, 1981 WIS. L. REV. 454, 461.

[19] For a thoughtful discussion of the occasions when paternalism might be justified, see
Duncan Kennedy, *Distributive and Paternalist Motives in Contract and Tort Law, With
Special Reference to Compulsory Terms and Unequal Bargaining Power*, 41 MD. L. REV. 563,
638-44, 646 (1982).

[20] *See* Robert S. Redmount, *Attorney Personalities and Some Psychological Aspects of
Legal Consultation*, 109 U. PA. L. REV. 972, 975 (1961).

Douglas Rosenthal in his classic study of lawyer-client relations found what may be a common client reaction to godfather lawyering. One client, after his lawyer had encouraged him to hedge on the truth says:

> [T]he lawyer is a reassuring presence who takes away your guilt feelings. He says, "Hey, this is the way the game is played; you take as much as you can get; it's what they expect; it's the way it's done." He takes upon his own shoulders the burden of your guilt — he's the professional.[21]

In our view, it is not the business of lawyers to shield clients from moral responsibility.

One of the greatest dangers of godfather lawyering is that no one will consider the moral issues that arise during the representation. The client turns his problem over to the lawyer, the lawyer assumes that his job is to be an advocate, to attack the other party, and ignore the interests of third parties. No one even considers the interests of other people.

§ 9-3.   CLIENT-CENTERED COUNSELORS: THE LAWYER AS HIRED GUN[22]

The hired gun lawyer, like the godfather, ignores the interests of others, but leaves it to the client to control the representation. The sole goal of the hired gun is the autonomy of the client. Within client-counseling circles, the advocates of hired gun lawyering are the "client-centered counselors."[23] Client-centered legal counseling focuses on the desires of the client. "Because client autonomy is of paramount importance, decisions should be made on the basis of what choice is most likely to *provide a client with maximum satisfaction.*"[24] The lawyer should not act in ways that would influence the client's choice. The lawyer should be "neutral"[25] and "non judgmental."[26]

When a decision is to be made in legal representation, the client-centered advocates suggest that the lawyer and client list on a sheet of paper all of the alternative courses of action and the "consequences to the client" of each.[27] The lawyer asks probing questions that will help lawyer and

---

[21] DAVID ROSENTHAL, LAWYER AND CLIENT: WHO'S IN CHARGE (1974) *quoted in* William H. Simon, *The Ideology of Advocacy: Procedural Justice and Professional Ethics,* 1978 WIS. L. REV. 117 n. 198 (1978).

[22] For a fuller discussion of the lawyer as hired gun and the client-centered counseling model, see SHAFFER & COCHRAN, *supra* note 2, at 15-29.

[23] *See* BINDER ET AL. (1991), *supra* note 3; BINDER ET AL.(2004), *supra* note 3; BASTRESS & HARBAUGH, *supra* note 3; *and* DAVID A. BINDER & SUSAN C. PRICE, LEGAL INTERVIEWING AND COUNSELING: A CLIENT-CENTERED APPROACH (1977).

[24] BINDER ET AL. (1991), *supra* note 3, at 261 (original emphasis). *See also* BASTRESS & HARBAUGH, *supra* note 3, at 256.

[25] BINDER & PRICE, *supra* note 23, at 166; BINDER ET AL. (1991), *supra* note 3, at 288.

[26] BASTRESS & HARBAUGH, *supra* note 3, at 57.

[27] BINDER & PRICE, *supra* note 23, at 184; BASTRESS & HARBAUGH, *supra* note 3, at 246-49; BINDER ET AL. (1991), *supra* note 3, at 307.

client to more fully understand the consequences for the client. The lawyer converts client statements into advantages or disadvantages,[28] and the client chooses from the options. Note that the most significant difference between the client-centered counseling method and the model we advocated in the previous chapter is that the client-centered counselors consider only "consequences to the client," whereas our model considers consequences to all people that might be affected by the client's decision.

Note also that despite the client-centered counselors' claims to neutrality, their framework steers the client toward a particular method of moral analysis, consequentialism. Decision-making under the client-centered model is a matter of cost-benefit analysis. But the client-centered counselors not only steer clients toward a particular method of moral analysis, they steer clients toward a form that is morally dubious. The client-centered counselors have clients consider only "Consequences *to the Client*." This ignores the importance of other people.

In the illustration that one client-centered book gives of the client-centered counseling method, a client is considering suing his neighbor for a zoning violation. On the decision sheet, among the listed "Consequences for Client" of filing suit are: "time and effort required," "money to pay for fees and expenses," "exposure to deposition and trial examination," and "strain on relationship with [the neighbor]." Under subjects to be probed, the book suggests that the lawyer ask, "How important to the client is his friendship with [the neighbor]?"[29] The client is to consider the consequences to the neighbor solely in light of the effect that those consequences will have on the client; the client-centered methods give the neighbor no independent moral significance. The counseling plan suggests that if the neighbor is not a friend or if the client's friendship with the neighbor is not important, the neighbor is not worthy of consideration.[30]

---

[28] BINDER & PRICE, *supra* note 23, at 168.

[29] BASTRESS & HARBAUGH, *supra* note 3, at 246.

[30] The client-centered counselors suggest that the lawyer might legitimately raise moral concerns when the client makes a decision which the lawyer believes is "morally wrong." The lawyer might try and persuade the client to change his mind. BASTRESS & HARBAUGH *supra* note 3, at 334-35, and BINDER ET AL. (1991), *supra* note 3, at 282-84. However, there are likely to be problems with moral discourse at this stage.

> First, client-centered counselors' moral discourse comes into play only when the lawyer feels that the client wants to do something that is "morally wrong." Morality (in and out of the law office) is not generally a matter of choosing whether to do something that is "morally wrong"; more often it is a choice between something that is better and something that is worse. It may not be often that the client will make a choice that the lawyer feels is "morally wrong," but clients constantly are faced with issues that have moral implications. We feel that those moral implications should be considered during the decision-making process.

SHAFFER & COCHRAN, *supra* note 2, at 23-24.

Second, the method of moral discourse suggested by the client-centered counselors is likely to be ineffective. After lawyers encourage the client to see things solely from the client's perspective and the client makes a decision, it will be difficult for lawyers to shift gears and reverse the direction of the counseling. *See id.* at 24.

The client-centered counselors argue that their methods are neutral, but we think that their methods influence clients to make self-serving choices. In theory, the client-centered counselors are hired gun lawyers, but in fact, maybe they are godfather lawyers. Client-centered lawyers *lead* clients to focus on their own interests, rather than the interests of others. They impose a framework of client selfishness.

The framework of the client-centered counselors is not neutral, but the problem is not merely that they fail to attain their goal of neutrality. Neutrality may be impossible in a counseling situation. The impossibility of neutrality was illustrated to one of us a few years ago by a story that a lawyer friend — we will call him "Sam" — told. We have changed aspects of the story to protect the privacy of those involved. The story involves Sam's relationship with his brother, but we think that it is instructive for the question of neutrality and influence with clients.

> Sam's brother called and told Sam that he had left his wife and children and moved in with a younger girlfriend. Sam was troubled. He felt that his brother was making a mistake, a moral mistake. But Sam was careful not to criticize his brother; he did not want to, as he said, "impose my values on my brother." He sought to remain neutral. The following day, Sam got a call from his mother. She was furious. "How can you support what your brother is doing? What about his wife and those children? This is one of the worst things that your brother has ever done, and he says that you approve." Sam was stunned. He had said nothing to support what his brother had done. He sought to remain "neutral." But Sam's brother had taken Sam's neutrality as approval and had used it to justify his actions to himself and to his mother.

One of the dangers of "neutral" counseling, whether with a brother or a client, is that when one is told of morally dubious actions, the failure to question can be taken as affirmation. It may be that it is impossible to remain neutral on moral issues. If the actions of a client are likely to injure a third person, to raise a concern about those interests is to suggest that they are important, but to not raise them (when the lawyer is raising all sorts of other factors) is to suggest that they are not important. It may not be possible for the lawyer to be neutral.

In an earlier portion of this book, we suggested that at the interviewing stage, the lawyer should remain non-judgmental about the client's descriptions of his past actions. As we noted at that time, being non-judgmental and accepting of the client at the interviewing stage may be an important part of establishing rapport and gaining information from the client. But at the counseling stage, it may be that the lawyer should be more willing to raise concerns about client actions. Though building rapport and obtaining information are important throughout the relationship, at the counseling stage they may not be as important as at the beginning. At the counseling stage, the lawyer generally will have already developed a relationship with the client.

More importantly, at the counseling stage, the client is generally trying to determine what to do in the future. The decisions of the client are likely to affect other people. The purpose of building the lawyer-client relationship was so that it could serve as the basis for wise decision-making. Hopefully, by the time that decisions have to be made, the rapport between the lawyer and client will be such that they can be candid with one another. The question is whether the lawyer can raise such issues without imposing her values on the client. We address that question in the following section.

Whereas the godfather and guru models of lawyering were authoritarian, the hired gun/client-centered model is individualistic. The client decides questions alone, the goal is to increase the interests of the client, and the focus is on the rights (not the responsibilities) of the client. Individualism is also reflected in client-centered lawyering in the notion that the lawyer is not responsible for what she does; the client controls choices and the lawyer is merely a tool in the hands of the client. In the words of one commentator, "When acting as an advocate for a client . . . , a lawyer is neither legally, professionally, nor morally accountable for the means used or the ends achieved."[31]

In some situations, it may be that the client-centered counselors' focus on client empowerment is justified. It seems that most of the advocates of client-centered lawyering came from legal clinic backgrounds, in which they represented poor people. Generally, poor people need empowerment. Lawyers representing poor people may tend to be paternalistic and may need the client-centered counselors' focus on client autonomy. In those cases in which the lawyer represents a poor client against a rich opponent, there is probably little need for the poor client to worry about the interests of the rich opponent — the rich opponent will be likely to have plenty of lawyers to look out for his interests. But when the lawyer represents the wealthy client against the (often unrepresented) poor party, the lawyer's exclusive focus on client autonomy is likely to result in injustice. If clients who produce dangerous products, have many employees, or have a great impact on the environment make decisions based solely on "consequences to the client" they can cause great harm to others.

As we argued previously, respect for client dignity includes allowing the client to make the important decisions within legal representation. But respect for client dignity also includes a willingness to discuss the morality of issues facing the client. Monroe Freedman is one of the leading proponents of client autonomy as the goal of legal representation. On the matter of the lawyer's role within the counseling relationship, however, Freedman is clearly on the side of moral counsel.[32] He recognizes that moral counsel is not inconsistent with client freedom. Moral counsel gives

---

[31] Murray Schwartz, *The Professionalism and Accountability of Lawyers,* 66 CAL. L. REV. 669, 673 (1978).

[32] *See* FREEDMAN & SMITH, *supra* note 3, at 53-55.

the client the benefit of the moral resources of the lawyer. The lawyer and client should be concerned with more than "consequences to the client."

§ 9-4.   COLLABORATIVE LAWYERS: THE LAWYER AS FRIEND[33]

The lawyering models that we have discussed thus far in this chapter are at the extremes of authoritarianism (the guru and godfather) and individualism (the hired gun). We believe that there is error for the lawyer in the extremes of either individualism or authoritarianism. Like the classic Aristotelian virtues, the good may be a mean between two extremes. Just as between the extremes of cowardice and recklessness is the virtue of courage, between the extremes of individualism and authoritarianism may be the appropriate mean, the collaborative model of lawyering. As to the moral issues that arise in legal representation, we believe that the lawyer should look for guidance to the analogy of the lawyer as friend.

The lawyer as friend can be compared with the other lawyer models with the following chart. Recall that the two questions that define the moral relationship between lawyer and client are: 1) Who controls the important decisions in the relationship? and 2) Are the interests of others taken into consideration in making those decisions? Each of the lawyers we have considered in this chapter gives a different combination of answers to those questions. The lawyer as guru takes control of the relationship and considers the interests of others; the lawyer as godfather also takes control of the relationship, but ignores the interests of others; the lawyer as hired gun defers to the client and ignores the interests of others; and the lawyer as friend defers to the client, but raises the interests of others for discussion with the client.

	Others Considered	Others Ignored
Lawyer Control	Guru/Authoritarian Lawyer	Godfather/Authoritarian Lawyer
Client Control	Friend/Collaborative Lawyer	Hired Gun/Client-Centered Counselor

In our culture, we generally think of friendship in terms of pleasure, but as sociologist Robert Bellah and his colleagues have suggested, central to the traditional notion of friendship was a moral component:

> For Aristotle and his successors, it was precisely the moral component of friendship that made it the indispensable basis of a good society. For it is one of the main duties of friends to help one another to be better persons: one must hold up a standard for one's friend and be able to count on a true friend to do likewise. Traditionally, the opposite of a friend is a flatterer, who tells one what one wants to hear and fails to tell one the truth.[34]

---

[33] For a fuller discussion of the lawyer as friend, see SHAFFER & COCHRAN, *supra* note 2, at 40-54 and 113-34.

[34] ROBERT N. BELLAH ET AL., HABITS OF THE HEART: INDIVIDUALISM AND COMMITMENT IN AMERICAN LIFE 115 (1985).

Of course, lawyers cannot become friends to every client, but they might discuss moral issues with a client in the way that they would discuss moral issues with a friend, not imposing their values on the client, but exploring the client's moral values, and not being afraid to influence the client. Imagine that a close friend comes to you and confesses that he has embezzled something from his employer. You are likely neither to push your friend to confess, nor to ignore the wrong that your friend has done. You are likely to try and help your friend think through the matter. You might offer an opinion, but you would be likely to do so in a tentative fashion, respecting the dignity of your friend. The lawyer as friend engages in moral conversation with the client but leaves decisions to the client.

The lawyer as friend has a long tradition within the bar. The initiation ceremony of the legal fraternity, Phi Delta Phi, founded in 1869 says:

> Not alone by brilliant triumphs as an advocate, but more often as the advisor and friend, does the lawyer find the sphere of largest usefulness. By discouraging suits and encouraging settlements, by aiding the prompt administration of the law, by making it profitable not to litigate, the able counsellor promotes the interests of the client and inculcates justice.[35]

The rules of the legal profession also encourage the moral discourse that is central to the lawyer as friend. The 1969 ABA Model Code of Professional Responsibility states:

> In assisting his client to reach a proper decision, it is often desirable for a lawyer to point out those factors which may lead to a decision that is morally just as well as legally permissible.[36]

The ABA Model Rules of Professional Conduct state:

> In representing a client, a lawyer shall exercise independent professional judgment and render candid advice. In rendering advice, a lawyer may refer not only to law but to other considerations such as moral . . . factors, that may be relevant to the client's situation.[37]

How would the lawyer as friend deal with the client of the Horsewhip Lawyer, with whom we began this chapter? It might be instructive for you to think about how you would deal with a close friend who was making such a decision. We suspect that you would neither ignore the matter, nor attempt to impose your values on her. If you are a good friend, we suspect that you would raise the issue and discuss it seriously with your friend.

In the following excerpt, Anthony Kronman discusses how a lawyer as friend might deal with a client who appears to be making an impetuous decision.

---

[35] INITIATION RITUAL, THE INTERNATIONAL LEGAL FRATERNITY PHI DELTA PHI 15-16 (1997).

[36] MODEL CODE OF PROF'L RESPONSIBILITY EC 7-8.

[37] MODEL RULES OF PROF'L CONDUCT R. 2.1.

ANTHONY T. KRONMAN, THE LOST LAWYER 129-132 (1993)[38]

* * *

[The lawyer's responsibility to help a client make a deliberatively wise choice] may be seen most clearly in the case of what I shall call the "impetuous" client — the client who, in the grip of some domineering passion like anger or erotic love, has made a quick decision to change his life in an important way, for example, by dissolving a long-standing partnership or rewriting his will for a lover's benefit. Let us suppose the client states his objective with lucidity and insists there is no need for a further clarification of his goals. He merely wants his lawyer's help in implementing the decision he has made. Most lawyers will agree, I think, that under theses circumstances it would be irresponsible simply to do what the client asks without first assuring oneself that his decision is a well-considered one. In determining whether it is, a lawyer is likely to begin by asking his client if he has thought the matter through and really wants to do what he now says he does. It may not always be clear that the client's decision is impetuous, but when surrounding circumstances suggest that it is, a responsible lawyer will test his client's judgment before accepting it, recognizing that in such situations the danger of regret is large and that a lawyer must protect his client from this familiar species of self-inflicted harm as well as the harm caused by others.

But it is not enough for a lawyer simply to ask his client whether, on reflection, he wishes to stick by his original decision, for the client's answer to this question may be as impetuous as the decision itself. If the lawyer's effort to determine whether the decision is impetuous or well-considered is to be at all meaningful, he cannot just accept his client's answer at face value. He must have some independent means of evaluating it. But from what vantage point is the lawyer to conduct such an independent inquiry? This is a difficult question, but one thing at least seems clear. It would be inappropriate for the lawyer to conduct this inquiry from the perspective of his own personal desires by asking whether he would want to do what the client has proposed, and to conclude that the client's decision is impetuous if the lawyer would not have made it for himself. After all, the client's desires may simply be different from those of his lawyer, and the fact that they differ in their wants is not itself a sign that the client is acting in a foolish or self-destructive way.

It is from the perspective of the client's own interests that his judgment must be assessed. To do this, a lawyer needs to place himself in the client's position by provisionally accepting his ends and then imaginatively considering the consequences of pursuing them, with the same combination of sympathy and detachment the lawyer would employ if he were deliberating on his own account. . . .

. . . Of course, if a lawyer continues to believe that his client is acting impetuously, but is unable to persuade the client of this, a time will come when he must decide whether to do the client's bidding nonetheless. A lawyer may elect to do so, assuming the client's objective is a legal one, without violating any norm of professional responsibility as these are at present defined. But he is likely to experience the decision as a difficult one, and to feel that he has not served his client as fully as he might. The lawyer who fells this way testifies by his feeling to the fact that he considers it his duty not merely to implement the client's decision, no matter how impetuous it is, but also to help him assess its wisdom through a process of cooperative deliberation in which the lawyer examines the decision with sympathy and detachment for the client's point of view.

The lawyer with an impetuous client must consider matters from the standpoint of the client's interests and desires. Once he has assumed this standpoint, however, he proceeds just as if he were attempting to answer a personal question for himself. To do this part of his job well, therefore, a lawyer needs the same capacities that he does in deliberations of a first-personal sort. Indeed, if anything, he needs them more. For, on the one hand, he may have to make a special effort at sympathy to take his client's interests with the seriousness the client rightfully expects. And on the other hand, he must work particularly hard to sustain an attitude of detachment when deliberating on the client's behalf, since this is just what an impetuous client cannot do. The detachment he brings to their cooperative inquiry is one of the main benefits a lawyer can offer such a client, and while it may be true that the client is paying for sympathy, it is also true that he is paying for calmness and distance as well. Only those lawyers who are able to combine the qualities of sympathy and detachment are thus able to give an impetuous client the advice he needs, even if it is not always the advice he wants.

These last remarks help explain the sense in which a lawyer may sometimes be said to act as his client's friend. Friends take each other's interests seriously and wish to see them advanced; it is part of the meaning of friendship that they do. It does not follow, however, that friends always accept uncritically each other's accounts of their own needs. Indeed, friends often exercise a large degree of independent judgment in assessing each other's interests, and the feeling that one sometimes has an obligation to do so is also an important part of what the relation of friendship means . . .

————

There are two places, in particular, in the client counseling process where we believe the interests of others should be a part of the decision-making process. The first is the point where the lawyer and client are considering the consequences of various alternatives. As noted previously, the client-centered counselors suggest that the lawyer and client consider only "consequences to the client." We suggest that the lawyer and client consider the consequences to others as well. Decisions should be made based on a recognition of the effects of one's actions on others. The lawyer and client should consider all of the consequences that might arise from various alternatives. This can be as simple as the lawyer asking the client what effects various alternatives will have on other people.

A second place at which we believe the lawyer and client should consider the interests of other parties is at the point of decision-making. The goal of the lawyer as friend is to help *the client* make this judgment. The focus of discussion should therefore be on how the client's ethics would address the question that they confront. A lawyer can raise this by merely asking a client what would be fair. The client's answer to that question is likely to draw on the client's moral values.

As noted in Chapter 1, a large part of client counseling is the exercise of practical wisdom. As Gerald Postema describes it:

> Judgment is neither a matter of simply applying general rules to particular cases nor a matter of mere intuition. It is a complex faculty, difficult to characterize, in which general principles or values and the particularities of the case both play important roles. The principles or values provide a framework within which to work and a target at which to aim. But they do not determine decisions. Instead, we rely on our judgment to achieve a coherence among the conflicting values which is sensitive to the particular circumstances. Judgment thus involves the ability to take a comprehensive view of the values and concerns at stake, based on one's experience and knowledge of the world. And this involves awareness of the full range of shared experience, beliefs, relations, and expectations within which these values and concerns have significance.[39]

§ 9-5. AVOIDING LAWYER DOMINATION[40]

The danger of not engaging the client in moral discourse is that the interests of other people will be ignored. But moral discourse carries with it the danger of lawyer domination. The danger is that the lawyer who thinks that he is engaging in moral conversation as a friend, will in fact be a guru, imposing his values on the client. Some of the most thoughtful students (and teachers) of the professional/client relationship have despaired of professional/client moral discourse. Martin Buber, who described better than anyone the joys of interpersonal relationships,[41] concluded that there is too much distance between the professional and the client for mutuality. He felt that the sides are too unequal: "I see you *mean* being on the same plane, but you cannot. . . ."[42] William Simon, who originally advocated that lawyers

---

[39] Gerald J. Postema, *Moral Responsibility in Professional Ethics*, 55 N.Y.U. L. Rev. 63, 68 (1980).

[40] The remainder of this chapter is adapted from Robert F. Cochran, Jr., *Crime, Confession, and the Counselor-at-Law: Lessons From Dostoyevsky*, 35 Houston L. Rev. 327, 383-85 and 391-96 (1998).

[41] Martin Buber, I and Thou (Kaufman trans., 1942).

[42] Martin Buber, The Knowledge of Man 171-72 (M. Friedman & R. Smith trans., 1965).

and clients resolve moral issues as partners,[43] has concluded that lawyers invariably will control the relationship; the focus of Simon's attention is now on how the lawyer alone (as guru) should resolve moral issues during representation.[44] Jack Sammons has questioned whether moral discourse is possible when the lawyer and client do not share the same values.[45]

Nevertheless, it may be that the lawyer's awareness of the power imbalance, of the tendency of the client to defer to the lawyer, and of the lawyer's own temptation to exercise power can be a start in overcoming the imbalance between the lawyer and client. We have two suggestions for the lawyer who wants to engage the client in mutual moral discourse.

The first is that the lawyer can seek to empower the client. As we have already noted, client empowerment begins at the earliest stages of the relationship. Client empowerment is in part a function of the way that the lawyer organizes the office. Friendly secretaries and accessible lawyers can help to place the client at ease. References to the client that convey *equality* (e.g., lawyer and client each refer to the other as Mr./Ms. or they each use first names) can signal the client that he is to be a partner in the relationship. The lawyer's manner with the client will also affect the client's willingness to be actively involved in decision-making. Active listening and looking the client in the eye convey to the client that the lawyer believes that what the client says is important. A lawyer can also empower a client by directly addressing the question of control. The lawyer can acknowledge to the client that the lawyer is not an expert on the life of the client, and that the thoughts, feelings, and values of the client will be most important in determining what they do during the representation. Client empowerment is not something that goes on only at the beginning of the relationship. Throughout the relationship, the lawyer must convey respect to the client. The lawyer empowers the client by asking him how they should proceed at important points in the representation, and by the way that she gives advice (often in a tentative manner), if she gives advice at all.

The second way that the lawyer can encourage mutuality is by regulating the intensity with which she engages the client in moral discourse. This serves as a significant qualification to the lawyer as friend analogy. With friends, one need not "measure words." But not measuring words within the lawyer/client relationship can create the danger of lawyer domination. Friends can be more direct with one another because there is less danger that they will overreach. A difference between the lawyer/client relationship and the friendship relationship is the imbalance of power. The lawyer's power can often overcome a client.

---

[43] William H. Simon, *The Ideology of Advocacy: Procedural Justice and Professional Ethics*, 1978 WIS. L. REV. 29 (1978).

[44] Simon argues that lawyers should look to the law's moral values to resolve legal issues. William H. Simon, *Ethical Discretion in Lawyering*, 101 HARV. L. REV. 1083, 1113 (1988); SIMON, *supra* note 13, at 138.

[45] Sammons' argument is addressed *infra* in text accompanying notes 47-48.

If a lawyer is too intense, she may overcome the client and there will be no mutual discourse. There is, however, also the danger that if the lawyer is not sufficiently intense, the client may not take the moral issue seriously. A lawyer should regulate the intensity with which she engages the client in moral discourse.

A lawyer can engage a client over a broad range of intensity levels. That intensity can be expressed both in the emotions that the lawyer displays and the statements that she makes. We believe that the level of intensity should vary, depending on the client and the circumstances. At one end of the intensity spectrum, a criminal lawyer who has been appointed to represent a poor woman charged with petty larceny might remain relatively neutral as to moral issues: expressing little emotion, asking non-leading questions ("Has anyone been affected by what you did?") and ("What do you think that you should do?"). This lawyer's primary concern might be empowering the client.

At the other end, a corporate lawyer who has learned that a corporate executive approved the sale of defective kidney dialysis machines[46] might be quite directive (using methods that border on those of an authoritarian lawyer): emotionally raising the interests of others ("Think what you might do to these patients!"), making a moral judgment ("You did a terrible thing!"), and directing the client ("You have got to stop those sales!"). This lawyer's primary concern might be influencing the client. There are, of course, a broad range of levels of intensity between these extremes.

Note that the factual context of the counseling greatly influences the intensity of the lawyer's moral counsel in these examples. Were the criminal lawyer to use the directive counseling with the poor woman ("You must confess!), he probably would not generate moral discourse — he would merely push the client to follow his wishes. If the corporate lawyer were to use the neutral counseling with the corporate executive ("What do you think you should do?"), she would probably not generate moral discourse — the corporate official would probably ignore her. The remainder of this section considers some of the factors that a lawyer might consider when determining the level of intensity with which to engage a client in moral discourse.

1. *Ability of the Client to go Elsewhere* — When the client has chosen the lawyer, and can easily go to another lawyer, the lawyer may feel free to engage the client in more intense moral discourse. If the client feels that the lawyer has pushed too far, he can go elsewhere. Of course, as the representation goes forward, it may be more difficult for the client to go elsewhere; there is greater risk that the lawyer's power will overcome the client. In the case of court-appointed counsel, the client generally will not have chosen the lawyer and would have a difficult time changing lawyers. When the client has not chosen the lawyer or would have a difficult time changing lawyers, the lawyer should be less directive in moral counsel.

---

[46] *See* Balla v. Gambro, Inc., 145 Ill. 2d 492, 584 N.E.2d 104, 164 Ill. Dec. 892 (1991).

2. *Power of Lawyer and Client Within the Relationship* — Much of what has been said previously in this book has assumed that the lawyer is the powerful player in the lawyer-client relationship and must empower the client. The lawyer's knowledge of the law will give the lawyer substantial power within the relationship, but in some situations most of the power will rest with the client. The client may have great financial power over the lawyer. The client could be the owner of a large business and the lawyer, little more than an employee. When one client provides a substantial portion of a lawyer or law firm's business, the power balance can be with the client.

The power within the relationship will also be a function of a host of other factors: age, education, experience, sex, social class, race, and status.[47] When these determinants of power are primarily on the lawyer's side, the lawyer should be more hesitant to push during moral discourse. When the determinants are equal or primarily on the side of the client, the lawyer is unlikely to overcome the client and can feel freer to address moral issues. The lawyer's natural instincts will, of course, be in the opposite direction. The powerful lawyer (with weak clients) is likely to feel comfortable asserting power and may overcome the client; the weak lawyer (with powerful clients) is likely to be hesitant to raise moral concerns and may fail to give the independent advice that the client needs. If the lawyer is to both involve the client in moral discourse and not overcome the client, she may need to act against her instincts. The powerful lawyer may need to work to respect the dignity of the weak client; the weak lawyer may need courage to confront the powerful client.

3. *Differences in Client and Lawyer Values* — As noted previously, the lawyer as friend addresses moral issues with clients in the way that she would address such issues with friends, based on Aristotle's notion of friendship as a moral relationship. Jack Sammons has thoughtfully questioned the use of Aristotle's ideal of friendship as a moral teacher in our multi-cultural world. Aristotle envisioned moral discourse within the Greek city-state among friends who shared a common moral tradition.[48] There is a danger that a lawyer who seeks to counsel one with different moral values may think that she is engaging the client in moral discourse, when she is merely imposing her values on the client.

Common experience testifies that moral discourse is more difficult across cultural boundaries, but that moral discourse is possible. We find it most easy to discuss moral problems with those with whom we share a common tradition; there are fewer misunderstandings. But most people also have the experience of learning from those who are different from them. For example, when most people view a film or read a book from a

---

[47] Our point here is not to suggest that these factors should affect the power in the relationship or that one cannot overcome a lack of power, but to suggest that lawyers should be aware that these factors are likely to affect the level of influence that the lawyer will have over a client.

[48] *See* Sammons, *supra* note 3, at 8-27.

different culture, parts seem strange and beyond their understanding and parts seem surprisingly familiar. We share significant moral values with even the most different cultures.[49] Some parts of films or books from another culture may seem odd, but may cause us to question and look beyond our own culture. We can gain insight from those who are different from us.

Lawyers should be aware that there may be differences in moral values between them and their clients and they should be sensitive to those differences. When there are differences, lawyers should make the moral values *of the client* the focus of the discourse, and be aware that they may be tempted to impose. When there are differences, the lawyer should be more hesitant to insert her values into the discussion. We provide a more extended discussion of dealing with differences between lawyer and client in Chapter 11.

4. *Danger to Other People* — Up this point in the analysis, the factors that we have suggested should be considered in determining the intensity of the lawyer's involvement have concerned the dignity of the client — the lawyer should have sufficient respect for the client to raise moral issues and sufficient respect not to overreach the client. A final factor that the lawyer should consider when determining at what intensity level to engage in moral discourse is danger to other people. If one of the client's options will create danger to other people, the lawyer should address the moral concerns with greater intensity. The greater the danger, the greater the intensity. If the lives of other people are at risk, the most directive moral counsel would be justified. (If such counsel fails, disclosure of confidential information may be justified.[50]) This concern for the interests of other people is based on a normative judgment that other people are important.

A consideration of the above factors makes it clear that there is not a rule for how to engage a client in moral discourse. Some of the factors to be considered are likely to suggest more intense engagement and some, less intense engagement. In determining how to engage the client in moral discourse, the lawyer must exercise judgment, and, as noted above, judgment can be a complex matter.

Of course, after this moral conversation, lawyer and client may disagree about what should be done. When lawyer and client disagree, so long as the lawyer does not believe that the direction that the client wants to go would be wrong, we believe that the lawyer should defer to the client. This, of course, is another matter requiring wise judgment on the part of the lawyer.

---

[49] As C.S. Lewis has demonstrated, there are many common moral values across cultures. *See* the appendix to his THE ABOLITION OF MAN 95-121 (1947).

[50] *See* FREEDMAN & SMITH, *supra* note 3, at 152-154.

CHAPTER 10

TO SUE OR SETTLE?: COUNSELING ABOUT DISPUTE RESOLUTION

§ 10-1. INTRODUCTION

Lawyers are in the conflict business. In the popular image, they are combatants — at times heros, at times villains — battling it out in court. In reality, more often, thankfully, lawyers serve as conflict avoiders, even conflict healers. At times, they engage in conflict avoidance when litigation is in view — they seek to settle or mediate cases that are set for trial. But just as often, good lawyers engage in conflict avoidance when litigation is not in view, often before anyone else has even considered the possibility of conflict. They draft a partnership agreement, a sales agreement, articles of incorporation, or even a will with an eye toward avoiding future conflicts. Clients often call on lawyers to negotiate and draft the terms under which they will live with their partners, employees, customers, spouses, and business associates. Resolution of conflicts, whether the open conflict of litigation or the — at times subtle, at times not so subtle — conflict of negotiation will be the subject of much client-lawyer discourse.

Law office counseling about dispute resolution was the subject of a lecture by one of the United States' greatest litigators (who was also one of its greatest presidents). Abraham Lincoln said:

> Discourage litigation. Persuade your neighbors to compromise whenever you can. Point out to them how the nominal winner is a real loser — in fees, expenses, and waste of time. As a peacemaker, the lawyer has a superior opportunity of being a good man. There will always be enough business. Never stir up litigation.[1]

Many of the issues that lawyers and clients must resolve concern dispute resolution. Whether to sue or settle? Whether to accept the proffered terms of a partnership agreement? Whether to make a counter-offer? What counter-offer to make? Increasingly, clients and lawyers must decide whether to pursue means of alternate dispute resolution (ADR) such as arbitration or mediation. Only a few decades ago, most lawyers had not heard of ADR. Today, it is an integral part of the practice of law; a lawyer who is not familiar with ADR and does not present the possibility of pursuing ADR options to a client may be subject to malpractice liability[2] or

---

[1]Abraham Lincoln, *Notes for Law Lecture,* July 1, 1850, *in* AN AUTOBIOGRAPHY OF ABRAHAM LINCOLN, CONSISTING ON THE PERSONAL PORTIONS OF HIS SPEECHES AND CONSERVATIONS 93 (Compiled and annotated by Nathaniel Wright Stephenson, 1926).

professional discipline.[3] ADR opens up another realm of issues for the law office. Do we pursue arbitration or mediation? Do we create our own dispute resolution mechanism? In drafting a contract, do we include a provision requiring mediation or arbitration of disputes that might arise under the contract?

In this chapter, we discuss how a lawyer might raise and discuss negotiation and ADR decisions with a client. Of course, negotiation and ADR are the subject of separate courses in law school, and each raises many issues. We will raise only a few of the most important issues, with a focus on how these issues can be discussed and resolved with clients.

§ 10-2.   COUNSELING CLIENTS ABOUT NEGOTIATION DECISIONS[4]

The outcome of negotiation, whether of a transaction or a dispute, is generally of great importance to clients. In negotiation of a dispute, avoiding litigation can limit uncertainty, speed resolution, and enable the parties to tailor a settlement to meet their special needs.[5] Many decisions that the attorney or client make during negotiations are likely to affect the outcome. Some alternatives enhance the likelihood that a settlement, if obtained, will be favorable to a client, but create a greater risk of deadlock.

As we noted previously, there is justification for leaving much decision making authority with the lawyer in litigation, where many of the decisions are technical or urgent, but, generally, these justifications do not apply to negotiation decisions. Negotiation choices may be difficult, but generally the client can understand the risks and benefits of various alternatives. The lawyer will play an important role in explaining the likelihood of various results under the bargaining alternatives, but lawyers should allow clients to control negotiation choices in light of the client's values and risk preferences.

---

[2] Robert F. Cochran, Jr., *Legal Representation and the Next Steps Toward Client Control: Attorney Malpractice for the Failure to Allow the Client to Control Negotiation and Pursue Alternatives to Litigation,* 47 WASH.& LEE L. REV. 819, 819-77 (1990).

[3] Robert F. Cochran, Jr., *Professional Rules and ADR: Control of Alternative Dispute Resolution Under the ABA Ethics 2000 Commission Proposal and Under Other Professional Responsibility Standards, in* "Symposium: ADR and the Professional Responsibility of Lawyers," 4 FORDHAM URB. L.J. 895-914 (2001); Robert F. Cochran, Jr., *ADR, the ABA, and Client Control: A Proposal that the Model Rules Require Lawyers to Present ADR Options to Clients, in* "Symposium: Emerging Professional Responsibility Issues in Litigation," 41 S. TEX. L. REV. 183-201 (1999); Robert F. Cochran, Jr., *Must Lawyers Tell Clients About ADR?,* ARB. J. 8, 8-13 (Vol. 46, No. 2, June 1993).

[4] Much of the following is adapted from Robert F. Cochran, Jr., *Legal Representation and the Next Steps Toward Client Control: Attorney Malpractice for the Failure to Allow the Client to Control Negotiation and Pursue Alternatives to Litigation,* 47 WASH.& LEE L. REV. 819, 859-861 (1990). Copyright © by The Washington & Lee Review Law Review. Reprinted with permission.

[5] *See* John T. Dunlop, *The Negotiations Alternative in Dispute Resolution,* 29 VILL. L. REV. 1421, 1423 (1984).

In many situations, the client may have advantages over the attorney in making negotiation decisions. The client may know the opposing party and know better than the attorney how that party is likely to react to various types of strategic behavior. The client may have greater knowledge than the lawyer of some aspects of the subject over which the parties are negotiating. This knowledge may enable the client to think of creative means of arranging a deal or settling a case in a way that will benefit both sides.

Cases clearly establish that the client must approve of settlement offers made by their attorneys[6] and that the client has the right to choose whether or not to accept settlement offers from the opposing side.[7] Other decisions during negotiation are also sufficiently important that they should be made by the client.

In conducting a negotiation, two basic questions will be what style and strategy to adopt. The style of negotiation is the interpersonal behavior of the negotiator in dealing with the other side, and may be either competitive or cooperative.[8] Both competitive and cooperative styles of negotiation can be successful. One study found that:

> [E]ffective competitive lawyers are dominating, forceful, attacking, aggressive, ambitious, clever, honest, perceptive, analytical, convincing, and self-controlled. Effective cooperative lawyer-negotiators, on the other hand, were found to be trustworthy, fair, honest, courteous, personable, tactful, sincere, perceptive, reasonable, convincing, and self-controlled.[9]

Though each style can be effective, each carries its own strengths and risks. A competitive style of bargaining may yield a more favorable result because it may intimidate the opposing side, however a competitive style "generates tension and encourages negotiator mistrust," creating a greater risk of deadlock.[10] On the other hand, the terms reached under a cooperative negotiating style often are not as favorable to the client, but a cooperative style encourages mutual understanding, reduces the risk of deadlock, requires less negotiation time, and generally produces a higher joint outcome for the parties.[11]

---

[6] See CHARLES W. WOLFRAM, MODERN LEGAL ETHICS 169-72 (1986) and cases cited therein.

[7] *See, e.g.,* Joos v. Auto-owners Ins. Co., 288 N.W.2d 443,445 (1979), *later appealed,* Joos v. Drillock, 338 N.W.2d 736 (Mich. 1983) (" . . . an attorney has, as a matter of law, a duty to disclose and discuss with his or her client good faith offers to settle."); Rubenstein v. Rubenstein, 31 A.D.2d 615, 615, 295 N.Y.S.2d 876, 877 (1968), *aff'd,* 25 N.Y.2d 751, 250 N.E.2d 570, 303 N.Y.S.2d 508 (1969) ("failure to disclose an offer of settlement and submit to the client's judgment for acceptance or rejection is improper practice"); Rizzo v. Haines, 555 A.2d 321 (Pa. 1986); Whiteaker v. State, 382 N.W.2d 112 (Iowa 1986).

[8] *See* ROBERT M. BASTRESS & JOSEPH D. HARBAUGH, INTERVIEWING, COUNSELING, AND NEGOTIATION: SKILLS FOR EFFECTIVE REPRESENTATION 390 (1990).

[9] *Id.* at 391 (*citing* G. WILLIAMS, EFFECTIVE NEGOTIATION AND SETTLEMENT (1981), a study of lawyer-negotiators in Denver and Phoenix).

[10] *Id.* at 392 (*citing* G. WILLIAMS).

[11] *Id.*

Whereas the style of negotiation is the manner of interpersonal behavior with the opponent, the strategy controls the substantive choices. There are two types of negotiation strategies, adversarial and problem-solving.[12] An adversarial strategy assumes that there is a given pie to be divided and that any concession to the other side will be a loss to the client; problem-solving negotiation attempts to resolve conflict in a manner that will create a bigger pie and enable both parties to win.[13] Problem-solving negotiators attempt to discover the needs of both of the parties and, together, create solutions that meet those needs.[14] Bastress and Harbaugh contrast adversarial and problem-solving strategies as follows:

> Adversarials proceed linearly to develop their plans, concentrating on creating and defending positions along the bargaining continuum. Planning by problem solvers, on the other hand, focuses on identifying needs and brainstorming to develop solutions for mutual gains. Adversarials engage in positional argument while problem solvers tend to explore interests. Adversarials make offers to which they appear to be committed. Problem solvers advance proposals that invite opponents to accept, reject, or modify based on how the proposals intersect with their interests. Adversarials are more likely to restrict information flow, problem solvers are more inclined to exchange data. Adversarials reject the opponents' offers summarily and make concessions along the continuum. Problem solvers explain why solutions are acceptable or unacceptable in whole or in part based on a needs analysis. They also seldom make concessions, as their adversarial colleagues do, but instead shift to another proposal that more completely addresses the parties' mutual problems.[15]

Adversarial and problem-solving strategies each have potential benefits and risks for the client. Problem-solving negotiation can help both parties if it enables the parties to develop a creative solution that is mutually beneficial. If the parties want to have a continuing relationship, it may be important to each of them that the other benefit from the ultimate resolution of the dispute. However, if the problem is such that the client's only goal is to obtain as much as possible of a pie of a given size, then adversarial bargaining is likely to produce the greater gain.[16] If problem-solving fails to produce a creative solution to the problem, either or both parties

---

[12] Adversarial and problem-solving strategies can be used in combination with either a competitive or cooperative bargaining style. *See id.* at 393-97; *see also* Carrie Menkel-Meadow, *Toward Another View of Legal Negotiation: The Structure of Problem Solving*, 31 UCLA L. REV. 754, 818 (1984).

[13] *See* ROGER FISHER & WILLIAM URY, GETTING TO YES, NEGOTIATING AGREEMENT WITHOUT GIVING IN (1981); *see also* BASTRESS & HARBAUGH, *supra* note 8, at 381; and Menkle-Meadow, *supra* note 12, at 783-85 & 809-13.

[14] *See* Menkle-Meadow, *supra* note 12, at 801-17.

[15] BASTRESS & HARBAUGH, *supra* note 8, at 383.

[16] *See id.* at 402.

may have revealed weaknesses to the other side that will be damaging. The choice of what strategy to employ during negotiation carries with it risks and benefits for the client, and the lawyer should explain them to the client.

Some law students (and lawyers) are enamored with the image of the hard-ball negotiator who uses both a competitive style and an adversarial strategy. As noted above, these methods can be effective, but carry a high risk of deadlock and a limited prospect of generating a creative alternative. The advantage of problem-solving negotiation is illustrated by one of our favorite cases, that of *The Highwaymen v. The Highwaymen.* Sounds like a case for hired guns, but it was resolved to everyone's satisfaction by some cooperative, problem-solving negotiation.

In the early 1990s country-western legends Waylon Jennings, Willie Nelson, Johnny Cash, and Kris Kristofferson decided to go on tour under the name, "The Highwaymen." After a substantial amount of tour publicity and preparation, they were sued by the lawyers for the 1960s folk singing group, The Highwaymen (singers of "Michael" and "Cottonfields") for trademark infringement. The folk singing Highwaymen (including, by the way, guitar player and Ninth Circuit Court of Appeals Judge Stephen Trott) were still around and attempting a comeback. At this point, you might pause to consider whether there are creative means of settling the case that would benefit both sides.

Competitive negotiators might have tried to settle the case for a figure based on the value of the name, but Waylon Jennings did a little creative problem-solving. He proposed a settlement under which both Highwaymen got to use the name, and the old Highwaymen served as the warm-up act for the new Highwaymen in their Los Angeles concert. Waylon, Willie, Johnny, and Kris got to keep the name and the folk singing Highwaymen got more exposure than they could have imagined. Both sides were pleased.[17] Our point is not that problem-solving negotiation will always generate such an attractive alternative, but that it may, and that lawyers should discuss such prospects with clients.

At an early point in the lawyer-client relationship, the lawyer should discuss with the client the advantages and disadvantages of different styles and strategies in negotiation. The lawyer should enable the client to make an informed choice as to such matters.

For example, assume that a client asks you to represent him in the creation of a partnership with another person. They want to open a flower shop together. Your client has experience running a successful flower shop. The potential partner has cash. They have agreed that the partner will provide the money; your client will provide the expertise; and they will split the profits. As is often the case, the parties are optimistic.

---

[17] Steve Hochman, *Highwaymen Solve Legal Wrangle Over Name,* Los Angeles Times, Oct. 1, 1990, at F12.

You and the lawyer for the partner begin to draft a partnership agreement. As good lawyers, you both quickly spot a potential conflict. The parties (being optimistic) have not considered how they will deal with potential losses. You take the issue to your clients. They disagree. Your client argues that the partner should bear the losses: "He is the one coming up with the money for the venture; losses are part of the money for the venture." The partner argues that they should share the losses: "We were to share the profits; we should share the losses. That's what a partnership is all about."

You and your client need a counseling session. There are several issues that you need to resolve. One issue is who should do the negotiating — you or the client. There are potential advantages either way. You are the experienced negotiator, and might be more skilled in persuasion. On the other hand, the client knows more about the business and the potential partner. In addition, if they are to be partners, they will need to learn how to resolve disputes together. Assume that your client is afraid to handle the negotiation of this issue and wants you to handle it.

Now come the issues of the style and strategy of the negotiation. As to style, you might say:

> We have to decide what style I should use in the negotiation. The style is the manner that I use with the other lawyer. We can list the possibilities and the advantages and disadvantages of each on this piece of paper. I can be either competitive or cooperative. If I am competitive, I will be aggressive, I will act like we don't care whether we reach an agreement or not. If I am cooperative, I will be more friendly, and let him know that we want an agreement and are willing to be reasonable. These are, of course, the extremes. We could decide that I should use something in between these two styles.

> Generally, when they are able to reach agreement, competitive negotiators get better results. I will list that as an advantage of competitive negotiation. But competitive negotiators are more likely to fail to reach an agreement. I will list that as a disadvantage. Cooperative negotiators are more likely to reach an agreement, but are not as likely to obtain an agreement that is as good for the client. I will list that advantage and that disadvantage of cooperative negotiation. You should also consider the effect that each of these styles might have on your future relationship with your partner. A competitive style may signal to him that he can't take advantage of you, but it may damage your relationship. How do you think your partner would react to each approach? Do you see other advantages or disadvantages to either approach?

As to the strategy of the negotiation, you might say:

> Now we have to decide what strategy to use. There are two basic strategies to choose from. One is adversarial. I will list it on our sheet. Under an adversarial strategy, we will probably resolve this issue by some compromise between what your partner wants and what you want. Our goal will be to get as close as we can to what

you want. We will probably wind up settling somewhere between you having to pay 50% of the losses (which is what he wants) and you paying none of the losses (which is what you want). If we employ an adversarial strategy, we will initially refuse to pay any of the losses, in hopes that he will give in. If we make concessions, they will be small, few, and far between. You, of course, will have the chance to decide whether to accept any of their offers and what counter-offers, if any, to give. An adversarial strategy is likely to generate the best amount if we reach a settlement, but it also carries a greater risk of deadlock than a less adversarial strategy. You may have a better sense in this case whether deadlock is likely. How badly do you think that your partner wants a deal?

After a discussion of adversarial strategy with the client, you might say:

A second strategy that we might employ in the negotiation is problem-solving. Under this strategy, we would work with your partner to see if we could come up with a solution to the problem that would be more acceptable to both of you than merely compromising somewhere between you paying 50% of the losses and you paying none of the losses. For example, it seems from what you have said that your partner has more money than you, but does not have as much expertise. Maybe he would agree to assume the business's losses if you would take on some additional responsibility in running the business. Maybe you could keep the books. Or, maybe you can think of some other way to reach a settlement. If we try a problem-solving strategy, we will seek with them to develop a new way to resolve the problem. We may come up with something together that none of us could come up with alone. An advantage of this strategy is that we may develop an idea that pleases everyone. It is also likely to help build your relationship with your future partner. A disadvantage is that if it fails, we may have shared information with them that will hurt us. For example, if we let them know that you would have a hard time paying for part of the business' losses, they may realize that you would have a hard time paying for a long series of negotiations over this issue. That might lead them to take a hard-nosed approach. Do you think that we might be able to come up with a creative way of resolving this problem if we work with them?

In a real session with a client, there would probably be more give and take with the client, but this gives you a rough idea how you might enable a client to make an informed decision between the different styles and strategies of negotiation.

Other important negotiation decisions include when to make offers and what offers to make.[18] These issues are especially important when you use

---

[18] Douglas Rosenthal found that less than 20% of attorneys discuss the initial settlement demand with the client. *See* DOUGLAS E. ROSENTHAL, LAWYER AND CLIENT: WHO'S IN CHARGE 113 (1974).

an adversarial negotiation strategy.[19] The closer your offer is to a reasonable settlement figure, the more likely it is that the case will be settled, but the less favorable is likely to be the final settlement figure.[20] The party to make the first concession usually does worse in negotiation,[21] and small, infrequent concessions are likely to yield the most favorable results.[22] However, toughness as to concessions may result in deadlock.[23] These options and their potential advantages and disadvantages can be laid out on a decision making sheet as we suggested in Chapter 8.

§ 10-3. COUNSELING CONCERNING ALTERNATIVE DISPUTE RESOLUTION[24]

Increasingly parties are resolving cases through alternative means of dispute resolution.[25] The two major alternatives to litigation and negotiation

---

[19] Rather than focusing on offers and counter-offers, the problem-solving negotiator proposes multiple solutions to the problems of the parties and then discusses with the opponent how each of them might meet the needs of the parties. *See* BASTRESS & HARBAUGH, *supra* note 8, at 501. Once the parties have agreed on the general outline of an agreement, however, they may shift to adversarial exchanges of offers and counter-offers to determine the final terms.

[20] *See id.* at 497-499 (unreasonable initial offers maximize the client's return, but create "an extraordinarily high incidence of deadlock") and 520 ("a grudging approach to the size and the number of concessions results in the maximum payoff to the negotiator," but extreme levels of toughness create a risk of deadlock).

[21] *See* GARY BELLOW & BEA MOULTION, THE LAWYERING PROCESS: NEGOTIATION 115 (1981) and studies cited therein.

[22] *See id.*

[23] The failure to make a concession could lead to a failure to settle because it carries with it:

> (b) the danger that the opponent will become discouraged and end the negotiation prematurely; (c) the danger that one's own side or the opponent will become so committed to an unviable position that agreement is impossible; (d) the danger that further maneuvering now will leave too little time in the future to work out an agreement . . .

Pruitt, *Indirect Communication and the Search for Agreement in Negotiation*, 1 J. APP. SOC. PSYCH. 205 (1971), *quoted in* BELLOW & MOULTON, *supra* note 21, at 108.

> If [an initial demand] is high enough it will (i) protect counsel from under-estimations of his or her opponent's minimal settlement point; (ii) conceal counsel's own minimal settlement point; and (iii) permit counsel to make concessions and demand counterconcessions which still perform these concealment/protective functions. . . . On the other hand, if the initial demand is too high, it may (i) be dismissed and have no effect on opposing counsel's decisions; (ii) cause opposing counsel to believe that threats or other cost-imposing tactics are necessary; (iii) produce an expectation of deadlock (opposing counsel might then begin preparing for trial, incurring costs which would later have to be recovered). . . .

BELLOW & MOULTON, *supra* note 21, at 100.

[24] Much of the following is adapted from Cochran, *supra* note 2 at 862-68.

[25] For helpful introductions and discussions of ADR, see JAY FOLBERG & ALISON TAYLOR, MEDIATION: A COMPREHENSIVE GUIDE TO RESOLVING CONFLICTS WITHOUT LITIGATION (1984); STEPHEN B GOLDBERG, ERIC D. GREEN & FRANK E.A. SANDER, DISPUTE RESOLUTION (1985);

are mediation and arbitration.[26] In mediation, the parties meet with a neutral third party, often chosen by the parties, who attempts to facilitate the negotiation of a settlement. The mediator controls the communication and information exchange between the parties, establishes a positive emotional climate, helps to define the problem, and develops procedures for generating options.[27] Mediation is like negotiation, in that the parties must reach agreement in order for there to be a resolution of the dispute. Sometimes mediation is conducted by the parties without the presence of counsel; at other times, the lawyers are present for the mediation. Generally, whether or not lawyers are present is a matter to be resolved by the agreement of the parties. When the lawyers do not participate in the mediation, agreements worked out by the parties often are subject to the review of counsel.

Some courts require the parties to engage in mediation, but courts can only have so much influence in mediation. They can lead the parties to mediation, but they can't make them settle. (When courts apply so much pressure that parties *have* to settle, it makes little sense to call the procedure "mediation" or the product of it "an agreement" — it is merely an imposed judgment by another name.)

In arbitration, an arbitrator, generally chosen by the parties, conducts a hearing.[28] The parties are represented by counsel. Arbitration is like litigation in that a third party, the arbitrator, makes the final decision. The ground rules of the arbitration generally are created by the agreement of the parties. They determine how many arbitrators there will be, how the arbitrators will be chosen, what rules of evidence will apply, and whether or not the decision may be appealed. In traditional arbitration, the decision of the arbitrator is binding. Courts have generally upheld agreements to binding arbitration.[29] Occasionally parties opt for non-binding arbitration. Under non-binding arbitration the decision of the arbitrator can

---

JOHN S. MURRAY, ALAN SCOTT RAU & EDWARD F. SHERMAN, PROCESSES OF DISPUTE RESOLUTION 247 (1989) [hereinafter MURRAY]; LEONARD RISKIN & JAMES E. WESTBROOK, DISPUTE RESOLUTION AND LAWYERS (1988); Owen Fiss, *Against Settlement*, 93 YALE L.J. 1073 (1984); Owen Fiss, *Out of Eden*, 94 YALE L.J. 1669 (1985); Louis A. Lavorato, *Alternative Dispute Resolution: One Judge's Experience*, 42 ARB. J. 64 (1987); Andrew McThenia & Thomas L. Shaffer, *For Reconciliation*, 94 YALE L.J. 1660 (1985); Jessica Pearson, *An Evaluation of Alternatives to Court Adjudication*, 7 JUST. SYS. J. 420 (1982); Leonard Riskin, *Mediation and Lawyers*, 43 OHIO ST. L.J. 29 (1982); Frank E. Sander, *Alternative Methods of Dispute Resolution: An Overview*, 37 U. FLA. L. REV. 1 (1985).

[26] Other forms of alternative dispute resolution include the mini-trial (lawyers present their cases to the principles of institutional clients, who then, with the help of an advisor, seek to reach agreement) and mediation/arbitration (begins as mediation, proceeds to arbitration if the parties do not agree). RISKIN & WESTBROOK, *supra* note 25, at 5, 173-88.

[27] *See* MURRAY, *supra* note 25, at 247-48; RISKIN & WESTBROOK, *supra* note 25, at 4, 83-90.

[28] *See* RISKIN & WESTBROOK, *supra* note 25, at 3-4.

[29] *See* Gateway Coal Co. v. United Mine Workers of America et al., 414 U.S. 368 (1974); Steelworkers v. Enterprise Corp., 363 U.S. 593 (1960); Bailey v. Bicknell Minerals, Inc., 819 F.2d 690 (7th Cir. 1987); O'Malley v. Wilshire Oil Co., 59 Cal. 2d 482, 381 P.2d 188, 30 Cal. Rptr. 452 (1963); Retail Clerks Union, Local 770, AFL-CIO v. Thrifti mart, Inc., 59 Cal. 2d 421, 380 P.2d 652, 30 Cal.Rptr. 12 (1963); Posner v. Grinwald Marx, Inc., 56 Cal. 2d 169, 363 P.2d 313, 14 Cal. Rptr. 297 (1961).

serve as guidance for the parties in their negotiation, but the parties are not bound by it.

Mediation and arbitration may differ from litigation in time required before resolution of the dispute, cost, effect on the future relationship of the parties, likely result, and procedural protections. There are risks and potential benefits to each means of dispute resolution. The decision whether to pursue an alternative means of dispute resolution is an important one and, just as medical patients are entitled to choose whether to pursue alternatives to surgery under the right of informed consent,[30] legal clients should be entitled to pursue alternatives to litigation. In order to enable clients to make such decisions thoughtfully, lawyers need to be able to explain the common means of dispute resolution and the risks and potential benefits of each. The remainder of this section discusses the advantages and disadvantages of various means of dispute resolution. As you read this section, consider how you would explain these to a client. For example, you might want to list the advantages and disadvantages of each means of dispute resolution on a decision-making sheet for the client.

Time and Attorneys' Fees — Mediation and arbitration may save the client both time and money. They can save the client time in two respects. First, the parties generally can arrange to have the dispute mediated or arbitrated at a much earlier date than they could have a trial. In litigation, the delay between the filing of a complaint and the trial of a case can be substantial. In arbitration or mediation the parties can begin to mediate or arbitrate a dispute as soon as they agree on a mediator or arbitrator and arrange for a meeting.

Mediation and arbitration can save the client time in a second respect. Once mediation or arbitration begins, it may require a shorter amount of attorney and client time than litigation or attorney negotiation. In some cases, mediation will resolve a dispute faster than attorney negotiation, in some cases it will not. Some characteristics of mediation may expedite resolution of a dispute, other characteristics may retard its resolution. When the parties meet directly with each other during mediation, they can answer each other's questions and make offers and counter-offers without delay. On the other hand, during mediation, the parties may spend time dealing with underlying emotional conflicts that are not related to the specific problem in dispute.

Arbitration generally will require a shorter amount of time than litigation. The arbitrator is typically an expert in the subject matter of the dispute, and it may require less time for the arbitrator to understand the facts of the case than a judge or jury.[31] Arbitration results also may not be subject to appeal, and this may prevent the long delay that may accompany appeal.

---

[30] *See, e.g.,* Custodio v. Bauer, 251 Cal. App. 2d 303, 59 Cal. Rptr. 463 (1967); Marino v. Ballestas, 749 F.2d 162 (3d Cir. 1984); Jacobs v. Painter, 530 A.2d 231 (1987). *See also* the following statutes which require disclosure of alternative methods of treatment, FLA. STAT. § 768.46 (1978); ME. REV. STAT. tit. 24. § 2905 (1988); N.C. GEN. STAT. § 90-21.13 (1977).

[31] *See* Jethro K. Lieberman & James F. Henry, *Lessons From the Alternative Dispute Resolution Movement*, 53 U. CHI. L. REV. 424, 431 (1986).

In addition to the potential savings of time, the parties may save attorneys fees through mediation or arbitration. In some mediations, the parties meet alone with the mediator. If so, negotiations that take place with the opposing party during mediation will require less expense on the part of the parties than negotiation for a similar amount of time by attorneys. Mediation without attorneys requires only one professional fee, the fee of the mediator, during the time of the mediation. This savings may be offset, to some extent, by the expense of having an attorney review the agreement. If the mediation is successful, the parties will probably save money. If the mediation is unsuccessful, however, the parties will bear the mediator's fees, as well as their attorneys' fees and litigation expenses.

Mediation creates the biggest savings of time and money in cases in which it is successful and attorney negotiation would not have been successful. Of course, it is difficult to tell whether any one case that has been resolved through mediation would have been resolved through attorney negotiation, but it appears that mediation is somewhat more successful at resolving disputes than attorney negotiation.[32] Therefore, if the parties mediate, the client is likely to save time and money if the mediation is successful. In cases in which the client knows the other party, the client may be the best person to determine whether mediation is likely to lead to an agreement.

The attorneys' fees in arbitration are likely to be somewhat less than the attorneys' fees in litigation. In arbitration, attorneys represent the parties in hearings that are like trials in many respects. The arbitrator is typically an expert in the subject matter of the dispute, and so the hearing may be shorter, requiring less attorney fees than a trial.[33] However, the parties will generally have to pay the expense of the arbitrator, and this may reduce the savings of attorneys' fees created by the shorter hearing. A big savings in time and attorneys' fees can come if the parties agree that the decision of the arbitrator will be final. The parties can thereby avoid the great potential expense of an appeal.[34]

The Future Relationship Between the Parties — Litigation discourages communication and encourages distrust.[35] In litigation, the parties are adversaries: one party wins, the other party loses, and victory is reduced to a money judgment. Litigation is likely to increase friction and animosity between the parties. The friction that litigation creates can be especially troublesome in commercial cases in which the parties want to maintain a future business relationship, and in child custody cases in which the parties *must* maintain a future relationship.[36]

---

[32] *See, e.g.*, Jessica Pearson & Nancy Thoennes, *Divorce Mediation: Strengths and Weaknesses Over Time, in* ALTERNATIVE MEANS OF FAMILY DISPUTE RESOLUTION 51, 57-58 (H. Davidson, L. Ray, and R. Horowitz eds. 1982).

[33] *See* Lieberman & Henry, *supra* note 31, at 431.

[34] GOLDBERG, GREEN, & SANDER, *supra* note 25, at 189-90.

[35] *See* Lieberman & Henry, *supra* note 31, at 427.

[36] *See* Lavorato, *supra* note 25 (Iowa Supreme Court Justice, Louis A. Lavorato discusses the damaging nature of litigation in family disputes).

Possibly the greatest value of mediation is that the parties are likely to have a better future relationship after mediation than after litigation.[37] One of the central goals of mediation is to create trust and communication between the parties.[38] Whereas litigation and attorney negotiation are likely to inhibit communication between the parties, one of the things that the mediator does is to try and open up lines of communication so that the parties can better understand one another. Maintaining a good relationship with the opposing party may be important to the client.

Results — The likely result if a client pursues a form of ADR may vary from the likely result if the client pursues litigation. In some cases, ADR is likely to lead to a better result; in some cases to a worse result. Whether in a particular case mediation is likely to lead to a more favorable resolution than litigation or attorney negotiation will depend on the client, the other party, the case, and the mediator. Clients with good negotiation skills, i.e., clients that are intelligent, articulate, forceful, and meticulous, are likely to do well alone in mediation; clients with poor negotiation skills are likely to do poorly. If the parties have had a relationship in which one party has dominated the other party, often the case in a domestic dispute, the dominant party may have a great advantage. The party with the greater knowledge of the subject of the litigation is likely to do better in mediation.[39] Some mediators attempt to equalize the bargaining strengths of the parties, others do not.[40]

In some cases, the results of mediation are likely to be better for both parties than a result reached through litigation or attorney negotiation. The parties may develop a creative compromise through mediation that differs from any remedy a court has the power to provide.[41] Attorneys, of course, may reach a creative compromise through negotiation, but the parties will often be more familiar than their attorneys with the subject matter of the dispute and may be more likely than their attorneys to develop a creative compromise. For example, assume that there is a contract dispute between two commercial parties. In litigation, a court may have only the option of determining which party breached and awarding damages to the other party. In negotiation, the attorneys may be concerned primarily with the dispute at issue and may attempt to settle it somewhere between the likely result if plaintiff wins and the likely result if defendant wins. However, in mediation, the parties may be able to structure a new agreement in a way that will be beneficial to both parties.

---

[37] A study comparing child custody agreements reached through mediation with other child custody arrangements found that a substantially higher number of those that had mediated agreements were in compliance. *See* Pearson & Thoennes, *supra* note 32, at 59.

[38] *See* Lieberman & Henry, *supra* note 31, at 427.

[39] *See* MURRAY, *supra* note 25, at 292.

[40] This advantage may be diminished if the mediator seeks to equalize the power between the parties, however, there is disagreement among mediators over whether this is a proper role for the mediator. *See* FOLBERG & TAYLOR, *supra* note 25, at 185; Lieberman & Henry *supra* note 31, at 431.

[41] Lieberman & Henry *supra* note 31, at 429.

Studies comparing the attitudes of parties toward litigation and mediation show that generally parties are more satisfied with the results they achieve in mediation than litigation.[42] They are more likely to comply with and less likely to litigate over agreements that they have reached through mediation than judgments rendered by courts.[43]

An advantage of arbitration is that an arbitrator may be more likely to give a correct decision than a judge or jury. The parties can choose the arbitrator based on experience, expertise in the subject of the dispute, and reputation for good judgment. The arbitrator's expertise may be especially beneficial if the resolution of the dispute depends on trade custom and usage. In a dispute concerning a complex area of business, it may be in the interest of a client who wants a correct decision to have an arbitrator with a background in the subject area of the dispute.

Privacy — A final advantage to the parties of ADR is privacy. Mediation sessions and arbitration hearings generally are not open to the public. In some jurisdictions, the information the parties convey in the meetings will not be a matter of public record unless the result later becomes the subject of a court proceeding.[44] In other jurisdictions, information conveyed during ADR sessions is confidential as a matter of law. Privacy can be especially important to parties to a domestic dispute, who consider the matters to be discussed to be personal, or to parties to a business dispute, who want to avoid releasing information that might damage their business.[45]

Lack of Procedural Protections — Since mediation often does not rely on rules of law, rules of procedure, or the other protections of the adversarial processes, less powerful individuals and groups may not fare as well under it as under litigation. In litigation, judges may lessen the impact of inequalities, for example by asking questions at trial or inviting *amici* to participate.[46]

As noted previously, arbitration cases generally cannot be appealed; this can be cheaper, but the client loses the protections of the appeal process.[47] As the Eighth Circuit Court of Appeals has stated:

> The present day penchant for arbitration may obscure for many parties who do not have the benefit of hindsight that the arbitration system is an inferior system of justice, structured without due process, rules of evidence, accountability of judgment and rules of law . . . No one ever deemed arbitration successful in labor conflicts because of its superior brand of justice.[48]

---

[42] *See* MURRAY, *supra* note 25, at 248.

[43] *Id.*

[44] *See id.*, at 391.

[45] *See* RISKIN & WESTBROOK, *supra* note 25, at 148.

[46] *See id.*, at 1077.

[47] *See* Pearson, *supra* note 25, at 440.

[48] Stroh Container Company v. Delphi Industries, Inc., 783 F.2d 743, 751 n.12 (8th Cir. 1986).

Lack of Precedent-Making Potential — In addition, cases resolved under ADR do not establish precedent. Some parties may want a case to establish a precedent, especially in public interest litigation; others may not. Removing cases from the judicial system may reduce the ability of the system to develop just rules of law. This can especially be a problem if ADR becomes the predominant route for cases involving the poor. If such cases are not litigated, courts will not be confronted with the opportunity and responsibility to develop precedents that will benefit the disadvantaged.[49] As to many issues, there is a genuine social need for an authoritative interpretation of law. These are factors that the client should consider in deciding whether to pursue ADR. Some clients may want their case to serve as precedent for those facing similar problems in the future.

Note that all of the factors to be considered in making a decision whether to pursue ADR do not point toward pursuing ADR. If ADR is unsuccessful, the client may bear the expenses of pursuing ADR, plus the litigation expenses. If the client is not a good negotiator, he may do poorly mediating a case without the benefit of a lawyer. ADR does not have the procedural protections afforded by the litigation system. If the party wants to establish a legal precedent in the case, ADR is not the answer. Clients should be aware of both the risks and potential benefits of forms of ADR before deciding whether to pursue them. It is your job as an attorney to make sure that the client is able to make an informed choice.

---

[49] *See* Edwards, *supra* note 25, at 679.

CHAPTER 11

DEALING WITH CLIENT-LAWYER DIFFERENCE

§ 11-1. INTRODUCTION

We are a global community. News from around the world flashes instantaneously across multiple media screens. The Internet provides immediate interpersonal connections as well as access to all types of information. Diverse communities exist not only in cyberspace and throughout the world, but even within local neighborhoods. Lawyers are called upon to work with all peoples. Across their differences, what brings people to lawyers is often the same impetus — conflict. Some of these conflicts involve interests and needs and some of these conflicts are created by or accentuated by differences between and among people. In order to competently take on their roles with such a diverse population, lawyers need to increase their cross-cultural understanding.[1]

In addition to becoming familiar with customs and perspectives of people from other countries, lawyers must become aware of the perspectives of many cultural groups in order to relate to diverse people within the United States. Because the goals of interviewing and counseling include building rapport, gathering information, helping clients make decisions, and acting on these decisions, lawyers must be able to create relationships in which clients feel safe to let down their guard and share their stories. The process of creating a secure interpersonal environment for disclosure requires knowledge of others' nonverbal and verbal etiquette.

Assuming the lawyer creates an appropriate environment and the client discloses information, there is still a danger of the lawyer misinterpreting the information if he is not cognizant of cultural concerns and convictions. Without sensitivity to cultural differences, information from and about a client lacks context. Failure to understand differences between lawyer and client will inadvertently undermine effective communication and distort the representation of the client. Knowledge and training can enable people to extend beyond their own perceptual structures in order to relate to others.[2] They can then more easily recognize communication gaps. When lawyers are unable to bridge cultural differences in perception or interpretation, it is useful for them to recognize divergence and to sensitively acknowledge communication gaps rather than to proceed as if the gaps do

---

[1] Earlene Baggett, *Cross-Cultural Legal Counseling,* 18 CREIGHTON L. REV. 1475 (1985).

[2] *See* Don Peters & Martha M. Peters, *Maybe That's Why I Do That: Psychological Type Theory, the Myers-Briggs Type Indicator, and Learning Legal Interviewing,* 35 N.Y.U. L. REV. 169 (1990), *and* Michelle S. Jacobs, *People from the Footnotes: The Missing Element in Client-Centered Counseling,* 27 GOLDEN GATE U. L. REV. 345 (1997).

not exist. Learning about diversity provides lawyers with information they can use in beginning to bridge cultural divides with diverse clients.

§ 11-2. THE IMPACT OF DIFFERENCES ON THE LAWYER-CLIENT RELATIONSHIP

Cultural, racial, ethnic, gender, sexual orientation, disability, religious, socioeconomic status, age, and other differences impact the issues clients bring to lawyers, their perception of events and interactions, and the remedies they seek. These differences compose and focus the lenses through which clients and lawyers experience the world. These lenses are embedded in the identity of people, constructing subjective understandings and forging meanings and interpretations.

These lenses also provide potential barriers to trust that affect both the client's comfort in revealing information and the lawyer's assessment of the client's story. They determine the facility with which the lawyer and client can develop congruent perceptions and interpretations. Whatever the lawyer's own characteristics, she is likely to be called upon in today's world to work with people who are different from herself.[3] These differences call for a sensitivity that only develops with a personal commitment to increase self-awareness and to become acquainted with cultural patterns, world views, and life experiences of diverse populations. This is not merely a matter of race and ethnicity, but of cultural context.

Building rapport with and gathering information from diverse clients requires lawyers to learn new skills. The underlying processes of connecting with clients, building relationships of trust and respect, and using communication strategies to help gather the client's full story and to explore the client's needs and interests apply across all groups and for all individuals.[4] Meeting these basic goals calls for lawyers to draw from different resources when communicating with persons different from the lawyer in personal experience and perceptual framework. The main requirements are

- Awareness of Cultural Encapsulation and its impact on the interviewing and counseling process;

- Sensitivity to different cultural patterns, beliefs, and experiences;

- Empathy to relate others' experiences to shared human understanding; and

- Caution not to stereotype by attributing group preferences to individuals.

---

[3] NICHOLAS A. VACC & LARRY C. LOESCH, A PROFESSIONAL ORIENTATION TO COUNSELING (2d ed. 1993).

[4] Mary A. Fukuyama, *Taking a Universal Approach to Multicultural Counseling,* 30 COUNS. EDUC. & SUPERVISION 6-17 (1990).

§ 11-2(a). CULTURAL ENCAPSULATION

Physical, psychological, social, and cultural dimensions of diversity touch every relationship. The more similar lawyer and client are, the more shared assumptions and meanings they will have. However, in an effort to relate to others it is often natural to assume similarity and to miss differences that influence perceptions and form perspectives about situations, events, and relationships. The first and perhaps greatest challenge in legal interviewing and counseling is to become *aware* of and *sensitive* to personal biases and subjective attitudes that unknowingly affect one's relationship with clients. Without this intimate self-awareness it is easy to rely on assumptions of similarity that result from "cultural encapsulation," a term coined by Wrenn[5] to describe counselors who are not able to adapt their habits, patterns, behaviors, and attitudes when working with diverse clients. By unconsciously applying their own cultural methods and strategies as if they were universal, culturally encapsulated professionals miss the opportunity to address clients in relevant ways.[6]

Clients' perceptions of competence are positively linked to cultural sensitivity, not culture-blind behavior.[7] The perception on the part of the client that the lawyer can comprehend his or her story and perspective is critical to a belief that the lawyer will be able to help the client. A lawyer's lack of awareness to cultural differences or an absence of sensitivity to diverse perspectives can not only threaten rapport, but can also undermine essential trust and respect, creating a risk of silence and withdrawal rather than self-disclosure.[8]

We must therefore work to step outside of our own strong perceptual fields in order to relate to the needs of diverse clients. Even in writing this chapter, we authors are aware that our own cultural learning and personal experiences will structure and limit this discussion. We ask you to extend and challenge your own learned attitudes across cultural, racial, gender, and other differences to apply this information and to thereby enhance your ability to understand your clients' perspectives. Regardless of your individual characteristics and irrespective of your ethnic background, you are likely to represent some clients who are similar to you and some who are different from you. Learning to communicate and work with diverse people is part of a lawyer's job.

---

[5] C. G. Wrenn, *The Culturally Encapsulated Counselor,* 32 HARV. EDUC. REV. 444-449 (1962).

[6] WOODROW M. PARKER, CONSCIOUSNESS-RAISING: A PRIMER FOR MULTICULTURAL COUNSELING (1988).

[7] Teresa D. LaFromboise & David N. Dixon, *American Indian Perception of Trustworthiness in a Counseling Interview,* 28 J. OF COUNS. PSYCHOL., Vol. 28, at 135-139 (1991) (American Indians); Ruth H. Gim et al., *Asian-American Acculturation, Counselor Ethnicity and Cultural Sensitivity, and Ratings of Counselors,* J. OF COUNS. PSYCHOL., Vol. 38, no. 1, at 57-62 (1991); Donald R. Atkinson et al., *Mexican American Acculturation, Counselor Ethnicity and Cultural Sensitivity, on Perceived Counselor Competence,* J. OF COUNS. PSYCHOL., Vol. 39, No. 4, at 515-520 (1992).

[8] Jacobs, *supra* note 2, at 374, 377.

Generally, the more characteristics a person has that are dominant within a society, the harder the person has to work to challenge his own assumptions. On the other hand, minority and subordinate groups must frequently confront the differences between their own cultural learning and the standards of majority and dominant cultures. To participate in a world controlled by a dominant culture one *must* learn the ways of that culture. Whether one goes with or against the dominant culture, one is confronted by the standards of the dominant culture. To survive and progress in the dominant culture, one must be adept at using the nonverbal and verbal patterns of the dominant culture.

It takes work to stay alert to others' perspectives and positions when they are different from one's default patterning. Knowledge of different cultures and perspectives can counter cultural-centrism and create a sensitivity to diversity that helps avoid default patterning by increasing awareness of unspoken processes and by unmasking assumptions that are taken for granted.

Differences inform much of each person's world view — that is, one's position in society influences the way a person sees herself in relation to the world, social institutions, other people, and physical and natural environments.[9] Growing up within a culture provides a person with a world view that frames and defines the meaning of events and actions. Life experiences within diverse societies at times confirm and at times challenge one's world view. This construct is basic to a person's perceptual sorting of information and to their interpretation of events, symbolic data, and personal interactions. Differences in world view affect the ways lawyers and clients converse. A person's world view exists beneath the words of a conversation as if the words were merely the tips of icebergs, with the greater part of the meaning lying below the surface. Much of the "conversation" happens beneath the surface, because clients and lawyers rely on learned verbal and nonverbal content and behaviors in assessing and creating trusting relationships.

Cultural judgment affects every step of the communication process. The process of creating a meaningful pattern of events results in screening in some information and screening out other information. Each person at an event will perceive and record the scene somewhat differently. Communication is based on perceptions. One person attempts to convey content and meaning to another to build a bridge of common understanding. The receiver decodes the information through her or his own screens, adding the flavor of her or his life experiences and personal style. Each of us uses our own cultural and experiential contexts in expressing ourselves and in evaluating another's communication. To some extent, we are each bounded or encapsulated by this personal interpretation.

In order to work effectively with clients, lawyers must be cognizant of their own cultural encapsulation. Clark Cunningham's interaction with

---

[9] DERALD WING SUE & DAVID SUE, COUNSELING THE CULTURALLY DIFFERENT: THEORY AND PRACTICE (2d ed. 1990).

his client Mr. Johnson, discussed in Chapter 2, is an example of the way encapsulation can complicate communication and distort the client's concerns. Cunningham's article also sensitizes each person who reads it to the potential for perceptual distortion due to cultural differences.

§ 11-2(b).   SENSITIVITY TO DIFFERENT CULTURAL RAPPORT-BUILDING RITUALS AND PATTERNS

The importance of the lawyer's relational skills to the client's perception of the lawyer's competency was introduced in Chapter 2. The client will appraise each of these skills in the context of his or her cultural background. The underlying principles will be the same: attending to the client, respecting the client as a human being, being genuine with the client, and putting the client at ease.[10] But there will be differences.

- For example, the informality of using a first name may be too intimate for some world views while others may find first names equalizing, reducing a hierarchical threat.

- Shaking hands is a gesture that varies culturally. In most cultures the right hand is used. In fact, it is a huge affront to offer the left hand or to give something with the left hand to a Moslem. In Asian cultures it may be presumptuous or even rude to offer a hand in greeting.

- The appropriate physical distance between lawyer and client for building rapport depends on the culture.[11] Generally, in white American culture, people seem uncomfortable when others get too close.[12] Hispanics, French, African Americans, Africans, Indonesians, and some others are likely to prefer to converse at a much closer range.[13]

- Making eye contact or averting the eyes are gestures with definite cultural connotations. In the United States, eye contact indicates openness, honesty, and attention to someone. However, there are differences between African Americans and White Americans. African Americans tend to maintain eye contact more when they are speaking and less when they are listening than do White Americans, who maintain eye contact more when they are listening and less when they are speaking.[14] On the other hand, making

---

[10] Fukuyama, *supra* note 4; GERARD EGAN, THE SKILLED HELPER: A PROBLEM MANAGEMENT APPROACH (1994).

[11] *See* SUE & SUE, *supra* note 9. *See also* B. T. HALL, BEYOND CULTURE (1976).

[12] L. Goldman, *Effect of Eye Contact and Distance on the Verbal Reinforcement of Attitude*, 111 J. OF SOC. PSYCH. 73-78 (1980).

[13] J. V. Jensen, *Perspective on Nonverbal Intercultural Communication, in* INTERCULTURAL COMMUNICATIONS: A READER (L. A. Samovar & R. E. Porter eds. 1985).

[14] SUE & SUE, *supra* note 9.

eye contact with someone of perceived higher rank or class is dis-
respectful in some Asian, Middle Eastern, and Native American
societies. Because of the perceived power associated with lawyers
as a professional group, many clients may avoid eye contact.
Nodding the head in different cultures has different meanings. In
some cultures "yes" is expressed by nodding the head from left
shoulder to right shoulder, but in the same plane as the shoulders.
This is similar to a signal of "no" in many western cultures and
may be misunderstood by a lawyer. Appearing warm, reactive, and
animated will not build trust in all cultural contexts. In many
Asian cultures, expression of emotions is considered immature and
a sign of weakness.[15]

Behavioral choices that will build rapport and gather information
require the lawyer to attend to the responses and cues of the client.
Attending to these signals, coupled with having some knowledge of cultural
differences, can help lawyers respond sensitively in rapport-building ways
to clients' nonverbal behavior. It is worthwhile to take the time to learn
about different cultural patterns and expectations, because a lawyer's
knowledge indicates to clients respect for their diversity, interest and concern for them and their identified group, and a commitment to learning
about their culture. When a lawyer is able to acknowledge his limited
acquaintance with the client's cultural protocols, it can signal that he cares
about being respectful to the client and the client's cultural traditions.

Remembering to ask the client about her perception of the meaning of
events, interactions, or symbols rather than assuming that she knows the
meaning is a sign of respect. The client's context gives important information to the lawyer. Similarly, when a client's response is different from that
expected, it is good to *ask* in order to clarify the significance to the client.

While being aware of cultural differences is important, it is also important not to assume them. Individuals do not always identify with their cultural connections. For example, one of the authors' grandfather's family
came from Ireland, but there is little specific to that culture that influences her social interactions. Similarly, many Japanese Americans may
identify more with the generic American culture than with their Japanese
heritage even though their names or facial features reflect their ancestry.

Although many of the differences described here are macro differences,
there are also micro cultural differences. For example, within the United
States there is a large group that might identify itself as historically or
ethnically Hispanic, but within that group there is much cultural diversity
that originates from different regional roots and from the blending of his-
torical traditions with adaptations developed within a dynamic evolving
cultural structure. It would be a mistake to assume only one cultural tradition for such a diverse group.

---

[15] J. Yamamoto & M. Kubota, *The Japanese American Family, in* THE PSYCHOSOCIAL
DEVELOPMENT OF MINORITY GROUP CHILDREN (J. Yamamoto, A. Romero & A. Morales eds.
1983).

Another example of intra-group differences is socioeconomic class difference. Socioeconomic differences operate across all racial and ethnic lines, although there are often differences within socioeconomic groups between different cultural groups.[16] Micro differences affect ways of interacting and the interests, needs, and concerns of clients within these groups.[17] One illustration is the difference in the way people deal with health care or medical emergencies, which is often based on whether one has medical insurance. Upper-class clients, middle-class clients, and working-class clients of different racial and ethnic groups relate to medical emergencies differently because of different resources and accompanying strategies for getting help. The presence or absence of resources is related to socioeconomic class, but the use of home remedies, beliefs in specific health practices, and choice of health providers may vary based on other cultural diversities.

§ 11-3. STEPS TO BECOMING MORE AWARE OF CULTURAL ENCAPSULATION

Becoming aware of one's own racial, cultural, gender, and other biases and attitudes are critical explorations for any lawyer working with clients. Paul Pedersen[18] lists frequent assumptions of those counseling others. The ones identified here seem most relevant to the lawyering context.

- There is a general cultural assumption in the United States that the individual is the basic unit of society and that if the welfare of individuals is provided, the social fabric will thrive. However, in many other countries and in many communities within the United States, the family or social group is the basic building block.

- There is an emphasis on individualism. In western culture, dependence is discouraged, and yet an interdependence within family and community is normal and healthy in many other cultures and some subcultures within the United States. Lawyers in America are likely to start from an assumption that clients are entirely self-focused. Lawyers may incorrectly believe that the individual "should" make decisions and that the best decisions are those that benefit individual clients. However, the needs of a family or the value of continuing relationships may be more important to a client than individual gain. We have observed lawyers strongly influencing clients against the clients' wishes to get the "best" outcome for the clients, not realizing the "best" outcome for

---

[16] One of the authors was challenged with a suggestion by the Urban League of a major eastern city to try to live on a poverty budget of a certain dollar amount. The letter included suggested budget allocations and a menu. At the time the author, who was living on a student budget, was spending no more than the suggested amount, but the menu items and budget allocations were very different, reflecting cultural traditions and class values.

[17] Alexandra Garcia, *Is Health Promotion Relevant Across Cultures and the Socioeconomic Spectrum?* FAMILY & COMMUNITY HEALTH, Supplement 1 to Jan.-Mar. 2006, at 20. Elizabeth D. Carlson et al., *The Black-White Perception Gap and Health Disparities Research*, 21 PUB. HEALTH NURSING 372 (2004).

[18] Paul B. Pedersen, *Ten Frequent Assumptions of Cultural Bias in Counseling.*, 15 J. OF MULTICULTURAL COUNS. & DEV. 16-24 (1987).

the clients may be different from the "best alternative" viewed from the perspective of the lawyer.

- The assumption that problems can be categorized by academic discipline can limit the lawyer to the detriment of clients whose issues often blur the boundaries. This fragmentation of issues into disciplines may impact clients who are operating from more holistic frameworks and traditions.

- The value of linear thinking over nonlinear thinking is an assumption that affects information gathering and decision making. Lawyers who are trained in linear thinking may become impatient with others who do not process their experiences in linear ways. It is easy for someone trained in the value of linear thinking to disregard the value of nonlinear processes. If the lawyer makes this assumption, not only may rapport be damaged, but the whole communication process can be compromised.

- A critical assumption to question is that the "problem" is with the individual and not with the system. The system is part of the cultural encapsulation of those who benefit from it. Questioning the system requires challenging basic cultural rules and processes. It is much easier to assume that the client needs to change than to confront questions about one's cultural context. Clients who are not benefitting from the dominant system may articulate challenges to this system. Lawyers may hear this as whining and dismiss the client instead of asking whether the best interests of the client might be better served by seeking change in the system, even in a small way. Jacobs[19] gives an illustrative example of this process in the account of a lawyer who worked to have lawyers present to explain legal rights to people who were receiving eviction notices. Clients would have been better served had the legal expertise worked to compel landlords to make repairs or to ensure the quality of these repairs. In this situation, the problem needing attention was systemic, not individual.

While any one difference between lawyer and client may disrupt communication and inhibit building a basic relationship of respect and trust, such disruption may be compounded or intensified by multiple differences between client and lawyer. Each difference has the potential of creating additional barriers because there are fewer shared definitions and there is a wider variety of experience, creating greater potential for different interpretations of events and of verbal and nonverbal communication. The more diverse the experience base, the more challenging it may be to build a bridge. On the other hand, sometimes when there are more apparent differences, it is easier for lawyers to recognize the potential for miscommunication. Without vigilance, lawyers may slide into assumptions of shared

---

[19] Michelle S. Jacobs, *Pro Bono Work and Access to Justice for the Poor: Real Change or Imagined Change?*, 48 U. FLA. L. REV. 509, 514 (1996).

subjective realities when they do not exist. Particularly when client and lawyer are both from the United States, but from different regions, social classes, or cultural heritages, there may be false assumptions of similar perception.

The necessary vigilance must be built on a foundation of self-awareness. Understanding one's own cultural perspectives and their impact on attitudes, communications patterns, interactional habits, and cultural assumptions is a beginning. How can one understand the impact of race without awareness of one's own racial identity? Racial identity has been described as an awareness of one's racial heritage and a conscious appreciation of the relationship between one's own racial group and other racial groups. Awareness of one's racial identity is the first step in a developmental process that progresses from a lack of understanding to a positive resolution of racial consciousness with an appreciation and acceptance of all races.[20]

These models indicate that there is individual variation within racial groups as people confront institutional and societal racism and oppression. There is predictably a stronger concept of racial identity for most people of color in the United States than for White Americans.[21] The lack of awareness among White Americans seems to be a byproduct of belonging to a dominant group. The standard of the dominant group is assumed and "others" are defined as different from the dominant standard. For those within the dominant race there may appear to be only individual variation within the group, and they may fail to confront issues of their own race. These developmental attitudes and beliefs influence lawyers' and clients' communication, particularly if they are from different racial groups.

§ 11-3(a). EXPECTATIONS

Lawyers' perceptions of their clients — influenced by culture, race, ethnicity, gender, class, and other attributes — can alter their expectations of the success of a case.[22] Expectations of success affect actual outcomes. Therefore, lawyers' cultural evaluations of their clients, beyond even the facts of the clients' cases or the communication of their needs and interests, have consequences for the clients. Awareness is the first step in changing the often unspoken and unquestioned evaluations that influence the behavior of lawyers.

People quickly assess each other in a number of different and mostly unconscious ways. The external presentation of the client and the lawyer is often the first layer of this process. What the person is wearing or not

---

[20] J.E. HELMS, BLACK & WHITE RACIAL IDENTITY: THEORY, RESEARCH, AND PRACTICE (1990). *See also* SUE & SUE, *supra* note 9.

[21] Haresh B. Sabnani, Joseph G. Ponterotto & Lisa G. Borodovsky, *White Racial Identity Development and Cross-Cultural Counselor Training: A Stage Model,* 19 THE COUNSELING PSYCHOLOGIST 76 (1991).

[22] Jacobs, *supra* note 2.

wearing, their jewelry or lack of jewelry, and the appropriateness of these for the context of the meeting are all cultural judgments. Haircut and style, adornment of fingernails, tatoos, body piercing, and makeup are some of a person's statement of group association. We notice the state of the person — hair combed or not, shaven or not, indications of stress or calm — as part of our impression. Smells are also part of the impression: perfume; soap and shampoo; cigarette, cigar, or pipe smells; food odors; and body fragrance. We match these against sensory and style cues that are familiar and those we have learned to value or to evaluate as distasteful.

People tend to evaluate the language or dialect of a person against a cultural standard in which different is seldom better. Voice quality, tone, and loudness are other clues about a person. One may use the congruency of tone or emotional expression with verbal content to evaluate truth and determine importance. These interpretations are based on the evaluator's cultural learning. There is much evidence that people attend better and faster to some of these characteristics than others and that a person's expectation influences personal performance as well as the responses of others. Again, self-awareness is a key. We can modify our reactions once we are aware of our less conscious, culturally learned reactions.

Another expectation that affects the lawyer-client relationship is the lawyer's perception of her role. Role development is influenced by observing others in this role. The lawyers you know, including your law professors, are models. Books, newspapers, magazines, television, and movies provide other models that influence this personal construct. Whether you seriously consider what is written in this chapter or in this book will depend partly on your own preconceptions of the role of lawyers, how concrete and clear your view of lawyering is, and how consistent the material in this book is with your view of the role of lawyers. In your perception of your role as a lawyer, what is the power relationship between you and the client? Who is in charge? What are the responsibilities of each? How does this change with the culture, race, gender, ethnicity, sexual orientation, age, class, or other individual characteristics of clients? Do you know yourself well enough to be aware if it did change?

It is important to remember that the client is also assessing the lawyer on the same kinds of cultural criteria. The client measures the lawyer against images and expectations. The client is also gathering information and assessing rapport. Everything the client sees and hears in the law office will be part of an impression of the lawyer. Clients form beliefs about lawyer-client working roles from previous personal contact with lawyers or from stories or descriptions of associates', friends', or family members' experiences with lawyers. Lawyers in the news, portrayals of lawyers and law firms in television series, and book and movie stories of lawyers all affect expectations. These impressions of lawyering roles influence clients' expectations of the relationship before meeting or speaking with you.

All these expectations will be weighed against the client's actual experience in meeting you. The client will notice how you treat your assistants, the state of your desk, and most of all, your reaction to him. Clients want to know you can relate to them. They want to feel they are a priority for you and that you care about their issues. They need to see you as competent. The client will be observing to decide if you are a person to be trusted with important, perhaps delicate, information.

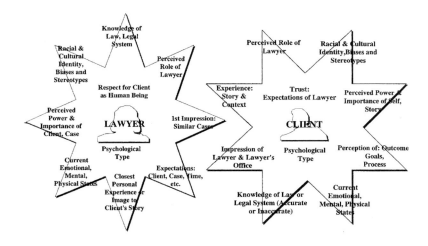

___

The Perceptual Fields of Lawyer and Client: Both lawyer and client bring expectations and history that influence the development of their relationship. Each will be consciously aware of only some of these factors.

Specific issues and needs motivate clients to contact a lawyer. These issues also create emotional responses in clients. Fear, stress, or defensiveness may be caused by the issues that motivate the client to contact the lawyer. They may also be influenced by preconceptions about lawyers. Clients assess the lawyer's skill partly on how well the lawyer can hear and understand the client's emotions.[23] Responding to emotions has both personal and cultural features. Unfortunately, the almost exclusive emphasis on analysis and rational thinking in many law schools dismisses the importance of emotions and the accompanying information.[24] Focusing on facts while blocking or skirting emotions may protect the lawyer from the discomfort of emotions, but may also separate the lawyer from the client. Michael Josephson[25] postulates that the excessive focus on analysis and denial of emotions in law practice has led to a societal anger that expresses itself in lawyer jokes that cast lawyers as cold and uncaring. Whether for the purposes of building rapport, gathering full information, or being seen as competent and skillful, learning to

___

[23] Stephen Feldman & Kent Wilson, *The Value of Interpersonal Skills in Lawyering*, 5 LAW & HUM. BEHAV. 311, 320 (1981).

[24] Martha M. Peters, *Bridging Troubled Waters: Academic Support's Role in Teaching and Modeling "Helping" in Legal Education*, 31 U.S.F. L. REV. 861, 864 (1997).

[25] Michael Josephson, *Unloved Lawyers: We Protect Rights and Safeguard the Legal System, So Why Don't People Like Us?*, 9 T. M. COOLEY L. REV. 293, 293-300 (1992).

understand emotional expression and developing comfort with emotional responses are part of being an effective lawyer.

For both the lawyer and the client, a first meeting can be laden with cultural learning. Although there may be only two people in the room, this means that there are two people *and* the personal and cultural history of each present. It takes conscious work to step outside of prejudgments and cultural conceptions, to meet a client as an individual, and to hear the client's story within the client's context. This work does not end with the first meeting, but continues throughout the lawyer-client relationship.

While nonverbal and verbal patterns are culturally learned, the influence of culture and personal world view goes beyond these patterns and permeates the meeting between client and lawyer, in the meanings given to the client's story by both client and lawyer and in the dynamic of the client-lawyer exchange. It is important to note that part of this influence extends beyond the essence of the individual's culture to the interactions between other cultural groups and the individual's cultural group. Dominant and minority clients frequently have had different experiences in encounters with members of other groups that relate to their dominant or minority status in the larger society. These interactions with individuals and with groups influence their interpretations of symbols and events. The client may or may not explicitly express these perspectives to the lawyer, but these beliefs are active factors in the rendering of the client's story and in the client's assessment of the lawyer's response.

Sociopolitical forces have affected minority races and cultures differently than majority races and cultures. Dominant races, genders, and cultures have very different sociopolitical experiences from those groups who are less influential or powerful. These differences may create incompatible interpretations of events and interactions, and when views expressed by lawyers match the views of the dominant group and conflict with the world view of the client, there is likely to be a breakdown in rapport and trust.

Such a breakdown in the lawyer-client relationship can put distance between lawyers and their clients and can leave clients feeling disempowered. Clients who feel disempowered may limit how much of their story they tell.[26] Thus, the perceptual divide that can result from the differing sociopolitical experiences and worldviews of lawyers and their clients can challenge lawyers' attempts to build the level of trust that is necessary for the type of collaborative client-lawyer teamwork that shares information and decision-making responsibilities.

When lawyers find their perceptions differ from those of clients, it is important to know when and how to challenge those differences. If the lawyer is in a rapport-building phase and does not yet have enough "capital" to challenge the client without risking trust, it is critically important that the lawyer be genuine with the client. That means that the lawyer

---

[26] Austin Sarat & William L. F. Felstiner, *Law and Strategy in the Divorce Lawyer's Office*, 20 LAW AND SOC'Y REV. 93 (1986).

must be honest and accurate in her response to the client. It is possible for a lawyer to acknowledge that the feelings, perceptions, values, and interpretations of her client are valid experiences without accepting them as her own — that is, a lawyer can agree that a client's description of the way he experiences the world is truly his experience without joining him in that perception.

§ 11-3(b). EMPATHY

The ability to relate to the client beyond cultural differences depends on the lawyer's ability to experience empathy. Empathy means being able to put oneself in the place of another. Empathy is a way for a lawyer to transcend differences by using his own humanness to understand the experiences of another. When a lawyer adopts an empathetic approach to a client, it means that, while he is aware of and values differences, he also looks beyond those differences to life experiences that can provide insight into the client's concerns, emotions, and choices. It is important for lawyers and law students to develop empathy in order to relate well to diverse clients.[27]

While it is important for the lawyer to understand clients, particularly across diverse cultures, it can be difficult for the lawyer to relate to a client's experience with respect for the client, especially when the lawyer may not respect the client's choices or behaviors. Empathy enables the lawyer to relate to clients genuinely. When the lawyer reflects on similar personal emotional reactions or personal life experiences, she may be able to connect to the client's experience on the level of shared human experiences.

However, the ability to empathize with clients does not remove the lawyer's need to be objective. The good lawyer brings both empathy and detachment to the relationship. She must keep a part of her evaluative process separate to observe and monitor the client's story and responses. It is important to be aware of discrepancies between one's own expectations and the client's responses as well as inconsistencies in the client's story or incongruence between the story and the nonverbal presentation. These are areas that need to be explored. The lawyer may experience a hunch or feeling that something is not right or that the person is telling the truth even when actual evidence contradicts his statements. These inconsistencies may indicate that you, the lawyer, are misunderstanding cultural cues or judging within your own framework and losing information; they may indicate that there is a part of the story that is difficult for the client to tell you; they may indicate the client is skirting around the truth; or they may tell you that something needs further clarification.

---

[27] *See* John L. Barkai & Virginia O. Fine, *Empathy Training for Lawyers and Law Students,* 13 Sw. U. L. Rev. 505, 526-7 (1983) (indicating that with instruction there was an increase in empathy as measured by the Truax Accurate Empathy Scale).

Sue and Sue[28] suggest a number of skills that can help lawyers who are interviewing and counseling diverse clients:

- Develop an array of verbal and nonverbal responses to give you flexibility in working with your clients. Minority groups may delineate problems differently than dominant cultural groups, and having a variety of encouragers and questioning strategies, as well as using silence sensitively, may help you get a handle on the full extent of the client's problem.

- Practice sending and receiving verbal and nonverbal messages. In sending a message, the goal is to have your meaning appropriately conveyed and accurately understood. One way to check on accuracy is to ask. "Ms. Lopez, I want to make sure I have communicated the process we will follow accurately. Would you, please, tell me, in your own words what you understood me to say?" Similarly, in receiving information, a content reflection to the client can clarify that you accurately understood. Use yourself as a monitor. When there is verbal or nonverbal communication that confuses you or that seems unexpected, ask your client. It is okay for you to not understand something your client is communicating during your appointment, but it is preferable not to have the client leave the interview or counseling session with *either of you* still feeling confused.

- Clarify with your client. A culturally skilled lawyer can be a helper. Your client may need more than legal advice. A client from a marginalized group may need help negotiating the system. As a lawyer you are within society's "system." Your educational background and all that got you to law school indicates that you can negotiate life systems. Your client may need help connecting to other helpers or understanding the ins and outs of societal structures.

- Be aware of your own limits and anticipate their impact on your client. Perfection is not an option, so knowing your weaknesses and areas of ignorance will be critical. Being able to recognize and admit limitations is an important signal of genuineness, openness, and honesty. Clients are then able to "help" you understand and give you information. This is an equalizing experience and can build an awareness in the client that the counseling process is a collaborative effort and that the client, as well as the lawyer, has something to contribute to the process.

The material people bring to lawyers is often intimate and interwoven with emotional meaning. Because lawyers are often challenged to perceive from the client's perspective, the ability to be empathetic and culturally sensitive is important to developing an effective lawyer-client relationship. As we noted earlier, cultural awareness conveys respect and helps clients feel safe enough to reveal their own experiences to their lawyers. Being culturally sensitive is much more useful than being culture blind.[29]

---

[28] SUE & SUE, *supra* note 9.

[29] Jacobs, *supra* note 2.

§ 11-4. CAUTION NOT TO STEREOTYPE BY ATTRIBUTING GROUP PREFERENCES TO INDIVIDUALS

Armed with self-awareness and some sensitivity to other cultures, the lawyer can engage in the initial contact with diverse clients without risking damage to rapport. Even then, there are hidden traps; it is important for the lawyer to know something of other cultures without stereotyping or assuming that a person shares the culturally defined attributes of his or her group. A client, although originating from a different group from the lawyer, may have learned the lawyer's or the dominant culture's nonverbal and verbal patterns and adopted these behaviors and attitudes. Building rapport requires approaching each client with respect and with a willingness to learn about the client as an individual who may or may not align with the general attitudes and values of his or her cultural group.

Stereotyping is a byproduct of the tendency to generalize. Stereotyping generally measures one group against the standards of another, yielding unfavorable comparisons for the different group. This process limits the ability of one to perceive other groups and individuals accurately and can lead to misinterpretations and rigid, negative attitudes that influence future perceptions of and behaviors toward a group or its members.[30] First impressions tend to create a stereotype both for the client and the lawyer. For both, continuing communication can develop a broader information base that includes understanding each person as a complex and unique individual. When this does not happen, the results can lead to some of the following behaviors described by J. A. Axelson.[31]

- *Patronizing the client:* This happens when the lawyer takes a superior position to the client and attempts to influence the client from this power position. When there are communication difficulties, lawyers must not attribute these differences in language or perception to a deficit on the part of the client and move into a role that presumes the client is less capable.

- *Insensitivity to the client's individuality:* This describes a process of treating a client as a member of a group rather than as an autonomous person. Unless the client is consulting the lawyer as part of a class action, the assumption of stereotypical group attributes over individual needs, interests, and concerns is demeaning, damages rapport, and decreases the amount of information the lawyer will either receive or comprehend.

- *Inability to relate to or understand the client:* This will be translated by the client as disbelief of his or her experiences. This happens most often when the lawyer's experience and the client's experience and world views are incongruent. Lawyers can guard

---

[30] J. A. Axelson, Counseling and Development in a Multicultural Society (1985).

[31] *Id.*

against prematurely judging the client's experience by staying in the information-gathering mode. The lawyer can further explore the experience through funnel questioning. (Discussed in Chapter 6) The lawyer must exercise caution to continue to gather data and not to move into challenging the client in an untimely interruption or with a cross-examination method.

§ 11-5.   DO'S AND DON'TS

- **Do attend to nonverbal information.**

- **Do be sensitive to the potential of cultural diversity even when there is no obvious cue.**

- **Do monitor yourself so that you do not fall into stereotyping clients.**

- **Do be genuine.**

- **Do clarify.**

- **Do use a written form with clients for elaborating on confidentiality and fee structures.** This is particularly valuable with clients whose primary cultural orientation, first language, or citizenship is different from the lawyer's. With all clients the key is to keep written forms simple and clear. Each profession has its own culture and language that creeps into any use of language. Taking the time to make sure that the forms used in your office are clear and to the point presents you to the client as straightforward and someone with whom the client can communicate. Forms that use the language of legal jargon will send different messages to clients than the ones you may intend. Allowing clients to take forms or documents with them means that these clients may consult those in their family or friendship circles whom they trust. For some clients and some issues, decisions may be made by a family group, not only by the individual with whom you are working most directly. Your openness to this process often builds rapport and trust. It is also particularly important to check with the client to make sure the client's interpretation of written materials matches yours. This can be a testing ground on which to measure some types of potential distance between you and your client.

- **Do not use humor inappropriately.** Be very cautious with the use of humor. It is one of the most difficult forms of communication to translate accurately across cultural contexts. We are accustomed to breaking tension with humor, so there may be a tendency to "lighten up the interaction" with a joke, a play on words, a twist on the situation that may seem funny to you. This is potential quicksand. It is very easy for a joke to seem to be at the expense of the client or the client's problem. One rule of thumb is to never make a joke about any group of which you are not an acknowledged member. However, there is then the possibility that your humor, aimed at yourself, could be seen as a lack of personal confidence.

- **Do realize that cultural diversity not only poses a challenge for building lawyer-client rapport, but also damages clients when differences are not understood and valued by legal decision-makers.** For example, maintaining eye contact is part of being truthful in the dominant cultures of the United States. Since direct eye contact is a sign of disrespect in some cultures, a client may look down or away from a judge when being directly questioned or when being addressed by lawyers before juries. Without realizing the cultural background of this nonverbal behavior, judges and jurors may interpret this as a lack of honesty.[32] Since most people give greater weight to what is done than what is said, most people process this nonverbal dissonance without addressing it directly — to the detriment of a client who has not learned the nonverbal signals of the dominant culture. It is the responsibility of lawyers who practice in diverse societies to become familiar with dimensions of diversity in order to bridge the cultural differences, build rapport, and present clients accurately to legal decision makers.

- **Do not be afraid to ask.** There is nothing more dangerous than a question you thought about and did not ask. When you think of a question, something within the client's story or the absence of something you expected to hear is generally the origin. Ask yourself why you are avoiding the question. If you are avoiding the question out of concern for damaging rapport, you may need to wait until later in the interview to ask your question or you may need to take special care with phrasing the question. It is important to ask questions in order to effectively represent your client. It is also important to ask respectfully and with the attitude of collaboration.

- **Do engage in role plays.** Role playing gives practice and increases skills development in a variety of settings and can be useful in learning to understand others' experiences.[33] Having the opportunity to engage with others in concrete situations whether provided by role playing or in actual life contacts helps make the experiences of others more real. Role playing also allows students to try out new behaviors by creating a situation where people can make mistakes safely and constructively learn from them. The development of all skills requires practice and simulation, and role playing opportunities provide solid contexts for learning.

- **Do increase personal contact with diverse communities.** This increases knowledge and decreases discomfort. This is not an

---

[32] Don Peters, *You Can't Always Get What You Want: Organizing Matrimonial Interviews to Get What You Need,* 26 CAL. W. L. REV. (1990).

[33] Carrie Menkel-Meadow, *Is Altruism Possible in Lawyering?,* 8 GA. ST. L. REV. 416 (1992). Menkel-Meadow argues that the most effective way to understand others is through participation in concrete situations provided by actual life settings, or in role-playing or simulation-based teaching.

easy process and can produce humility. One of the authors recalls a situation in which a small amount of courage would have gone a long way. A few of the white members of the law school community attended a predominantly African American church in order to participate in a worship service conducted by one of the ministers who was a personal friend. Near the end of the service visitors were invited to introduce themselves. Wanting to be "inconspicuous" and feeling somewhat uncomfortable with the customs in this different setting, the visitors did not stand and introduce themselves. Of course, there was no way to be "inconspicuous." The visitors appeared to be unsociable. However, upon attending services on later occasions, comfort increased, and the visitors introduced themselves. Learning did take place. The "awkwardness" of accepting and acknowledging racial difference disappeared with repeated visits to the church, but the only way to get past the awkwardness was to experience it and work through it.

- **Do seek cross-cultural training.** Student counseling centers or student services offices often sponsor multicultural training for individuals and groups. Many resources are available, just waiting to be discovered. Jacobs recommends one that would provide cross-cultural lawyer and student self-awareness training (CCLASS).[34]

- **Do expose yourself to broad cultural opportunities.** Books, both non-fiction and fiction, are a way to learn. Develop a culturally diverse reading list. Of course, as with any area, one book or books by one author will not be sufficient to express the diversity or subtleties of a culture, but each can teach you something. One caution: Be aware of stereotyping. Learning to recognize this tendency to generalize is, in itself, educational. Films are another way to learn of other cultures. Many wonderful films provide insight into different cultures, and some deal with the challenges of interacting across cultures. Also keep an eye out for cultural events sponsored by different interest groups in your school or community. Mutual sharing with classmates can enhance communication and learning.

§ 11-6.   SUMMARY

Lawyers need to be able to work with all people. There are many ways that people differ. Some of the people with whom a lawyer works — both colleagues and clients — will be similar to the lawyer and some will be different. Cultural encapsulation, or being unaware of the ways one's own culture influences beliefs, values, experiences of the world, and interactions with others, is natural. However, unchecked cultural encapsulation can impede effective interviewing and counseling.

Communication across differences requires attention because cultural learning is so intimate to the person that it is sometimes difficult to

---

[34] Jacobs, *supra* note 2, at 405.

recognize and identify miscommunications as having cultural origins. The more one is acculturated into the dominant group, the harder it is to recognize cultural components to interactions. The group standard becomes the norm. Therefore, lawyers who are from dominant groups may need to work harder to be aware of communication differences. Sensitivity to different cultural patterns, beliefs, and experiences is important because it enables lawyers to understand clients and relate to their interests, needs, and goals.

The development of empathy — the ability to relate to others' experiences on the basis of shared human understanding — is a way to bridge the gap across differences. This important human ability can be learned through experience — either real experience or that attained through role playing.

In learning about diversity and becoming sensitive to others, it is important for lawyers to remember that each client is an individual. While clients and cases may be similar, a good lawyer looks for what is unique in clients and their cases and avoids the tendency to stereotype. One way to combat this tendency is to learn about other cultures. This knowledge of diverse groups will make it easier for lawyers to relate to clients.

CHAPTER 12

LAWYERS, CLIENTS, AND PSYCHOLOGICAL TYPE THEORY

§ 12-1. INTRODUCTION

At first glance, Carl Jung's psychological types[1] theory may seem to belong in a psychology text and not in a practically oriented legal interviewing and counseling book. However, "practical" describes what works, and type theory works. Use of type theory increases effective communication with clients, colleagues, and others. In order to apply this theory to interviewing and counseling, it is necessary to understand the terminology and essence of Jung's theory. Once you are acquainted with the basics, we will apply this theory to the collaborative model of interviewing and counseling.

§ 12-2. AN OVERVIEW OF PSYCHOLOGICAL TYPE THEORY

Jung's theory explains three opposing ways of being that influence lawyers and clients as they communicate with each other and make collaborative decisions about clients' problems and the possible solutions or strategies they will pursue. Each of these three ways of being describes a different process and contrasts two approaches. People use all six of these processes, but their natural preference for a particular approach to each of these three ways of being can influence their perception, assessment, emphasis, and transmission of information. Understanding the influence of these psychological type dimensions increases effective collaboration through increasing lawyers' ability to monitor their own responses and biases and by providing insights into clients' ways of operating that build rapport and appreciation for clients' perspectives.

Two of these dichotomous ways of being describe the basic mental functions of perception, gathering and processing information, and judgment, evaluating information and making decisions.[2] The third dimension is an *attitude* that directs the ways we use these mental functions. Each of these dimensions has a direct influence on lawyers and clients as they engage in legal interviewing and counseling.

Perception describes ways of gathering, using, and storing information — the essence of the process of a legal interview. The perceptual process engages when the lawyer is gathering information and using it to build

---

[1] C. G. Jung (1921/1971). Psychological Types (H. G. Baynes, trans. Revised by R. F. C. Hull). Volume 5 of The Collected Works of C. G. Jung. Princeton, NJ: Princeton University Press. (Original work published in 1921.)

[2] Isabel Briggs Myers (With Peter B. Myers), Gifts Differing (1980).

rapport and to learn and understand clients' stories. However, the mental function of judgment is also operating as lawyers assess the nonverbal and verbal information provided by clients to learn about their situations, needs, and goals. This judgment function is a rational appraisal process that, while used in interviewing, is more apparent in legal counseling when lawyers and clients examine options and strategies. This process of evaluating generates more information through clarification of interests and goals. To summarize, the purpose of interviewing — gathering information — primarily requires use of the perception function and uses the judgment function secondarily. Counseling primarily uses the judgment function and secondarily uses the perception function. Lawyers must move flexibly between judgment and perception so that the two processes are used in both interviewing and counseling.

The third category, or scale, delineated by Jung, the *attitude*, or direction of energy scale, indicates a person's favorite field of attention — either an internal focus in the field of ideas and reflection, or an external focus in the outer field of people and actions. This dimension describes the location and manner in which the mental functions are used and relates to ways clients and lawyers draw upon, communicate, and apply information throughout this collaborative deliberation process.

Jung's theory is the basic construct of the Myers-Briggs Type Indicator (MBTI), an instrument designed by Isabel Briggs Myers and Katharine Cook Briggs to help identify psychological type.[3] The MBTI contributes a constructive framework for understanding Jung's descriptions of these different ways of being. It also develops and uses a fourth scale which is implicit in Jung's theory in order to identify the dynamics Jung described as occurring among the functions and in their different expressions in the directions of energy. This scale describes *lifestyle* orientations, defining them as ways people organize themselves in the physical world and the ways people appear to others. This orientation also influences the lawyer-client collaborative deliberation process during interviews and counseling sessions. Lifestyle influences the choice to continue gathering information or to move to closure with strategic decisions. It also influences perceptions of time and deadlines as well as tendencies toward structure or flexibility in all aspects of communication.

As you read the following descriptions of the different preference scales from Jung's theory as expressed through the structure of the MBTI,[4] you may find yourself guessing at your type. As you work to understand each

---

[3] Mary H. McCaulley, *The Myers-Briggs Type Indicator in Counseling*, Chapter 5 of TESTING IN COUNSELING PRACTICE (C. Edward Watkins, Jr. and Vicki L. Campbell eds., 1990).

[4] ISABEL BRIGGS MYERS & MARY H. MCCAULLEY, MANUAL: A GUIDE TO THE DEVELOPMENT AND USE OF THE MYERS-BRIGGS TYPE INDICATOR (2d ed. 1985) [Hereinafter cited as MBTI MANUAL (2d ed.)]; ISABEL BRIGGS MYERS, MARY H. MCCAULLEY, NAOMI L. QUENK & ALLEN L. HAMMER, MBTI MANUAL: A GUIDE TO THE DEVELOPMENT AND USE OF THE MYERS-BRIGGS TYPE INDICATOR (3d ed. 1998). [Hereinafter cited as MBTI MANUAL (3d ed.)]. All of the information about the Myers-Briggs Type Indicator relies on the material in these two editions of the MANUAL.

of the contrasting dimensions that make up each scale or way of being, you are likely to find yourself identifying more with one than with the other. It may help for you to think about which characteristics describe your preference when you are "being yourself," when you are not changing yourself for others or for work. This is one way to determine your psychological type.

According to psychological type theory, you will prefer one or the other category that together make up each scale. In this theory, being in the middle is not better nor is it a real option. Jung felt that people are born with a psychological type and that constellation of preferences is consistent over a person's lifetime. Finding one's psychological type preferences can be a challenge. Preferences for some dimensions may be easier to identify than for others. One reason it is sometimes difficult for people to clearly identify all of their preferences is that people must use all of these dimensions daily. Depending on environmental circumstances, it may be necessary to use non-preferred dimensions, frequently developing skills and strategies that will be familiar and can compete with clarity about a preference. For example, a person may have a natural lifestyle preference to explore options and gather information before making decisions. This preference might push the person to put off making decisions or to have difficulty making deadlines that are not clear and definite. However, if the person's supervisor or profession has strong sanctions against those who miss deadlines, the habits of work may override a choice for flexibility that the person would manifest in non-work situations. In determining psychological type, look for the dimension that is easier to use, takes less concentration and effort, and feels more natural than its opposite. Choose the characteristics that best describe you as you most naturally are, not the ones that you most want to develop. This choice becomes a working hypothesis for determining your psychological type.

The MBTI is the basic instrument for determining psychological type and is widely used. If you want to take the Indicator, you will need to find someone with whom to work who is qualified to administer and interpret the instrument with you.[5] For our purposes it is sufficient for you to understand the theory of type and to apply this theory to legal interviewing and counseling.

§ 12-2(a). TWO MENTAL FUNCTIONS: PERCEPTION AND JUDGMENT

Psychological Type Theory describes two basic mental functions or cognitive processes — perception and judgment — and two equally useful and valid ways of accomplishing each.[6] One of the mental functions —

---

[5] Most schools have access to counseling centers with qualified users of the MBTI. You may also call the Center for Applications of Psychological Type in Gainesville, FL or contact their website, http://www.capt.org, or Consulting Psychologists Press, Palo Alto, CA., the publisher of the instrument, for referrals to qualified administrators of the instrument.

[6] MBTI MANUAL (3d ed.), *supra* note 4.

perception — is the process that involves information gathering, use, and storage. Perception uses either a sensing process, which focuses on specific details, practical uses, and sequential learning, or an intuitive process, which focuses on themes and patterns, theoretical constructs, and associative learning processes.[7] People prefer one over the other. People can and do use both, but one process is more natural, more spontaneous, and used more than the other. Perception identifies and describes basic differences in the ways people use mental processes to take in information in legal interviews. Interviewing is a perceptual process focusing on building rapport, which requires attention to the verbal and nonverbal messages of clients. Interviewing requires gathering information through listening to the client's story; using the information to come to a common understanding of the client's story, needs, interests, and goals; and storing information for easy recall when reviewing the case, developing strategies and options, and counseling the client.

The other mental function — judgment — involves evaluation and decision-making. There are two ways of applying a judgment process — thinking or feeling. Thinking judgment is a process involving objective appraisal. When using thinking judgment, a person metaphorically steps outside situations in order to observe them objectively. This process assumes the need for distance to gain perspective and to evaluate information using objective criteria.

When using thinking judgment, lawyers or clients apply classic logic to weigh options against criteria, applying either those criteria established by legal rules or by social policy. The litigation system reflects this form of decision-making, using precedent, rules, and objective standards to determine admissible evidence and using uninvolved evaluators in the form of judges or juries to make decisions. Thinking judgment is what is taught in law school as the traditional form of legal analysis. Most lawyers and some clients prefer to use thinking judgment during interviews and counseling sessions.

Feeling judgment operates differently. Feeling judgment gives priority to options on the basis of values. Feeling judgment requires first stepping into situations and identifying with the people involved, and then evaluating, by determining and prioritizing the values and relationship issues. When using feeling judgment, lawyers and clients look at the principles behind decisions and assess the effect of a decision on involved parties and on relational factors. Feeling judgment assumes that fair treatment requires subjective assessment to identify the needs, values, and interests of the parties. Many of the criteria used in thinking judgment are considered in feeling judgment; however, they are weighed within the context of their influence on client's needs and relationships.

Feeling judgment is reflected in the move toward using mediation for resolving disputes. Mediation encourages parties to interact, either directly or through a mediator, to develop solutions that acknowledge needs and interests. The mediation process provides more flexibility than

---

[7] GORDON D. LAWRENCE, PEOPLE TYPES AND TIGER STRIPES (3d ed. 1993).

litigation, allowing the parties to go outside traditional criteria to solve problems in more subjective ways. It does not emphasize what has worked before, but rather explores how something might work for these parties. Some lawyers and some clients tend to use feeling judgment in assessing options either because it reflects their personality type preferences or because they have developed skills that reflect feeling judgment.

If lawyer and client use the same form of judgment, they often proceed through the counseling session fairly quickly. Because the lawyer's process of analysis and the client's are congruent they may have few conflicting concerns. However, if both of their judgment preferences are for thinking, they are more likely to miss the subjective analysis than if their preferred judgment functions differ or if they share a preference for feeling judgment. When both lawyer and client prefer feeling judgment, they may miss some important aspects supplied by objective analysis. Having one preferred type of judgment or the other does not mean the lawyer will necessarily miss an interest or potential solution, but the lawyer may have to work harder to consider the perspectives inherent in the non-preferred dimension. Both judgment processes are rational operations that consciously evaluate criteria. Both judgment processes are ways people evaluate options and make decisions — the core of legal counseling.

It is unfortunate that Jung chose these words — thinking and feeling — because they have different meanings in common usage. In Jung's use of the terms, thinking judgment uses classical logic methods; feeling judgment is a subjective evaluative process, not to be confused with "having feelings" or with emotional, nonrational decision making. Both people who prefer thinking judgment and people who prefer feeling judgment have feelings. There are times when people, whether they prefer thinking judgment or feeling judgment, make emotional, nonrational decisions. In those cases, decisions are being made without effectively using either process described by the judgment function in Psychological Type Theory. In legal counseling it is useful to call on both processes in order to consider all the options and to make effective decisions. This must be done sequentially since only one of each pair is used at a time.

§ 12-2(b). TWO DIRECTIONS OF ENERGY: EXTRAVERTING OR INTROVERTING

Psychological Type Theory posits that people use at least one of the four mental functions primarily in the outer world of people and things. Type theory calls this extraverting the function — that is, using a mental function in the outer world. When we extravert a function, others see us employing that function as our mental activity. For example, a lawyer using the intuition function in the outer world of counseling a client would likely be generating options, perhaps devising new possibilities even as she explains the ones she had prepared prior to the counseling session. She would be engaged in fitting together pieces (facts, interests, goals) in new ways to create a pattern, plan, or strategy to further the client's goals. A lawyer who is extraverting thinking would look different to the client. That lawyer might present some prepared options, but quickly move to focus on evaluating the options objectively using the client's or society's criteria.

People also use at least one of the mental functions in the inner world of reflection, the realm of thoughts and ideas. In psychological type terms, this internal use of a function is the process of introverting the function. If the lawyer were to introvert sensing perception in an interview of a client, the lawyer would be likely to reflect on the details of the story to enrich the mental picture of what happened and notice the order of the story. She might be noticing the nonverbal behavior of the client and filing that away as part of the information from the interview. A lawyer introverting feeling might be attending to the same information, but focusing somewhat differently on an assessment of the emotional nature of the story and the relational dynamics of involved parties. Evaluations of the relative importance to the client of different parts of her story, interests, or goals might occupy the reflections of this lawyer during the interview. Function preferences influence the follow-up questions the lawyer is likely to ask the client as the interview continues. When a lawyer is introverting a mental function, clients or colleagues will be unaware of this internal process unless they ask or are told by the lawyer. The introverting process is not visible to others.

Just as people prefer one type of perception over the other and one type of judgment over the other, we prefer one direction of energy. Jung described these directions as either an external orientation he called extraversion, or an internal orientation he called introversion. These terms have become part of generally used language, but popular usage has modified the terms from Jung's original definitions and intentions Jung coined the term extravert from the Latin *extra- + vertere*, meaning "to turn out." Similarly, introvert means "to turn in." (His original spelling has also been modified so that we often spell it as "extroversion." The proper spelling of Jung's concept is "extraversion.") These terms were defined by Jung to refer not just to the popular definition of social extraversion or introversion, but to sources of mental and emotional energy and the favored site of the strongest or most preferred mental process, which is called the dominant function.

Extraverts' preferred world is the external stimulation of people and things found in the world around them. They are energized by interactions with others and do their easiest mental processing when they are communicating with another. "Talking through" is their mode of deepening thought. Extraverts respond more quickly than introverts, because they tend to explore ideas by talking about them. Introverts must go inside and process ideas and then come back to an extraverting process to talk about their thoughts. These extra steps take more time; however, their ideas are more refined as a result of the time they spend thinking through ideas.

While introverts can be socially extraverted, performing "life of the party" roles, an extended time of extraverting takes a great deal of energy from introverts. They recharge by spending time alone or in an internally focused process such as reading, thinking, or listening to music. Introverts need to access their internal mode to do work through most mental processes. They need to think about data or evaluate and weigh options internally. When introverts share their thoughts, their comments reflect this internal processing. Introverts bring depth to a discussion or interaction.

People gravitate toward a favorite direction of energy when they have a choice. They use their favorite mental function or process in that direction, either introverting or extraverting. When surprised or unguarded the favorite function is naturally activated in the preferred direction of energy.

In both interviewing and counseling, there are times when it is most appropriate to extravert our mental functions and times when it is most appropriate to introvert our mental functions. When we are talking or expressing ourselves to clients we are extraverting, and when we are listening or thinking we are introverting. In interviewing, when we ask questions and respond to a client's story, we are extraverting. When we listen and attend to a client, pondering and considering rapport, information, or options, we are introverting. A good interviewer has the ability to do both. Each person has a preferred process, but is not limited to using only that preference. It just takes greater effort to use the nonpreferred tendency, particularly when a lawyer is tired or stressed.

§ 12-2(c).   TWO LIFESTYLES

Lifestyles can be either primarily judging or primarily perceiving. The lifestyle preference scale reflects which mental function — judgment or perception — a person extraverts or uses when engaging with people, things, and activities in their external world.[8]

A judging lifestyle influences behaviors that seek order and structure. The person preferring a judging lifestyle likes to make decisions and move to the next challenges. Those who have a judging orientation are inclined to be decisive and somewhat resistant to changing schedules, plans, or decisions. Someone who prefers a judging lifestyle constructs a planned and organized life. He or she accomplishes this by following schedules and having systems that keep materials in the places they belong. Everything important has a place or it is not important and should be sorted into the recycle or trash bin.

Persons who prefer a judging lifestyle like to spend less time gathering information so they can finish one issue efficiently and quickly and then move on to others. Judging prefers a lifestyle that is ordered; decisions are made and followed. Observers see them as orderly, structured, and attentive to time schedules. For people who prefer judging, time is linear, and energy is spaced in regular intervals. These people are generally on time for appointments and sensitive to their own time and to the time of others. They are aware of deadlines and prefer to have their work products completed in a timely way. They are usually more comfortable when their work is completed sufficiently ahead of deadlines so that external factors will not cause them to be rushed. This type of organization can push a lawyer to complete interviews or counseling sessions within allotted time schedules and may create

---

[8] MBTI MANUAL (3d ed.), *supra* note 4, at 6.

stress if clients do not operate with a similar time sensitivity or if more time is needed than has been scheduled for an appointment.

When a person prefers the lifestyle preference perceiving, he likely displays a greater focus on gathering information and exploring new ideas than on coming to conclusions and resolutions. A person preferring a perceiving lifestyle typically demonstrates adaptability by trying different approaches and displaying a willingness to reconsider or change decisions. These are "go with the flow" people and they typically gather a lot of information in an interview. In fact, they may have difficulty ending the information gathering process in interviews. On the other hand, it is a common experience in interviewing and counseling clients that the most critical information is often not disclosed by the client until near the end of an appointment. Lawyers who prefer perceiving may find that accommodating new information in later stages of interviews is natural. They typically can move from later stages in the interviewing process back to open questions as new information arises. Lawyers preferring perceiving may generate more options for clients in counseling sessions, and have a more difficult time moving to closure or evaluation stages without examining all options.

Timing is often an issue for a perceiving lifestyle. Even when they have developed schedules, people who prefer perception may use these more as a general guide than a strict time table because they tend to work in bursts of energy and need to take advantage of these focused times. People who prefer a perceiving lifestyle are seen as spontaneous and as moving flexibly through life. They may create stress for clients and colleagues who have a different preference and may see their flexibility as lack of conviction and their approach to deadlines as bad planning.

§ 12–3.   REFLECTING ON YOUR TYPE PREFERENCES

We have now examined the four preference scales. You may have an idea of what your own type is. If so, you will have chosen four of the eight possibilities as those you prefer and that describe your tendencies and experiences. The first letter of each of your four preference choices makes up a type code. For example, ISTJ is the type code for someone who chooses Introversion, Sensing, Thinking, and Judging. The combinations of these choices make sixteen types. Each type has its own dynamic interaction between the different preferences. In the code, the first letter reflects the person's favored direction of energy — E for extraversion or I for introversion. The second letter is the choice between the two perception functions — S for sensing or N for intuition. (Note that the "I" letter has already been used for introversion.) The third letter reflects the preference of the judgment function — either T for thinking or F for feeling. The fourth letter indicates lifestyle patterns that mirror what a person extraverts, either a J for judging or a P for the perceiving. Each of the sixteen types has its own approaches and ways of negotiating the world. While we can use any of the processes, those that we prefer and their unique interactions compose our psychological type.

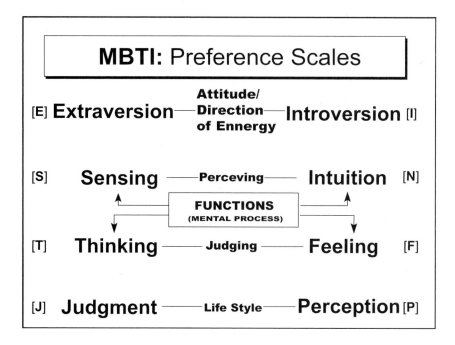

§ 12-4. VALUE OF TYPE KNOWLEDGE

In becoming aware of type theory, we gain self-awareness, which leads to greater control over our own cognitive processes and their expressions. By knowing our natural or habitual behaviors, we can become more purposeful in our choices. When a person identifies her own psychological type, she knows her default mode or basic processing style. This is invaluable information for a lawyer. There are many times when the default mode takes over, particularly when we are pressured, placed in new situations, or surprised. Much of a lawyer's job involves pressure, new situations, and dealing with the unexpected.

This knowledge can also give a better understanding of others, particularly those whose preferences are different from our own. In understanding how and why others make choices and act as they do, most people use themselves as their frame of reference. Unconsciously we assume that others' minds operate on the same principles as our own.[9] Psychological type gives insights into a variety of human processing methods, expanding the frame of reference to include multiple combinations of cognitive processes and their applications to human choices and expressions in human behaviors.

Psychological type preferences are thought to be inborn, like handedness or talents.[10] In this theoretical construct, all preference combinations

---

[9] MBTI MANUAL (2d ed.), *supra* note 4, at 11.
[10] *Id.* at 14.

do not have the same talents, but all have value. Each preference and combination of preferences has strengths and challenges. Together these preferences represent the full range of cognitive processing within both fields of energy applied in organized and flexible lifestyles. For lawyers working with clients, type knowledge can expand their ability to build rapport by sensitizing them to client dynamics. For example, being aware of the different directions of energy, lawyers can be more prepared for clients who process their own thoughts and reactions by talking through their concerns and for clients who need to have time during their interview or counseling session to reflect on their lawyer's questions and suggestions. Collaboration is enhanced when type is added to a lawyer's knowledge of human behavior. In § 12-6 ("The Four Preference Scales Applied to Interviewing and Counseling"), we have included additional applications of type theory to client interactions.

An analogy may help define and describe type. Imagine a working computer. There is a concrete structure to the computer, including the external container, the monitor, the mother board, memory chips, hard drive, sound and video cards, keyboard, mouse, etc. We call this the hardware of the machine, the physical body of the computer, rather like the human body — brain, eyes, ears, nose, mouth, etc. To make the computer work there must also be an operating system that interacts between the hardware and the software. It tells the parts how to gather information, how to store it, how to do complex tasks and to move from one task to another. There are set procedures for shutting down and for moving from one software system to another. The different operating systems sort and process data in their own ways. Psychological type is like the brand of operating system in a computer. In this theory, though, there are sixteen equally competent operating systems. These each have rules about the ways information from the basic physical system is sorted, the way experiences are stored, the structure of meaning, and future access to information. Psychological type organizes decision-making processes, influencing how decisions are made. (Type does not dictate which decisions are made, but it has a default process of analysis.) The factual situations will vary, but the processes for evaluating information and the weight of choice criteria are constant within operating systems and in psychological type. In computers there are backup systems and alternative ways of getting information or making decisions, but these require more time and more effort, just as using non-preferred type influenced skills can require more concentration and patience, but can be learned and practiced for greater ease of access.

While no analogy fits perfectly, the key concept with type is that it functions within each person as a basic system influencing fundamental mental processes and how they are expressed. Therefore, type is an important part of the communication process between lawyers and clients. The type preferences of a client and those of a lawyer do affect the interviewing and counseling processes.

This chapter began by discussing the value of type for self-knowledge. While knowledge of type is useful in dealing with others, its greatest value is for a lawyer's self awareness. If a lawyer can work to develop methods for learning and being that are consistent with his psychological type preferences he will feel confirmed and validated in his personal process. When a lawyer is clear on his own processes it is easier to adapt when clients or environmental factors require different methods than those preferred by the lawyer.[11]

Once conscious of the basic lens of type, this knowledge identifies potential strengths and weaknesses in interactions and helps lawyers to develop hypotheses for modification when communications become blocked or strained with clients and colleagues. Without an understanding of psychological type theory, requests from clients and colleagues for clarification of information or strategies may result in a repetition of the same words spoken louder and slower. However, psychological type theory helps expose that confusion may be resolved more effectively by using a different approach or analysis. Type provides a practical way to identify communication differences and to increase one's options of conveying information and evaluating alternatives. Armed with alternative communication methods, lawyers engaged in the processes of interviewing and counseling gain access to new arenas for collaborative communication and deliberation.[12]

§ 12-5. TYPE AND SKILL DEVELOPMENT

Psychological type development happens throughout a person's life,[13] and the influence of type affects all experiences. While psychological type does not measure or pre-determine skills development, some skills may be easier for one type to acquire than for another. In examining students' questioning and active listening responses in actual legal interviews, one study found that type preferences have an influence on questioning and listening.[14] However, skills development is not tied to type. People of different types can learn skills related to their nonpreferred indices. They may even become more proficient at these skills than someone for whom the skill is more consistent with type preferences, but who has not practiced the skill. Knowledge of type seems to increase the development of skills that are not related to type-predicted strengths. Law students often report having increased patience and persistence once they know the areas that come more easily and those that pose more challenges within the context of type theory.

The tasks and skills involved in legal interviewing and counseling, for example, encompass all eight processes measured by the MBTI and can be

---

[11] Don Peters & Martha M. Peters, *Maybe That's Why I Do That: Psychological Type Theory, the Myers-Briggs Type Indicator and Learning Legal Interviewing*, 35 N.Y. L. REV. 169 (1990).

[12] Peters & Peters, *supra* note 11.

[13] Mary H. McCaulley, *supra* note 3.

[14] Peters & Peters, *supra* note 11, at 184-195, where the authors give numerous examples of type-related interview behaviors.

accomplished by all sixteen types. Each person will prefer half of the processes that are needed and each can learn skills that use the nonpreferred processes. Examining just one of the preference scales — perception — illustrates how legal interviewing activates both processes of perception — sensing and intuition.

Legal interviewing requires a lawyer to pay attention to nonverbal signals from the client. Noting the specifics of the client's demeanor, sound of voice, appearance, comfort distance, eye contact, etc. are sensing strengths. Putting those pieces together into a pattern with implied meaning, such as noting the client's anxious or calm conduct is a combination of the sensory factors and an intuitive process of extracting meaning from a sensory pattern. Similarly, noticing the cold and flat tone of voice with which a client relates information about a particular person may trigger the intuitive to put these details together to hypothesize anger with the person, an avenue to be explored further as the interview develops. Attending to the gathering of known facts from the client's story involves sensing perception. Examining these facts to comprehend meanings, patterns, and implications uses intuition. Listening to the client's story requires the lawyer to stay in the perception mode to gather information. Chapter 2 provides a description of the ways the lawyer can distort the client's case by starting to evaluate the information before the client tells the full story. Asking questions appears to be a perceiving process, but distortion can happen when the form of the questions moves the answers toward conclusions influenced by a switch to one's preferred evaluation mode.

Legal interviewing and counseling and traditional legal analysis require a continual shuttling from specifics to general meanings and back again. Lawyers use sensing perception when dealing with specifics by determining and using facts and details. They use intuitive perception when they construct meanings and perceive implications to develop theories about these specifics. Then they must return to specifics by verifying whether the elements of these general theories exist. Similarly, options in counseling flow from not only the specific, existing legal rules requiring more of the exercise of the sensing function, but also from creative ideas about new ways to proceed from intuition.

Alternation between thinking judgment and feeling judgment occurs when the lawyer helps the client assess options from both an objectively distanced perspective and from a subjectively identified personal perspective. There are times throughout this process that the lawyer extraverts and the client introverts and vice versa. Extraverting and introverting appropriately require discipline and the development of listening and communicating skills.

Lifestyles also influence interviewing and counseling skills. There are times when lawyers must move to closure and when structured decision making is required. However, even beyond the interviewing process, new information may arise that requires lawyers to be flexible and to move from evaluation back to a perception process. It is important for lawyers to be able to make this shift from one process to another. Development of both the movement toward closure and the ability to move flexibly between perception and evaluation are skills for lawyers to develop in their quest to become effective interviewers and counselors.

Of these eight preferences, there is one — thinking judgment — that lawyers use more heavily than the others. Thinking judgment is taught in law school almost exclusively in the form of classical legal analysis. Its impersonal, objective weighing of factors strives to replicate classical logic in evaluating information. Available data suggest that the vast majority of law students — 70% of female law students and 82% of male law students[15] — prefer this type of decision-making. The other type of rational judgment process — feeling judgment, in which choices are ranked on the basis of values, particularly values that reflect their effect on people — is also found in law, but in less obvious and direct ways. Often policy and occasionally judicial decisions use a thinking decision-making structure to validate a rational feeling, value-ordered judgment, particularly when the policy or decision impacts the rights of people and clashes with impersonal, objective precedent.

Once again, a combination of these decision-making preferences facilitates successful law office practice. The general population studies[16] indicate that 50% of the population prefers each of these judgment functions and that, of those, 60% of males prefer thinking and 60% of females prefer feeling judgment. Clients may prefer either form of judgment. Communication may be enhanced with the development of skills that give the lawyer the facility to use both forms of decision-making in counseling clients. Even when the client and lawyer share a preference for thinking judgment, it is a useful exercise for the lawyer to spend time using a feeling judgment analysis to examine the impact of decisions on relationships and to identify subjective consequences and options for the client and other parties.

§ 12-6.   THE FOUR PREFERENCE SCALES APPLIED TO LEGAL INTERVIEWING AND COUNSELING

Since legal interviewing and counseling call on lawyers to use capacities from all eight processes, even though they prefer four, they will find some processes feel more natural and happen spontaneously, while others require conscious attention. Each preference is influenced by the other preferences; so any generalization about one preference must be understood within a range of expressions of that preference.

---

[15] Unpublished study of law student type frequencies gathered in 1984-85 on 602 students at the University of Florida, Levin College of Law, by Martha M. Peters, and sponsored by the Law School Admission Council.

[16] CHARLES R. MARTIN, ESTIMATED FREQUENCIES OF THE TYPES IN THE GENERAL POPULATION [Training Handout, Center for Applications of Psychological Type.] (1995).

Interactions between lawyer and client involve the type influences of both the lawyer and the client, making analysis of type influences quite complex. We will address type influences primarily on lawyers' behaviors since one's own type will be more known and one's own behavior is easier to modify. We will discuss client tendencies in less depth. Our statements are intended to describe general tendencies of type and not to predict any individual lawyer's or client's behavior. Self-knowledge can help any person override his or her type tendencies with purposeful behavioral choices and skills. When we make generalizations related to type it is with the understanding that we are talking of natural tendencies without the intervention of skills training or the decision of the lawyer to change natural tendencies with more effective behavioral choices.

§ 12-6(a). THE PERCEPTION FUNCTIONS: SENSING OR INTUITION

Sensing lawyers tend to ask many more questions than intuitives.[17] They like to get all the facts. If they can restrain themselves through the initial recounting of the client's story and limit themselves to open questions early in the interview, they will be more likely to receive a full story without distortion. Sensors need to look for the themes of the case and beware of too narrowly framing cases. They need to look for implications, for what lies behind the given facts.

Lawyers who prefer sensing like to hear a story in sequence. The first time through, the sensing preferring lawyer may be tempted to stop the client when the client diverges from the sequence of the story. However, there is a benefit to letting the client set the agenda and tell the story in her own sequence. It is important to pay attention to the client's order and ask what you can learn from the client's order of topics. Once the client has told her story, one of the sensing preferring lawyer's strengths is going back and helping the client put the story into sequence and asking questions of the client in order to fill in missing details.

Lawyers preferring intuition may jump ahead of the clients, filling in facts that their clients have not yet told them. Their quick anticipation of the story may take them from the client's story to one they partially create or, more likely, to a story that they later realize is missing details or specific sequential information. These lawyers may err on the side of gathering too little data, since it is their natural tendency to create pictures from small amounts of data.

Lawyers preferring sensing will look to their own experiences to verify clients' stories. "Does this make sense?" means "In my experience could this be true?" Their focus is on present reality. They seek pragmatic problem solving.

Lawyers preferring intuition will look for internal consistency in a story and may be swept away by their own interpretation of the story, missing

---

[17] Peters & Peters, *supra* note 11.

some inconsistent or incongruent aspects of the story if the general theme holds together. These lawyers think very quickly and tend to move to future implications, sometimes missing gaps in the story until they reconstruct it later. Intuitive preferring lawyers may miss nonverbal information that sensing preferring lawyers pick up easily, although they seem better at picking up on implied meanings. Intuitive preferring lawyers may jump quickly into strategies and potential solutions. While these are useful skills, they need to make sure they know all the facts first. Then their penchant for themes and possibilities can benefit the process. One of their strengths is seeing possibilities and constructing theories of the case.

Clients who prefer sensing may get caught up on tangents. It is sometimes difficult for them to sort through all the facts for those that are most important. To sensing clients, all facts may seem equally important. They store information as snapshots. Recall may be stimulated by asking about the sensory experiences related to the snapshot. For example, a lawyer might ask a sensing client, "Recreate the scene for me. Who was standing where? What time of day was it? What were people wearing?" It can also be helpful to cue a sensing client with sequence. "How did this incident begin? What happened next?" Combining physical sensory cues with sequence will be even more powerful for sensing clients. Be aware that this client will be looking for pragmatic and practical solutions that give him or her something tangible in the present. These clients may prefer things to revert to the way that worked before, as opposed to finding a new method. These clients are likely to want to have all the details spelled out, including the steps of the legal process.

Clients who prefer intuition may skip over facts and give general themes. They may edit out facts that conflict with the way they want to see the story without being aware that they have reconstructed the information in the story. They store their information by associations and may inadvertently fail to recall information if questions do not trigger the relevant association. Sharing strategies may influence them to bend facts to fit, rather than having the facts dictate the strategies, because the strategy may become a consistent frame and the associational structure for the client's memory. These clients will generally appreciate new and creative solutions as long as the principles underlying their goals are not compromised. They may be helped with alternative ways of framing solutions by using appropriate analogies. Even though some pragmatic outcomes may meet these clients' stated goals, they will be particularly sensitive to symbolic meanings that could undermine a pragmatic resolution. They may care a lot about potential future outcomes and need to know what the future steps will be if the settlement breaks down.

§ 12-6(b).   THE JUDGMENT FUNCTIONS: THINKING OR FEELING

Most lawyers prefer thinking judgment. It is the process that is most in evidence in the legal system and in legal training. Their strength is their kinship with this evaluation and decision-making process. Their weakness is the same. The thinking judgment process has been so reinforced that it is difficult for thinking preferring lawyers to understand the value of feeling judgment. When confronted with clients who use feeling judgment, there may be conflicts over the "rational" decision or the "best" decision. The thinking judgment lawyer's process is objective. He steps back from the information to evaluate it logically using set criteria. These lawyers critique spontaneously, so it is their natural tendency to question the strength of a case, to push clients on weak points. This can be a useful process, *but may strain rapport.*

Lawyers who prefer feeling judgment are usually also skilled at thinking judgment. They have had to learn the steps and procedures of this mental system in order to negotiate legal education. Their strength is in being able to also use feeling judgment, including evaluating a situation subjectively from the client's perspective and from the perspectives of the other parties. This is particularly helpful during legal counseling sessions. These lawyers also seem particularly skilled at learning listening skills and facilitative interventions.[18] They tend to spontaneously appreciate clients, but they run the risk of over-identifying with their clients. They can have difficulty standing back and objectively critiquing the case or challenging the client on difficult issues or inconsistent facts. They will look for solutions that meet the needs of their client.

For both thinking preferring and feeling preferring clients, it is useful for the lawyer to consider subjective, values-oriented evaluation and decision-making. For example, a client who prefers thinking analysis may miss the personal and relationship issues and be surprised later when there are negative consequences that last beyond the legal battle. For a client who prefers feeling judgment, it is important to have the lawyer use the client's type of analysis in evaluating issues because that method is easier for the client to follow and the client will be more comfortable with the decision.

Clients who prefer thinking judgment may be more comfortable with legal analysis and what are likely to be their lawyer's thinking judgment processes. They are more likely to appreciate an objective assessment and a counseling model that pushes for impersonal and logical evaluation of consequences and standards. Lawyers may need to push these clients to see the subjective feeling judgment analysis, particularly in order to understand the impact of decisions on other parties. Decisions in the law office are likely to have an impact on future relationships that may be important to the client but that the thinking preferring client may miss.

Clients who prefer feeling judgment may find the system of using precedent and objective standards cold and impersonal. They may feel disillusioned by systematic failure of the system to address individual needs or to structure solutions that meet the needs of the people involved. They like to witness and experience justice that addresses issues that affect people.

---

[18] Peters & Peters, *supra* note 11, at 192.

The lawyer may have to work hard to enable this client to understand what the "objective" legal system is likely to do with her case. Mediation may be an especially effective direction to move in for these clients, because it can enable the parties to create a solution that meets the needs of both parties, irrespective of what the law might have provided them.

§ 12-6(c). DIRECTION OF ENERGY: EXTRAVERSION OR INTROVERSION

Extraverted lawyers bring considerable energy to their interactions with clients. Since the external world is their favorite setting, it is natural for them to work through information out loud. Extraverts must monitor a desire to jump into the client's narrative with questions or comments that disrupt the flow of the client's recollections. Interruptions and interjections, although aimed at gathering additional information, may change topics and skew or distort the client's associations and memories. Note the number of ways lawyers' questions and interruptions caused distortions in Chapter 4.

Quick responses to clients may result in questions that are less purposeful and more directive. Learning to stay with open-ended questions, particularly as clients tell their stories, is a skill extraverts may need to learn.[19] Brainstorming is a strength of the extravert's tendency to think out loud. This collaborative process can help lawyers during the counseling process to engage their clients in generating options. Extraverted intuitives have a natural talent for this procedure.

Extraverts may be challenged by silences, particularly emotional pauses. They may be tempted to respond or interject content or humor in order to break emotional tensions. Often this is an ineffective response. Honoring silence in emotional contexts is respectful and allows the client to continue narrating difficult revelations. A nonverbal acknowledgment, a minimal encourager such as "yes," or other brief verbal confirmation, or a facilitative listening response addressing or acknowledging the feeling the client expressed, keeps lawyers connected with clients in this emotional space without disrupting emotional disclosures. In addition, there is research that indicates that extraverts can easily learn facilitative listening skills involving reflecting feelings, an excellent way of showing empathy.[20]

Introverts have a natural tendency to pause, reflect, and plan before responding to clients.[21] This natural tendency may help introverts avoid interruptions and respond facilitatively more often.[22] Theoretically, introverts are more comfortable with silence. Their own internal processing

---

[19] Peters & Peters, *supra* note 11, at 192.

[20] Hogan, *Development of an Empathy Scale,* 33 J. CONSULTING & CLINICAL PSYCHOLOGY 307, 312 (1969).

[21] Peters & Peters, *supra* note 11, at 193.

[22] *Id.* at 192.

makes them more familiar with taking time to work through thoughts and feelings in silence. Introverts use the time during silences to assess and plan.

Introverts' tendency to think about rather than talk out loud may lead them to consider more than they say. They may feel at the end of the interview that there are questions they did not ask that they wish they had asked. On the other hand, they may find that even without their asking, clients eventually disclose material in their own order and time.

Introverts tend to prefer different collaborative processes than extraverts. Without the benefit of knowledge of psychological type, as introverts hear and judge the extravert's process of developing understanding by talking out the information, they may assume that extraverts have less innate ability or are unable to refine their thinking. Introverts may assume that extraverts do not have the ability to think through the options since they often talk about possible solutions without scrutinizing them first.

When the client is an extravert, it may be easy for the lawyer to get the client to disclose information. On the other hand, the information may be less focused and contain more extraneous material than the lawyer wants. It is helpful to reflect content to extraverted clients who are processing data as they speak so they are able to further evaluate their expressed ideas. It is said that when you are talking to extraverts, if you do not know what they think, you were not listening.[23]

When the client is an introvert, it may be more difficult to gather information. The client may edit material as he thinks through what he will say, discarding important information on the cutting room floor of his mind. Introverts may be helped with the use of more open questions and verbal and nonverbal encouragers. It is said that when you are talking with introverts, if you do not know what they think, you did not ask.[24] By looking for extraversion/introversion influences, the lawyer may find clues that will enable more effective rapport building.

§ 12-6(d).   LIFESTYLES: JUDGMENT OR PERCEPTION

Lawyers who prefer a judgment lifestyle must beware not to make decisions about their clients' cases while still listening to the story. It is easy for lawyers (in their planned and scheduled worlds) to reach premature closure on clients' stories, calling this efficiency. The tendency of these lawyers is to move to a decision, to stay on schedule, and to create order in life. The weakness of these lawyers may be in not seeing the possibilities during the interview or not generating enough options during counseling.

---

[23] According to Dr. Mary McCaulley, this was the gist of a comment by Isabel Briggs Myers at a training workshop.

[24] *Id.*

Their strengths are in their organization and their clear time consciousness that help them meet their time commitments and deadlines.

Lawyers who prefer a perception lifestyle generally gather all the information and then some. They are apt to focus well on the information in the interview. They listen to clients in open ways, staying with the client's story, although simultaneously testing it against their own experience if they prefer sensing or against the consistency of the information if they prefer intuition. In counseling clients, they like to generate possibilities either through adaptive proposals if they prefer sensing or through creative new possibilities if they prefer intuition. They seek information to create solutions. They focus on alternatives. They like change and tire of routine. They look for a new twist in the facts or the themes. If not careful to move to judgment when appropriate, they may generate so many options that it is difficult to consider them all. They may seem inconsistent to others. Their time orientation, which is flexible, may be difficult for some colleagues and clients unless the lawyer applies time management skills.

Clients who prefer a judging lifestyle will expect a similar order and timeliness in their lawyers. If their lawyer does not demonstrate organizing skills or is late for meetings, the client may question the lawyer's competence, a decision that once made is difficult to counter. Clients who prefer a judging lifestyle may have already decided where their case *should* go and how it *should* be handled before they walk into their lawyer's office. Lawyers will be most helpful to these clients by systematically analyzing the legal situation with logic and with values. (These clients will certainly be on time and often arrive early for appointments.)

Clients who prefer a perceiving lifestyle may frustrate their lawyers with not having the structure in their lives that leads them to keep and file important documents. They may bring many possibilities to the counseling table and want to consider *all* options. Perceiving clients may also go back and question decisions after they have been made or begin to generate yet more possibilities. These clients may be challenged by time, thinking that they can do more in a given amount of time than is possible. (They may arrive late for meetings and appointments.)

§ 12-7. TYPE DYNAMICS

In her chapter on using the MBTI in counseling, Mary McCaulley reminds us that

> Both poles of the four preferences are valuable and necessary. Everyone uses E, I, S, N, T, F, J and P [extraversion, introversion, sensing, intuition, thinking, feeling, judgment, and perception] daily. Types sharing letters share those qualities in common. However, in each of the 16 types, the pattern of interests and skills associated with one preference is modified by the other three preferences. For example, the extraverted attitude appears differently

in ESTJ (a tough-minded executive type) and in ESFJ (a helpful, sociable type.)[25]

Each of the sixteen types represents a dynamic interaction of mental processes and use of energy. All types use the four functions — sensing, intuition, thinking, and feeling — routinely. Types differ in the priorities they give to each function and in the attitudes, extraversion or introversion, in which they typically use each function.[26]

One of the four functions will be the favorite one; this is called the dominant function and is used in the favorite attitude or preferred direction of energy. Myers referred to the dominant as the "captain of the ship" with undisputed authority to set the course and maneuver the ship safely.[27] Since the four functions direct conscious mental activity toward different goals, the lawyer's dominant function will influence the focus of work. People usually prefer to spend more time on activities that use their dominant function. For example, a person whose dominant function is a perception process, either Sensing or Intuition, may invest more time gathering information in the interviewing process while a person whose dominant is in the judgment scale, either Thinking or Feeling, may use more time on the evaluative and decision-making processes of counseling. A dominant sensing type may spend more time gathering facts, a dominant intuitive type may spend more time developing themes and possibilities, a dominant thinking type may spend more time on the objective logic, and a dominant feeling type may spend more time attending to identifying and setting priorities among the client's needs. We say "may" because part of the practical value of this knowledge is to be able to conduct effective interviews and counseling sessions using knowledge of type together with counseling models. Then lawyers can be purposeful in their behavioral choices and not just rely on their natural tendencies, the processes that have been modeled for them by others, or habits they have developed.

The four functions have different strengths, with the dominant function being the strongest, the auxiliary the second strongest, the tertiary the third strongest, and the inferior function the least conscious function and usually the area of the least developed skills and most challenge for a person. The dominant and auxiliary functions must operate in different attitudes to give a person access to both the inner and outer world. For example, if a person extraverts a perception function, then that person will introvert a judgment function. If a person extraverts a judgment function, then a perception function will be the one used in the inner world. The dominant or strongest of the four will be in the favored attitude of the person. The dominant function for an extravert will operate in the outer world of people, things and actions, and that person's auxiliary function will operate in the inner world. The dominant function for the introvert will

---

[25] McCaulley, *supra* note 3, at 95.

[26] MBTI MANUAL (2d ed.), *supra* note 4, at 12.

[27] MBTI MANUAL (2d ed.), *supra* note 4, at 13.

operate in the inner world of thoughts, ideas, and reflection, and that person's auxiliary function will operate in the outer world of interaction.

For lawyers this means that they always have access to both the external world and the inner world and that they have one of their two strongest functions operating in each field. Looking at the skills of interviewing and counseling through the lens of type dynamics is difficult, but it can be very helpful. The ordering and application of these cognitive processes helps lawyers understand their own cognitive processes and gives insight into the ways clients may work with lawyers. These dynamics open greater understanding of the ways people process and evaluate information which can enhance collaborative decision making.

For example, the lawyer whose dominant function is a perception function and whose favored field is extraversion may find that the process of interviewing is energizing. The perception process will stimulate active engagement of lawyers who prefer to use perception in the outer world, although which perception process the lawyer prefers will flavor the way he engages the client. If the lawyer prefers sensing, then he may focus on facts and gathering detailed, sequential information in an active way. If the lawyer prefers intuition, the interview is likely to look different, because the lawyer's tendency to perceive the story quickly may result in questions and comments aimed at generating strategies and possibilities interactively. For both of these lawyers, the tendency to use perception in the outer world may require them to "bite their tongues" or consciously monitor their extraverting process in order to respect the client's narrative process. When these lawyers who prefer extraverted perception move into a judging process, whether they prefer thinking or feeling judgment, they may find that they need more time to reflect. Their evaluative process will be introverted, because their perception process is extraverted.

For lawyers who extravert judgment and introvert perception the process would be more active in the evaluation phases and more reflective in the perception processes. This is also true for clients. One might observe a client who is reflective and concise in telling a story, actively engaging the lawyer in the evaluative process whether using thinking or feeling judgment. The decision-making process may be naturally more directed by a client who prefers extraverted judgment. This client may also have a difficult time telling a story without interjecting judgment into the process.

Another factor that can influence behavioral choices and that relates to type dynamics is stress. When a person is under a great deal of stress it is possible that the least conscious or the inferior function can emerge. This function is the least used and people often find themselves feeling almost childlike when it takes over. The inferior function may be any of the four functions. It is the one that is the polar opposite of the one most used, the dominant function. The inferior function has been described as the source of both our fool and our genius. For lawyers, the importance of being acquainted with the inferior function is to help clients under stress and to engage empathy instead of judgment when dealing with clients who are losing their objectivity or perspective. When this function emerges under stressful conditions, the person will be less in control and may say or do things that are out of character. If lawyers are aware of this type-related response to stress, they can use it to understand that the uncharacteristic behavior is an indication of the client's stress level. They can then help clients who are caught in the grip of their inferior function.[28]

There are many ways lawyers can help clients who are experiencing stress. Gaining a perception of control, framing a situation as a challenge, helping the client have an accurate understanding of what to expect, and reminding the client of the progress that has been made to date are all useful means of helping clients decrease the stress response.[29] Just listening to a client has a positive effect. Being able to respectfully and empathetically acknowledge the client's feelings also has healing dimensions and helps clients of all type preferences let go of their stress. Often these stressful feelings are wound up with either fears or anger. Having a respected other who will listen without interjecting judgmental comments can help a person gain perspective. When a client is under stress, the value of having built rapport and a relationship of trust will help client and lawyer negotiate this difficult time. The collaborative patterns developed in the interviewing and counseling stages will help them through stressful times. If stress responses occur early in the relationship, how the lawyer handles the emotions of the client will either build or damage trust. Knowledge of type dynamics and the inferior function can help lawyers handle these difficult situations in useful ways.

§ 12-8.   USING TYPE IN PROBLEM-SOLVING

Type-based problem-solving can be used in legal counseling. Myers described a method that can be used regardless of the type preferences[30] of the lawyer or client. Since all four functions are involved in good problem-solving, they can be systematically and consciously accessed. In this model, there is an appreciation for the importance of gathering both *sensing* information, including the facts and details of the situation, and *intuitive* information, recognizing the pattern and meaning dimensions of the problem. When applied to legal interviewing and counseling, this problem-solving process helps the lawyer and client work collaboratively. They can check to make sure that all the facts of the case and the specifics of the problem are known to both. They can then share the meanings they derive from these facts. This process can generate alternative ways of looking at information. The lawyer and client, through collaborating in the intuitive process of seeing patterns and creating strategies or options, may understand the situation in ways that neither one alone could have.

---

[28] Naomi L. Quenck, Beside Ourselves (1993).

[29] Martha M. Peters, *"Teaching Stress Management in the Law Office," in* Living with the Law: Strategies to Avoid Burnout and Create Balance (Julie M. Tamminen ed., American Bar Association, Section on Law Office Management, 1997).

[30] Myers, *supra* note 2. *See also* Mary H. McCaulley, *The Myers-Briggs Type Indicator: A Jungian Model for Problem Solving, in* Developing Critical Thinking and Problem Solving Abilities (J. Stice ed., 1987).

Once the lawyer and client agree that the pertinent facts have been explored sufficiently, and once options have been generated and possibilities have been developed, the lawyer and client move to the domain of the judgment functions. *Thinking* judgment requires that they collaborate in looking at the objective criteria for evaluating the information and possibilities. They need to step away from the situation and assess from an impersonal perspective using objective criteria. The client needs to weigh the information against his criteria. The lawyer contributes an analysis by weighing the information against her knowledge of legal criteria. Together they use their thinking judgment to evaluative objectively. Having fully explored these evaluations, the lawyer and client must not stop. It is time to move to the subjective, *feeling* evaluation process, stepping into the situation to be sure they have considered all of the personal and relationship aspects of the situation. They must prioritize the client's values and access the lawyer's perspective on the interests of all parties.

Only when all four functions have been used in a collaborative way will the client be fully ready to make a decision. These processes complement each other in the problem-solving process.[31] By working through this process in an active way, the lawyer and client collaborate, using the knowledge, skills, and type dimensions of each to create a synergistic process of helping, and to comply with the collaborative deliberation counseling model.

§ 12-9. CONCLUSION

Type does not explain everything. In addition to the variations found in the sixteen different dynamic types, there is infinite individual variability related to culture, race, religion, gender, sexual orientation, class, experience, and other dimensions of difference. However, type seems to be such a basic part of the universal human system that people across cultural differences report that they are more similar to those of their same type in the ways they process information and make decisions than they are to those in their own cultural group.[32] Because legal interviewing and counseling, particularly when using the collaborative decision-making model, involves information processing by the lawyer and client together, psychological type can give lawyers an understanding of potential differences between themselves and their clients that will facilitate rapport building, information gathering, and decision making. Knowledge of psychological type can therefore aid lawyers in working collaboratively with clients, increasing client satisfaction, and improving their own skill with interviewing and counseling clients.

---

[31] Martin, *supra* note 16.

[32] Oral communication with Gerald MacDaid, CEO of the Center for Applications of Psychological Type (CAPT) in Gainesville, Florida, following the first CAPT International Conference in Hawaii held in January, 1996.

INDEX

[References are to pages.]

[References are to pages.]

D

[References are to pages.]

[References are to pages.]